IMAGES
of America

SEATTLE'S HISTORIC HOUSES OF WORSHIP

ON THE COVER: Bishop Edward O'Dea celebrates his golden jubilee at St. James Cathedral around 1932. The celebration was attended and celebrated by thousands as his 50 years of service in the priesthood were honored. Bishop O'Dea built dozens of churches, hospitals, and schools and led the diocese through 50 years of good and bad times. (Courtesy of Archdiocese of Seattle.)

IMAGES
of America

Seattle's Historic Houses of Worship

Marilyn Morgan

ARCADIA
PUBLISHING

ISBN 978-1-4671-2638-0

Published by Arcadia Publishing
Charleston, South Carolina

Printed in the United States of America

Library of Congress Control Number: 2016962178

For all general information, please contact Arcadia Publishing:
Telephone 843-853-2070
Fax 843-853-0044
E-mail sales@arcadiapublishing.com
For customer service and orders:
Toll-Free 1-888-313-2665

Visit us on the Internet at www.arcadiapublishing.com

*To Christine, Joyce, Rae, Tonia, Sureta, Milan, Darius, and Gavin—
thank you for your support and caring; because
of you, I can reach for the stars.*

Contents

Acknowledgments 6
Introduction 7
1. St. James Cathedral 9
2. Immaculate Conception Church 27
3. Trinity Parish Episcopal Church 37
4. Temple de Hirsch Sinai 49
5. Seattle Betsuin Buddhist Temple 61
6. Mount Zion Baptist Church 73
7. Seattle First Baptist Church 87
8. Plymouth Congregational Church 97
9. First Church Seattle 113

Acknowledgments

I wish to acknowledge all the Seattle houses of worship that participated in this book project for allowing me access to their historical files and photographs. I extend my thanks to Jim Collier of Temple de Hirsch Sinai; Claire Gebbens, historian for First Church Seattle; Rev. Phyllis Beaumonte, historian of Mount Zion Baptist Church; Rev. Aaron Williams, senior pastor of Mount Zion Baptist Church; Richard Baxendale, historian of Trinity Parish Episcopal Church; Corinna Laughlin, historian of St. James Cathedral; Alan Hoshino of Seattle Betsuin Buddhist Temple; Dorothy Cordova, historian of the Immaculate Conception Church; Janice Randall and Robert Turner, historians for Plymouth Congregational Church; and Diana Jones, historian for Seattle First Baptist Church. I also want to thank the University of Washington Special Collections Department.

INTRODUCTION

This book feature churches that are at least 100 years old. Throughout the years, these churches have guided their parishioners through the transformation of Seattle from a frontier town to a major metropolis, brought them through such events as the Great Seattle Fire, the Great Depression, and the civil rights movement. Their history is America's history, which I think is unique about this book on churches.

The churches have been the guiding force and the beacon of hope for their parishioners and an example and standard bearer for the city. For example, in 1909, when no church would marry an interracial couple, Rev. Herbert Henry Gowan of Trinity Parish bravely ignored the threats and backlash and performed the ceremony for the couple at the church. During the 1960s, when Dr. Martin Luther King Jr. came to Seattle to speak on human rights, jobs, and equal education, most churches shied away from the iconic civil rights leader because at the time he was deemed too controversial; however, Temple de Hirsch gladly opened its doors so their worshipers could receive King's message. Also, well before *Brown v. Board of Education*, the sisters from St. James Cathedral and the Immaculate Conception made it their mission to seek out a diverse student body.

These historic churches are unique because they have always been in the forefront of spiritual enlightenment and social change.

Trinity Parish is the oldest Episcopal church in the Greater Seattle area. The original church was built in 1871 but was destroyed by the Great Seattle Fire in 1889. It was rebuilt but burned down again in 1902 and rebuilt in 1903 at its current location. In its first 10 years, the church established five mission churches, and continues to be a mission church today. In 1885, Trinity Parish established Grace Hospital, one of the first hospitals in Seattle. The church was designated a national historic landmark in 1976. The church has a 700-member congregation.

The Immaculate Conception Church is the oldest standing Catholic church in the Greater Seattle area. The building was constructed in 1904. The beautiful interior has frescoes that were hand-painted by Jesuit priests who founded the church and a grotto that is an exact replica of the grotto at Our Blessed Mother in Lourdes, France. In fact, many of the artifacts in the church are priceless, and many of the statues date back as far as 1890 and are irreplaceable. Immaculate Conception was declared a historic landmark in 1974. The church has always had a strong community outreach and diversity programs. The church has a 500-member congregation.

Mount Zion Baptist Church is one of the oldest churches in the state of Washington with a predominantly African American membership. Founded in 1891, it is currently celebrating its 125th anniversary. The church has always been a haven and advocate for blacks, poor people, and other minorities seeking social and political justice and employment opportunities. Under the spiritual leadership of Rev. Samuel McKinney, the church's social and political activism flourishes. Dr. McKinney was a roommate and friend of Dr. Martin Luther King Jr. while attending Morehouse College in Atlanta, Georgia. Dr. McKinney was Dr. King's lieutenant for the civil rights movement in the Pacific Northwest. The church has a 1,000-member congregation.

Temple de Hirsch is a Reform Jewish temple that was founded in 1899. During its history, it has had three locations. The third and current location was built in 1960. Samuel Goldfarb was the musical director from 1930 to 1967, and he composed "I Have a Little Dreidel," a Hanukkah musical staple. Since its formation, the temple has welcomed all. The temple has a 1,400-family congregation.

St. James Cathedral was constructed in 1907 and opened its doors for the first time in December 1907, with the occasion being an organ recital performed by the newly hired musical director Dr. Franklin Palmer. The church has a rich history of spiritual guidance, education, and community outreach. Soon after the church opened in 1911, the Sisters of the Holy Name of Jesus and Mary founded the cathedral school. The school was open to all, including poor and minority families. The sisters sought out a diverse study body—Japanese, African Americans, Germans, Italians, and many others shared the same space. In its first 100 years, St. James had only eight pastors, all with Irish surnames—Daniel Hanley, William Noonan, James Gordon Strafford, William Henry O'Neill, John Gallagher, Thomas Gill, William Gallagher, and Michael Ryan—and each left an indelible imprint on the church. The cathedral has a 3,500-member congregation.

First Church Seattle was founded in 1853 and is Seattle's oldest church. It survived the Great Seattle Fire and is a progressive Methodist church.

Seattle First Baptist was founded in 1869 by 11 people. It has been the mother of several churches, including Scandinavian Baptist (1883), Japanese Baptist (1891), and Chinese Baptist (1892).

Plymouth Congregational Church was founded in 1869 and is a member of the United Church of Christ denomination. The church is known for its historical social justice advocacy, its music programs, and its work with the homeless.

Seattle Betsuin Buddhist Temple was founded in 1901 in the Jodo Shinshu tradition, and is affiliated with the Buddhist Churches of America.

These nine churches have endured for well over 100 years. They have preached spirituality and fought for the rights of the poor, equal rights and treatment for minorities and immigrants, and equal housing, education, and basic human rights for all during times when it was unpopular to do so. Dr. Martin Luther King Jr. once said, "there comes a time when one must take a position that is neither safe nor popular nor politic, but he must take it because conscience tells him it is righteous."

One

St. James Cathedral

St. James is a beautiful cathedral, the mother church of the Archdiocese of Seattle. In the late 1890s and the early 1900s, Seattle was rapidly growing from a frontier town to a booming city. With the gold rush and its lumber and shipping industries, Seattle was rapidly outgrowing the larger and more established towns of Vancouver and Olympia. Sensing that Seattle would soon become the bigger city in population and wealth, Bishop Edward J. O'Dea purchased property in the city's First Hill neighborhood.

Bishop O'Dea was born in Boston, Massachusetts, and was named the third bishop of the Diocese of Nesqually in 1896, based in Vancouver, Washington. He petitioned Rome in a heartfelt letter for permission to move the diocese from Vancouver to Seattle. Moved by the letter, Rome granted Bishop O'Dea permission, and in 1903, he purchased property at Ninth Avenue and Marion Street to build what he hoped would be a great cathedral.

Bishop O'Dea had considerable previous experience building churches, orphanages, and even hospitals, but this was his first opportunity to build a cathedral from the bottom up, and he imagined a "magnificent cathedral that would surpass anything in the West."

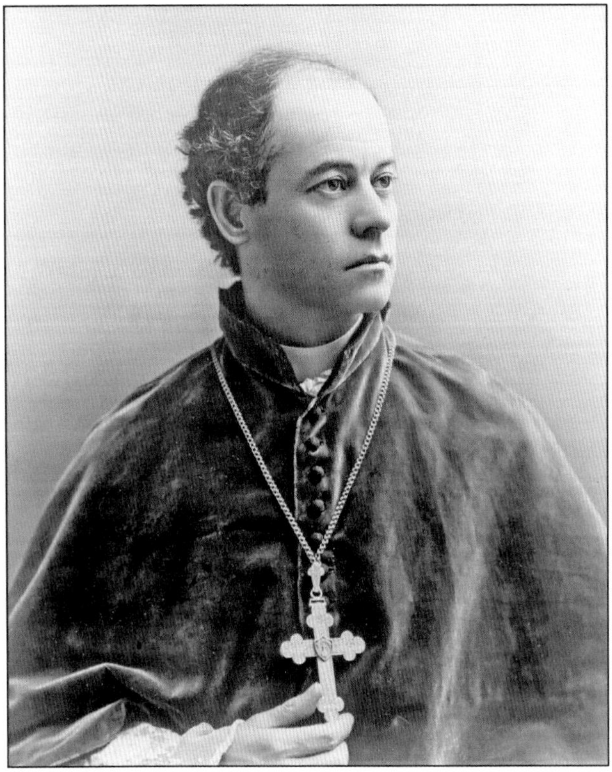

Bishop O'Dea hired the prestigious New York architectural firm of Heins and LaFarge to design a magnificent Italian Renaissance structure with twin towers 167 feet high. In October 1903, Bishop O'Dea held a week-long cathedral fair and raised more than $20,000 for the building fund. Construction began in 1904; the cornerstone was laid on November 12, 1905, with more than 5,000 people in attendance, the largest religious gathering in Seattle at that time. (Courtesy of Archdiocese of Seattle.)

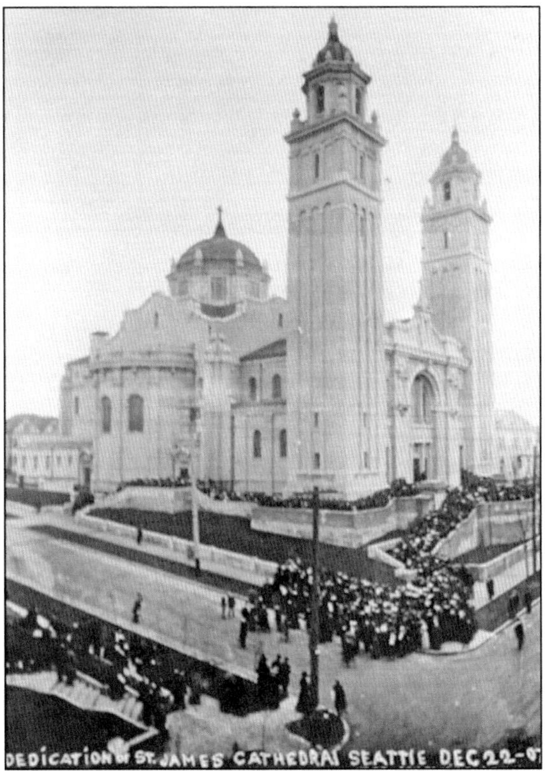

The church was dedicated in December 1907 and featured state-of-the-art electrical and ventilation systems. One of the unique features of the cathedral was a beautiful central dome constructed of steel, terra cotta, and brick covered with copper that was thought to be effectively indestructible. The dome allowed natural light to stream through and sat 40 feet above roof level. It was a beautiful sight to behold and could be seen from all over the city. (Courtesy of Archdiocese of Seattle.)

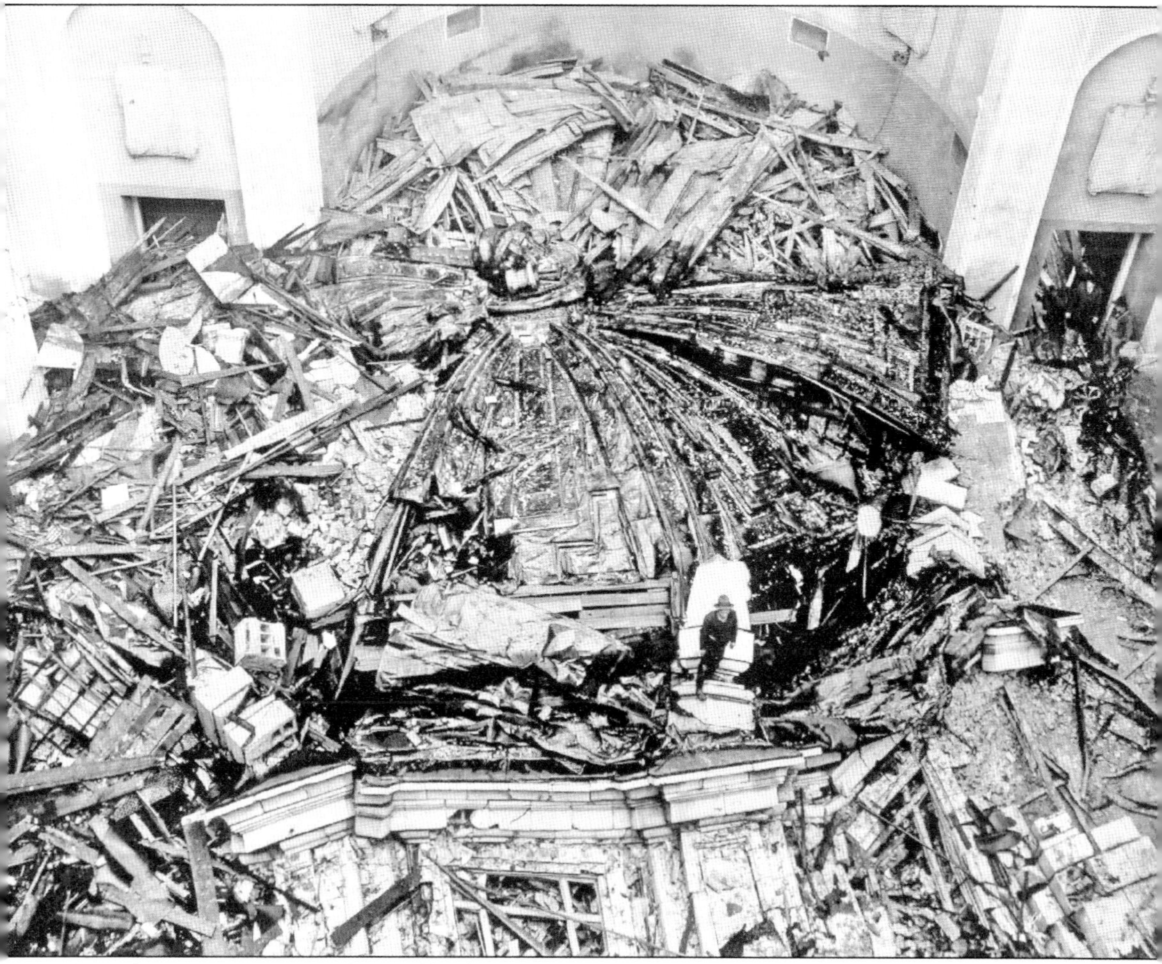

On February 2, 1916, Seattle was blanketed with a major snowstorm. It snowed heavily all day, a somewhat unusual occurrence in Seattle. The dome was weighed down with at least two feet of snow and collapsed under the weight, crashing to the floor. No one saw the dome fall, but the sound was heard for blocks. Luckily no one was in the nave at the time, as the children had been dismissed from class; the sisters were busy preparing for the next day's class, and the priests were busy with other matters. When the priests, nuns, and some neighbors rushed to the nave, they witnessed the damage. The dome collapse brought down about 80 square feet of ceiling, shattered all the windows, and destroyed the pulpit. Glass and mortar were everywhere. (Courtesy of Archdiocese of Seattle.)

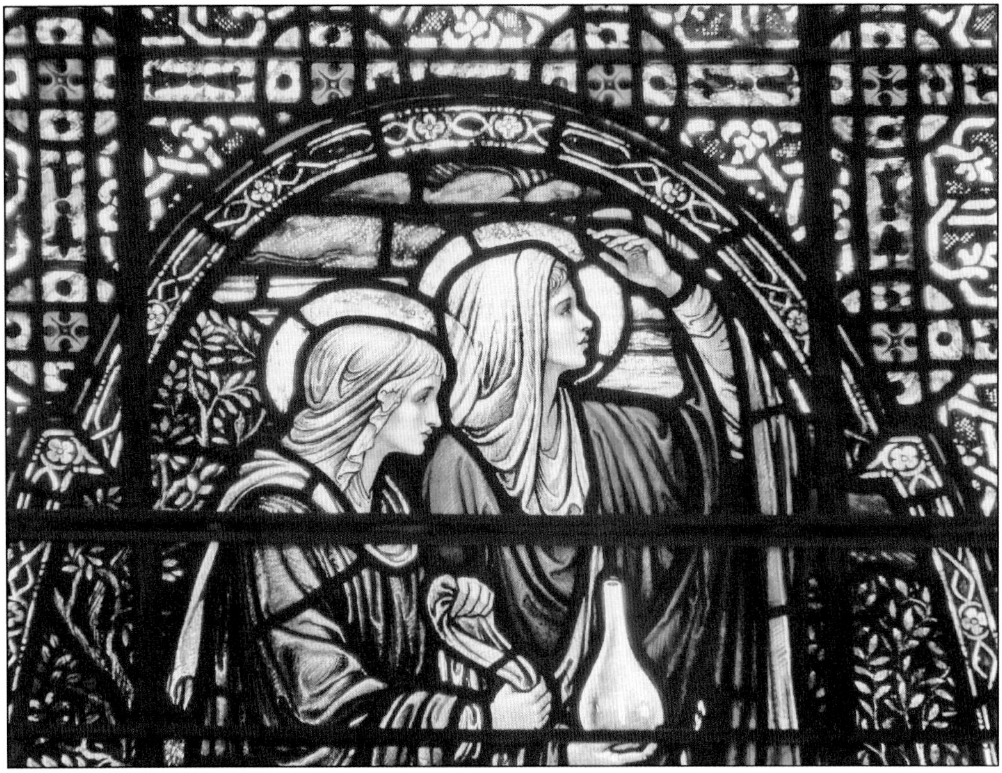

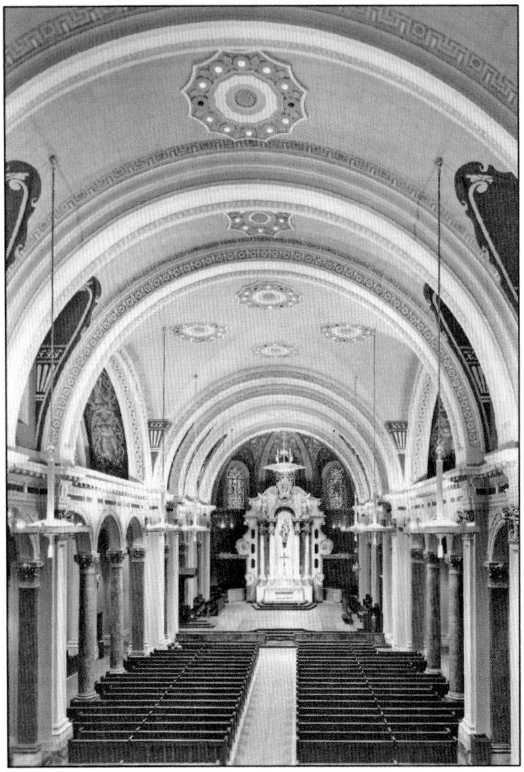

The destruction was so extensive that the church was closed for renovations for more than a year. It reopened on March 18, 1917, with a flat roof replacing the dome. With the flat roof, the acoustics had greatly improved. The shattered windows were replaced by a collection of stained-glass windows by prominent artist and muralist Charles Connick. Some of the windows on the lower level include images of Mathew, Mark, Luke, John, St. James, and St. Patrick. Ten windows on the clerestory level represent the Ten Commandments. In the north transept are three Christmas scenes, with Jesus, Mary, and Joseph in the center window. (Courtesy of Archdiocese of Seattle.)

In 1950, the church underwent a major remodel. The interior was transformed with a new altar, vibrant colors, statues, and a new window. There have been other renovations—in 1994, changes included moving the altar to the center of the building, removing the dust and grime from the exterior, and installing a skylight. (Courtesy of Archdiocese of Seattle.)

Monsignor Daniel A. Hanley was the cathedral's first pastor and served from 1906 to 1910. He was born in Baltimore in 1873. He studied at Loyola and Gonzaga Universities and was ordained in 1906. While serving at St. James, the monsignor built the first mission church (Holy Rosary) in West Seattle. After leaving St. James, he went on to pastor the Sacred Heart Church in Bellingham, Washington. (Courtesy of Archdiocese of Seattle.)

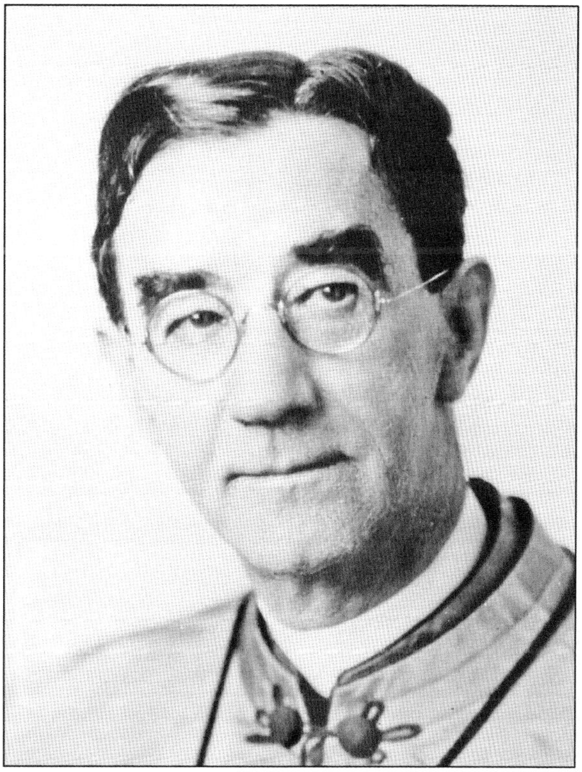

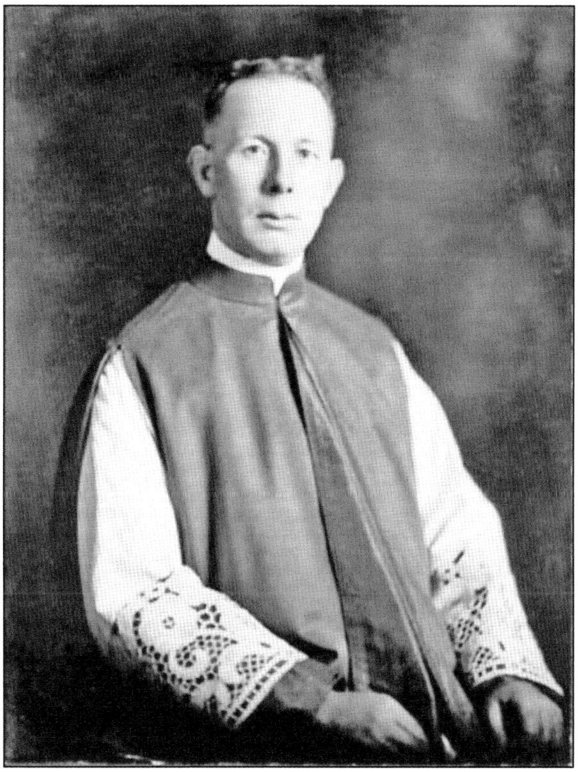

From 1910 to 1919, Monsignor William J. Noonan pastored St. James. He built the cathedral school, bought land to build the O'Dea School, and had the task of overseeing the renovation of the church after the dome crashed through the ceiling. He personally selected much of the church's exquisite stained-glass collection, which replaced the windows shattered in the crash. Monsignor Noonan was born in 1878 in Ireland and came to the diocese from Ireland in 1906. He spent 11 years at St. James before moving on to St. Patrick's in Tacoma, where he stayed for 34 years. He died in 1953. (Courtesy of Archdiocese of Seattle.)

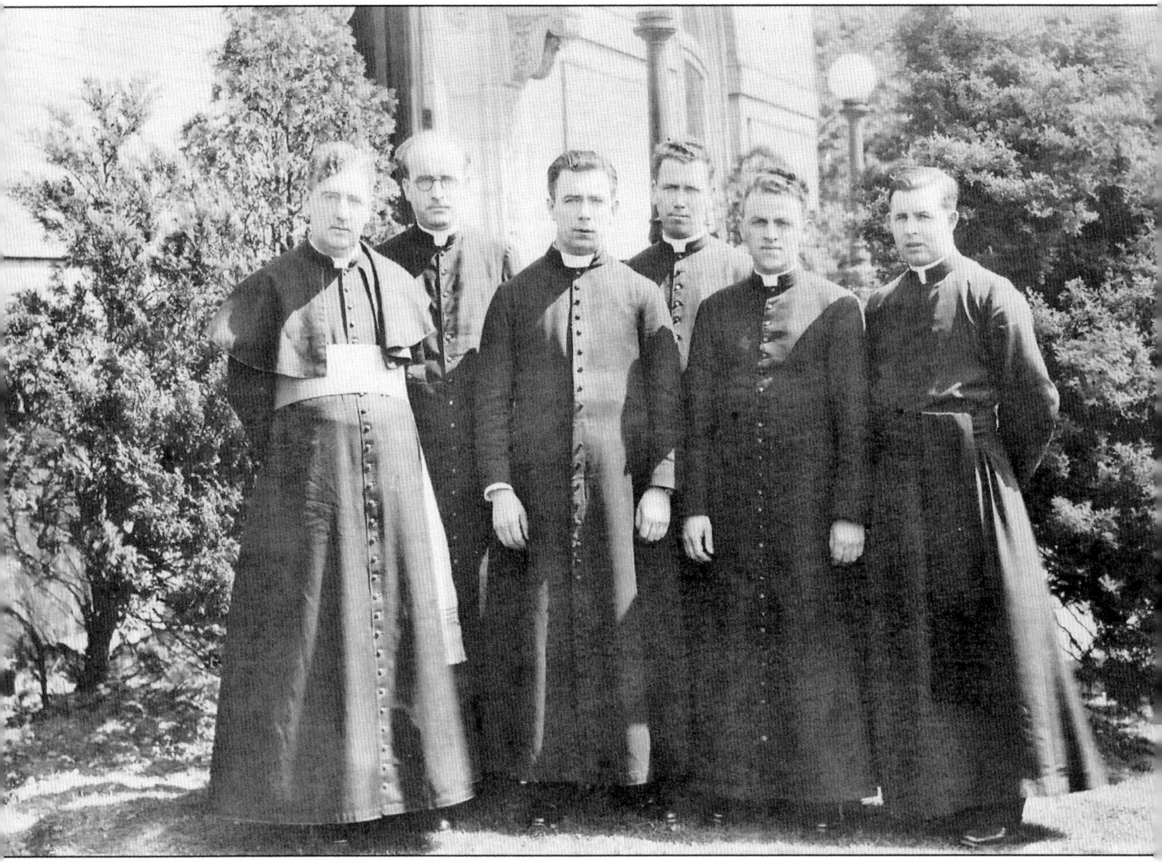

Monsignor James Gordon Stafford (far left) was the church's third pastor and became a monsignor in 1925. He was the spiritual leader of St. James from 1919 to 1935. He was born in Auburn, New York, in 1882 and studied in Maryland and at seminary in Paris before being ordained in Baltimore in 1910. Father Strafford was appointed to St. James by Bishop O'Dea in 1919, but he first served at St. Mary's and St. Margaret's. Monsignor Strafford was beloved and proved to be a prolific fundraiser. Within his first year of service, he raised more than $100,000 to pay off the repairs resulting from the dome collapse. He raised an additional $80,000 to build O'Dea High School. He also raised money to build a new convent for the Sisters of the Holy Names of Jesus and Mary. Monsignor Strafford also introduced the envelope system to the West Coast. The monsignor loved music and liturgy and how it enhanced the church experience. He partnered with Dr. Franklin Sawyer Palmer, the church's music director, to create a music program producing a regular radio broadcast of the Sunday mass beginning in 1925. The innovative program became nationally known. Monsignor Strafford celebrated his silver jubilee on May 24, 1935, with a noble celebration at a church. He left St. James five days later to take a new position at Assumption in Bellingham, where he served as pastor from 1935 until his death in 1949. He is pictured here with, from left to right, Fr. William O'Neill, Fr. Michael O'Callaghan, Fr. Edmund Hayes, Fr. Hugh Gallagher, and Fr. Edward McFadden. (Courtesy of Archdiocese of Seattle.)

Fr. William Henry O'Neill, the church's fourth pastor, was born in 1900 in Butte, Montana. He moved with his family to Seattle when he was 16 years old. He studied at Seattle College (now Seattle University) and at St. Patrick's Seminary in California. He was ordained by Bishop O'Dea when he was only 24. Father O'Neill served at St. James as an assistant before attending Catholic University to receive his doctorate in canon law. (Courtesy of Archdiocese of Seattle.)

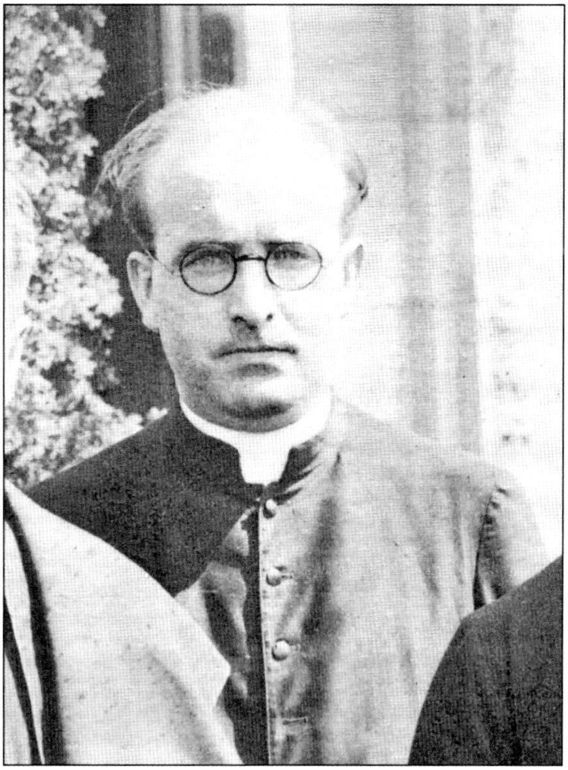

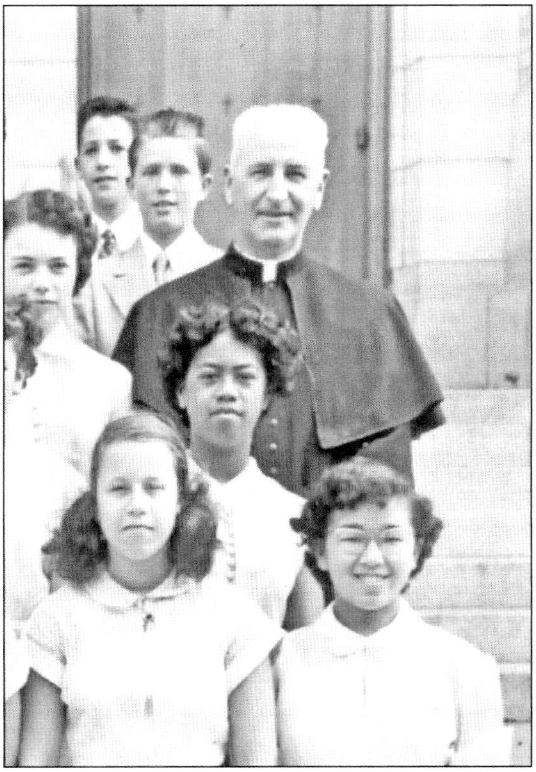

Monsignor John Gallagher, the fifth pastor, served from 1943 to 1954. He was born in Cleveland, Ohio, in 1900 and studied at St. Patrick's in California. After serving at St. Mary's Cathedral in San Francisco, he came to St. James, where he was an assistant for five years specifically helping Bishop O'Dea before leaving; he returned as pastor in 1943. He held a special interest in education and was very devoted to the cathedral school. He remained at St. James until his death in 1954 while visiting his parents in Cleveland. (Courtesy of Archdiocese of Seattle.)

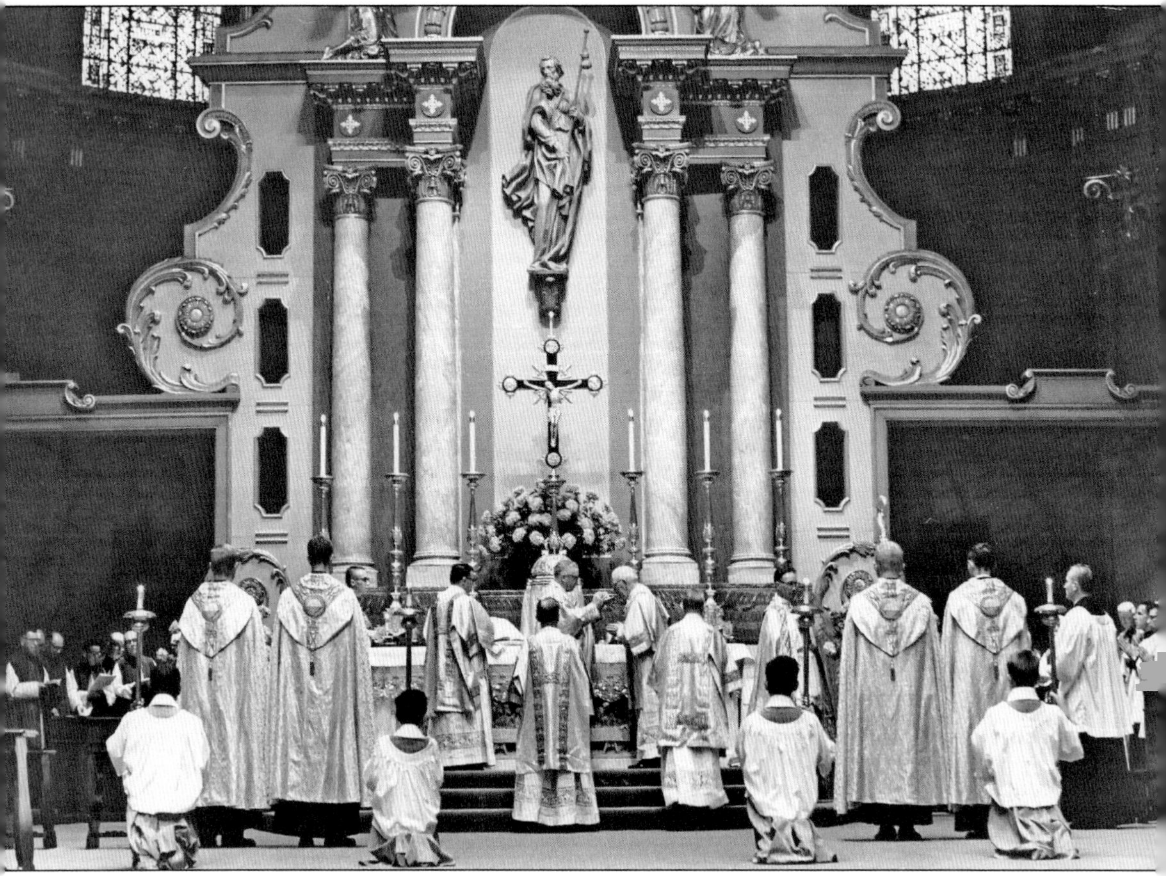

Bishop Thomas E. Gill was the cathedral's sixth pastor (1955–1973) and was the first to be a Seattle native. He was born on March 18, 1908, and attended St. Joseph's Parish on Capitol Hill. After serving assignments at St. Patrick's in Tacoma and St. Mary's in Seattle, Father Gill attended Catholic University in Washington, DC, where he received his master's degree in social work. He returned to St. James, where he managed Catholic Children's Services, which later evolved into Catholic Community Services, a charitable organization that aids people who need help regardless of their religion, race, or economic or social standing. Bishop Gill was known as a tireless worker. He carried out the duties of administrator, pastor, and later bishop. He remained at St. James until his unexpected death on November 11, 1973, of a heart attack while at a bishop's conference. Bishop Gill guided the church through some of the country's most turbulent times—the upheaval over the war in Vietnam and the civil rights movement, which explored issues of racial discrimination, segregation, poverty, jobs, and fair treatment for minorities and the poor. During his tenure, the nation's first (and still only) Catholic president, John F. Kennedy, was also assassinated. The parish has had only two other pastors—the modern pastors are Fr. William E. Gallagher, who served from 1973 to 1988, and Fr. Michael G. Ryan, who served from 1988 to the present. (Courtesy of Archdiocese of Seattle.)

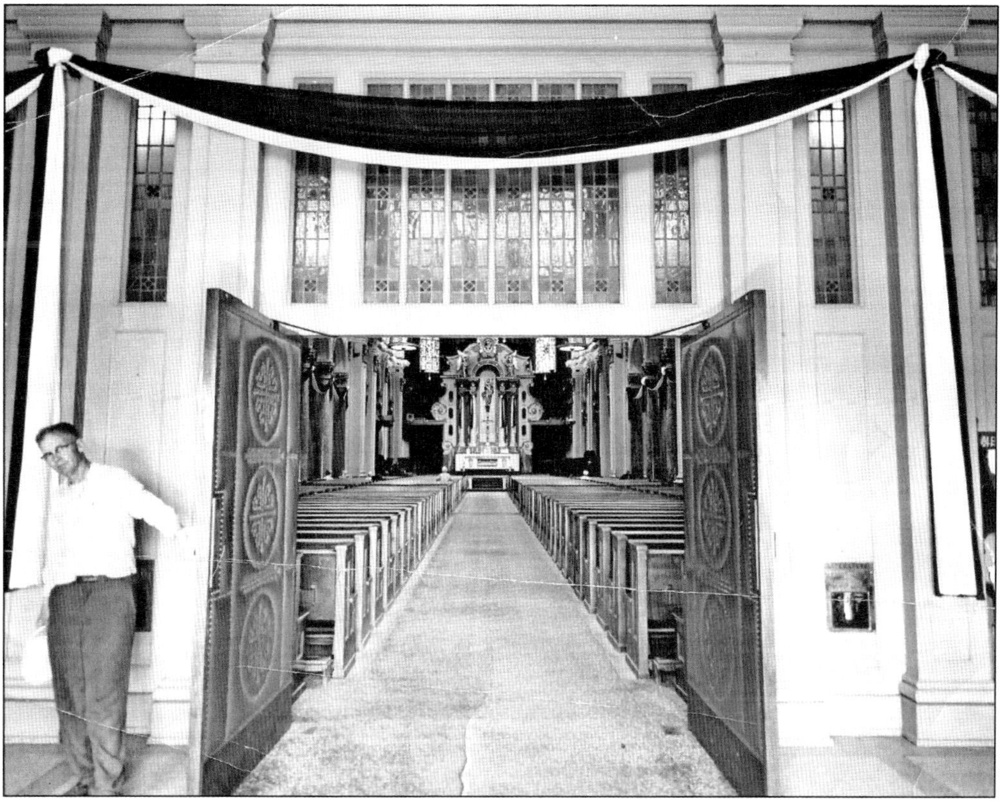

The assassination of President Kennedy was undoubtedly a devastating blow for the country, but for members of the Catholic community, it was especially heart-wrenching. This photograph shows the church's bunting for President Kennedy. (Courtesy of Archdiocese of Seattle.)

The bells of St. James rang out, and the church, as well as others in the area, was filled with mourners. The church held a requiem mass for President Kennedy (with a simulated casket draped with the American flag) attended by more than 1,500 people. St. James and other churches were a source of comfort in a world that suddenly made no sense. (Courtesy of Archdiocese of Seattle.)

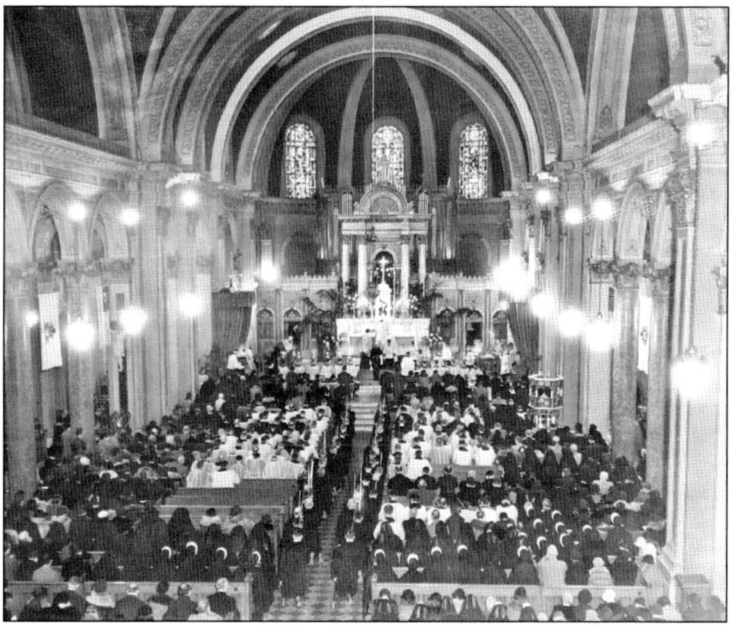

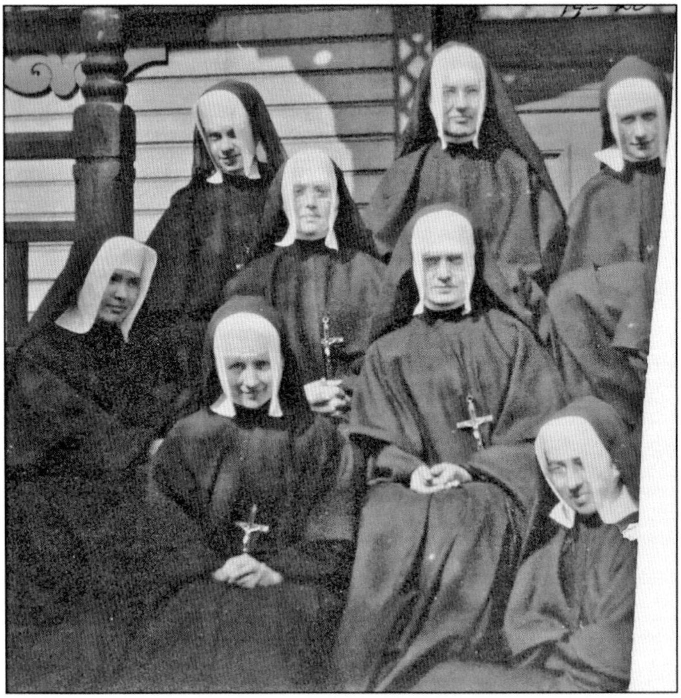

St. James has always been dedicated to education, and in 1911, not long after the church opened, the Sisters of the Holy Name of Jesus and Mary founded the cathedral school. The sisters consisted of Mary Everildis, Mary Flora, Mary Rosella, Mary Roswitha, and Mary Cyril. They have played a vital role in the cathedral since its inception as teachers, directors of religious education, and bookkeepers. (Courtesy of Archdiocese of Seattle.)

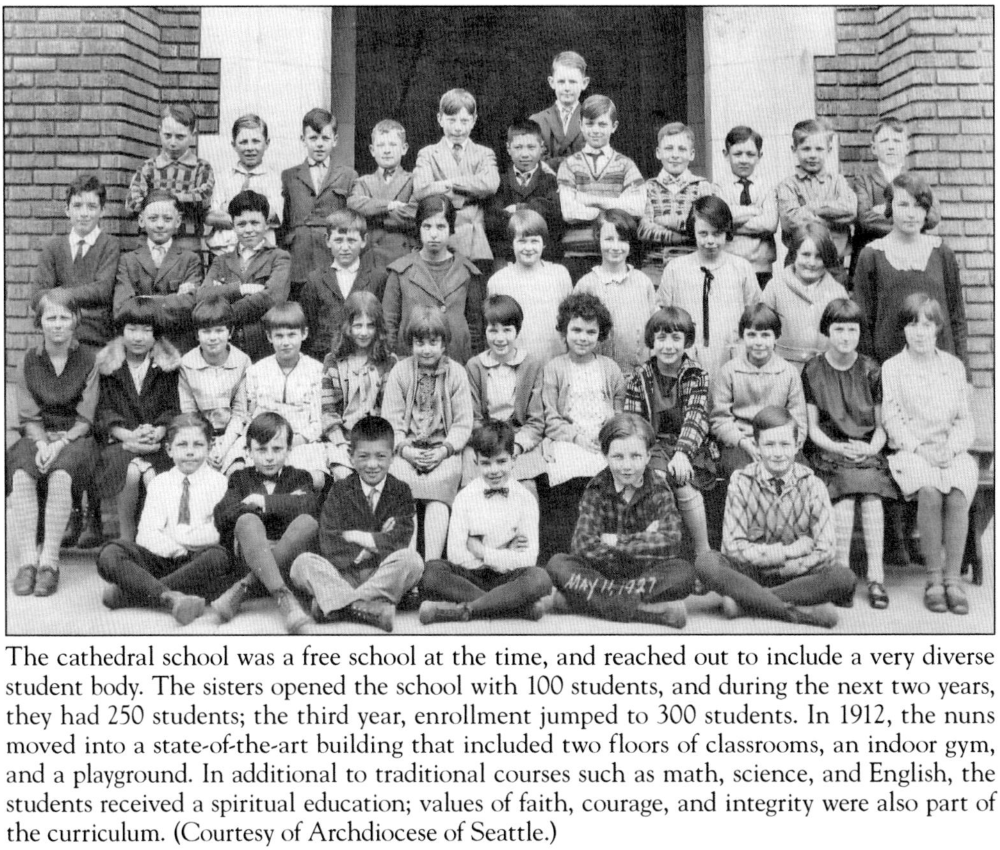

The cathedral school was a free school at the time, and reached out to include a very diverse student body. The sisters opened the school with 100 students, and during the next two years, they had 250 students; the third year, enrollment jumped to 300 students. In 1912, the nuns moved into a state-of-the-art building that included two floors of classrooms, an indoor gym, and a playground. In additional to traditional courses such as math, science, and English, the students received a spiritual education; values of faith, courage, and integrity were also part of the curriculum. (Courtesy of Archdiocese of Seattle.)

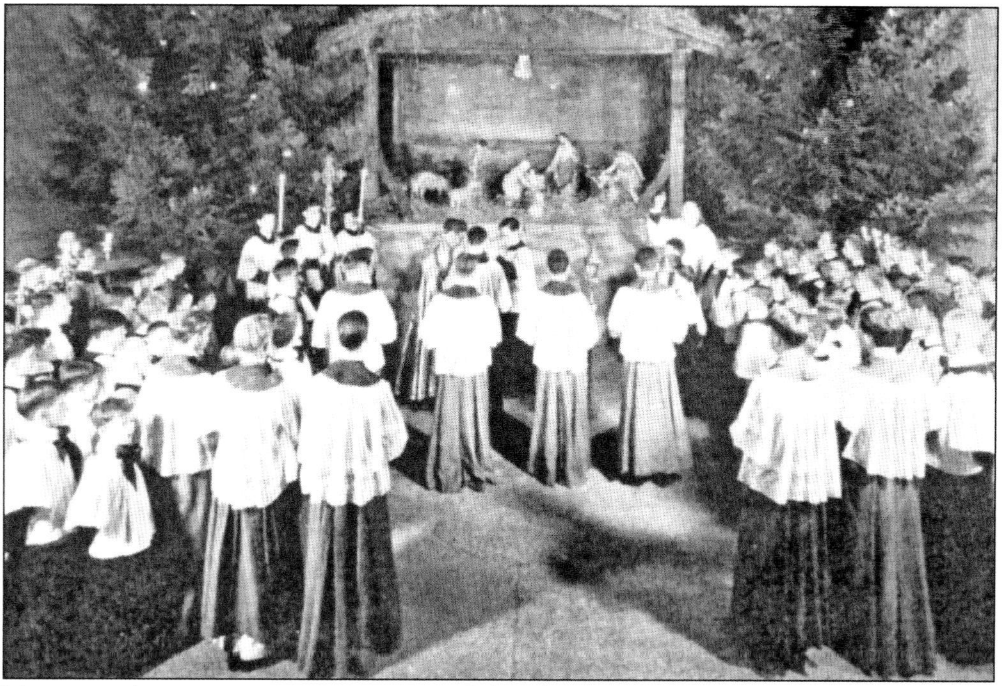

Music was also an important component of the school's teachings. The students sang at the liturgies and at some of the masses, and of course sang carols at Christmas. The school remained open for more than 60 years, but with more of its congregation moving to the suburbs, it closed in 1972. The building became a high school for Immaculate Conception Church. (Courtesy of Archdiocese of Seattle.)

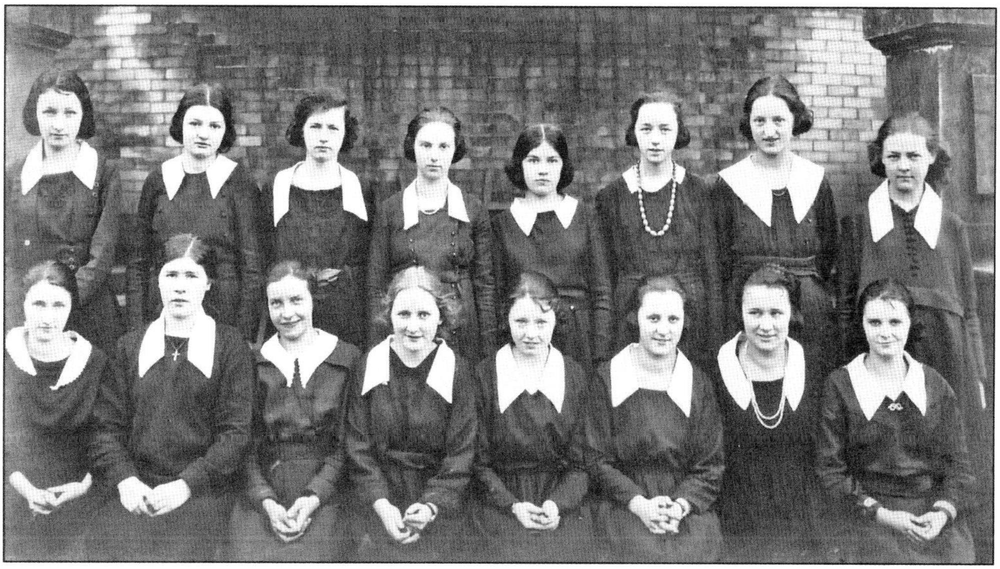

Even though the school closed in 1972, the Sisters of the Holy Name remained pivotal to the church. They continued to provide religious education to the young people of the congregation, developed an outreach program by providing in-home mass for the elderly and shut-ins, coordinated with social service agencies to make sure that their needs were met, and provided special programs and opportunities for poor kids. (Courtesy of Archdiocese of Seattle.)

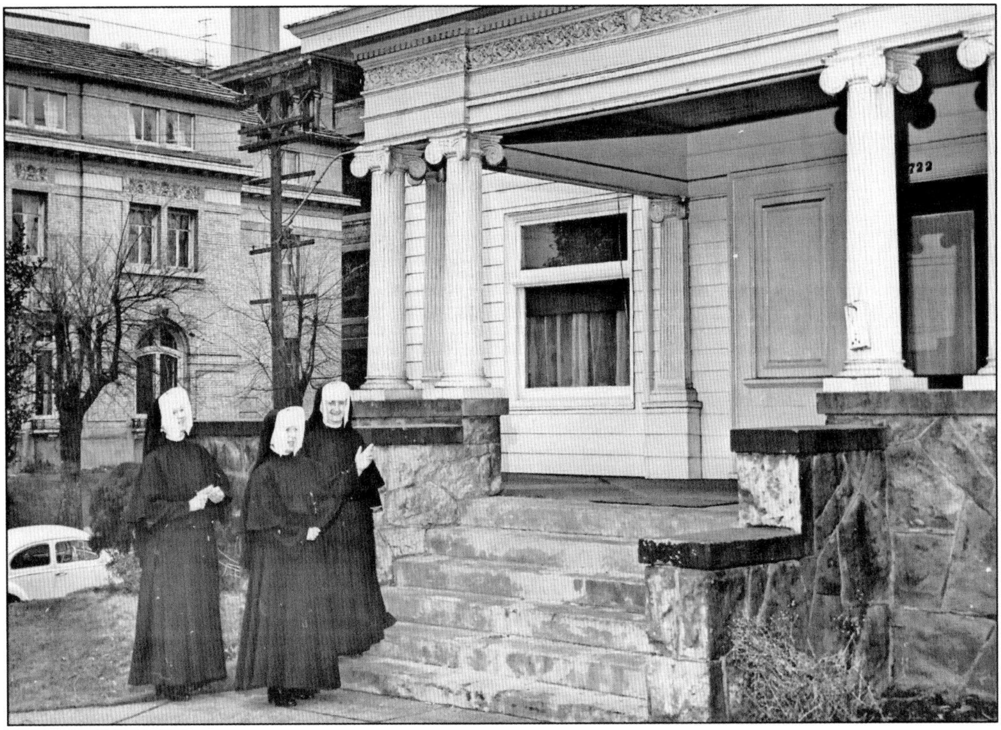

In 1975, during the Vietnam War, Seattle received many Vietnamese refugees who were anxious to learn how to read and write English. The sisters founded the St. James ESL Program (English as a second language), and the first class consisted of 25 students. The program continues today with students from more than 37 countries around the world. (Courtesy of Archdiocese of Seattle.)

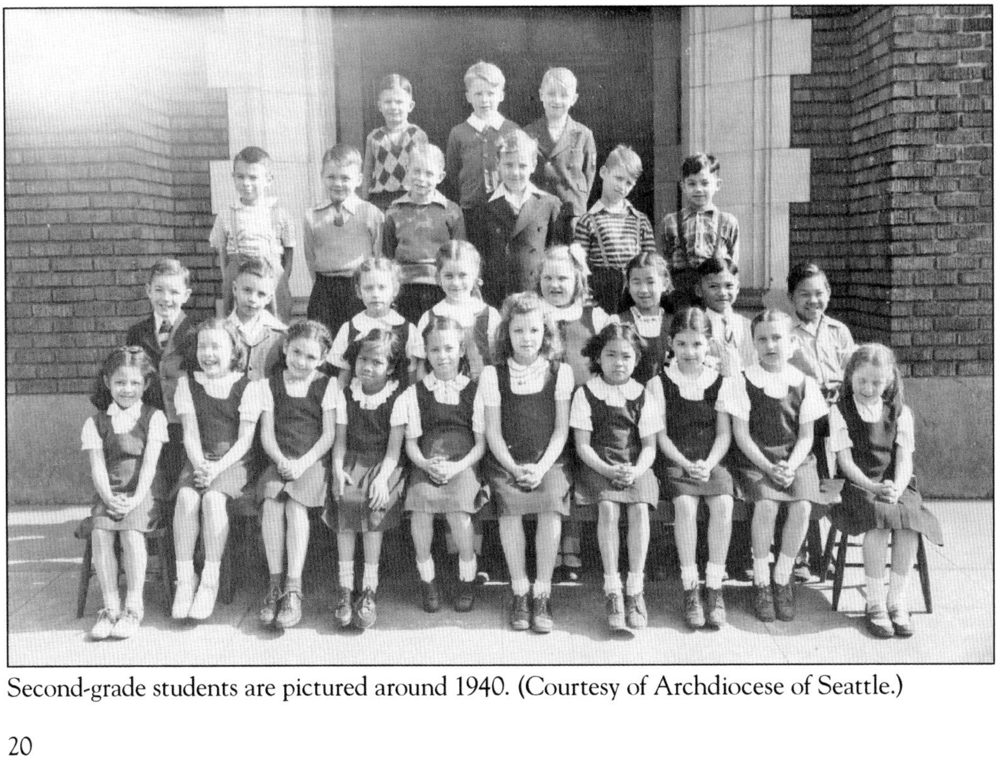

Second-grade students are pictured around 1940. (Courtesy of Archdiocese of Seattle.)

One of the unique features of St. James has always been its music. When Bishop O'Dea envisioned St. James Cathedral, music was an important component. He wanted a state-of-the-art organ and a world-class organist to lead the music program. Dr. Franklin Sawyer Palmer was the kind of person he had in mind. Dr. Palmer was a Harvard-trained physician and a talented and creative musician. He was hired in 1907 and remained at St. James as music director for almost three decades until his death in 1935. He worked diligently with a Boston firm on the specifications for the organ that was installed in the west wing of the cathedral. That organ is still used at the church today. (Courtesy of Archdiocese of Seattle.)

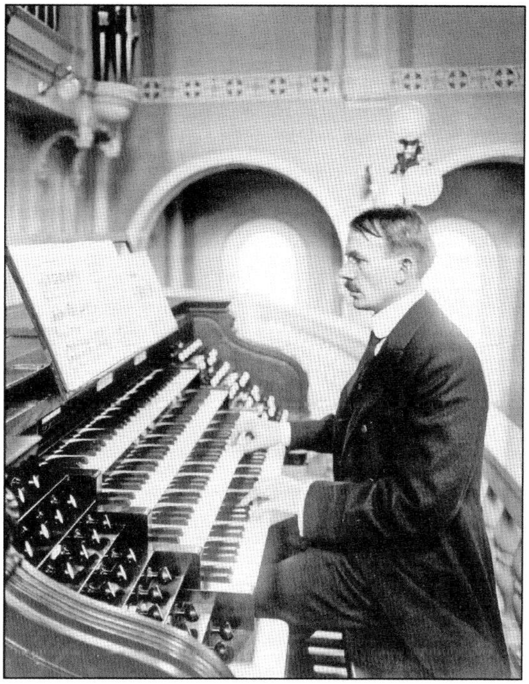

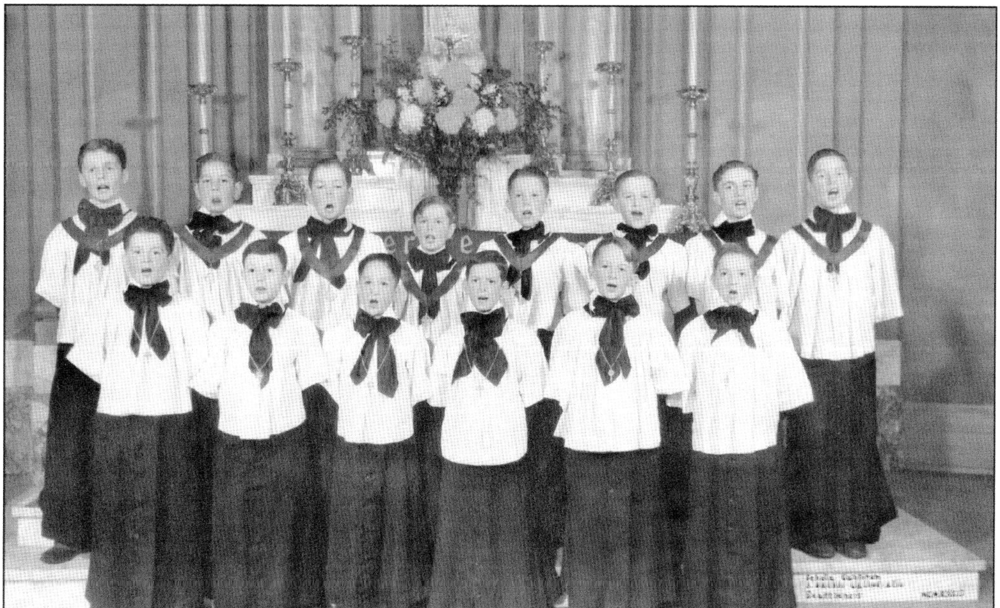

Dr. Palmer partnered with Monsignor Strafford to produce a radio program broadcasting the church's Sunday mass, a unique and innovative endeavor during those years. The initial choir consisted of men. At the time, there were no coed choirs; boys and girls and women and men did not sing together. That changed in 1922, when the church incorporated the Justine Ward system, which was set up to teach children to sing. With the help of Palmer's assistant, John McDonald Lyon, and the Sisters of the Holy Names of Jesus and Mary, many boys and girls were trained and sang beautifully at mass. The choirs were a big part of why the cathedral's music became renowned. (Courtesy of Archdiocese of Seattle.)

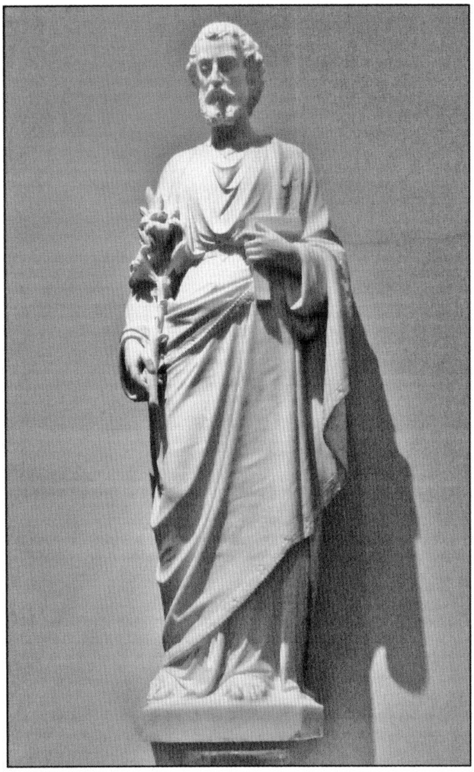

St. James, like most Catholic churches, has artifacts and statues of saints and relics that date back to its beginnings. A statue of St. James, of course, is prominently displayed above the north door of the cathedral. A marble statue of St. Joseph (pictured) dates to 1907, as does a statue of the Virgin Mary. (Courtesy of Archdiocese of Seattle.)

This Renaissance painting depicting the Madonna and Child surrounded by Saints Luke, Bartholomew, Lawrence, John the Baptist, Martin, and Sebastian dates to 1456. It is a rare and irreplaceable art piece by Neri di Bicci of Florence. (Courtesy of Archdiocese of Seattle.)

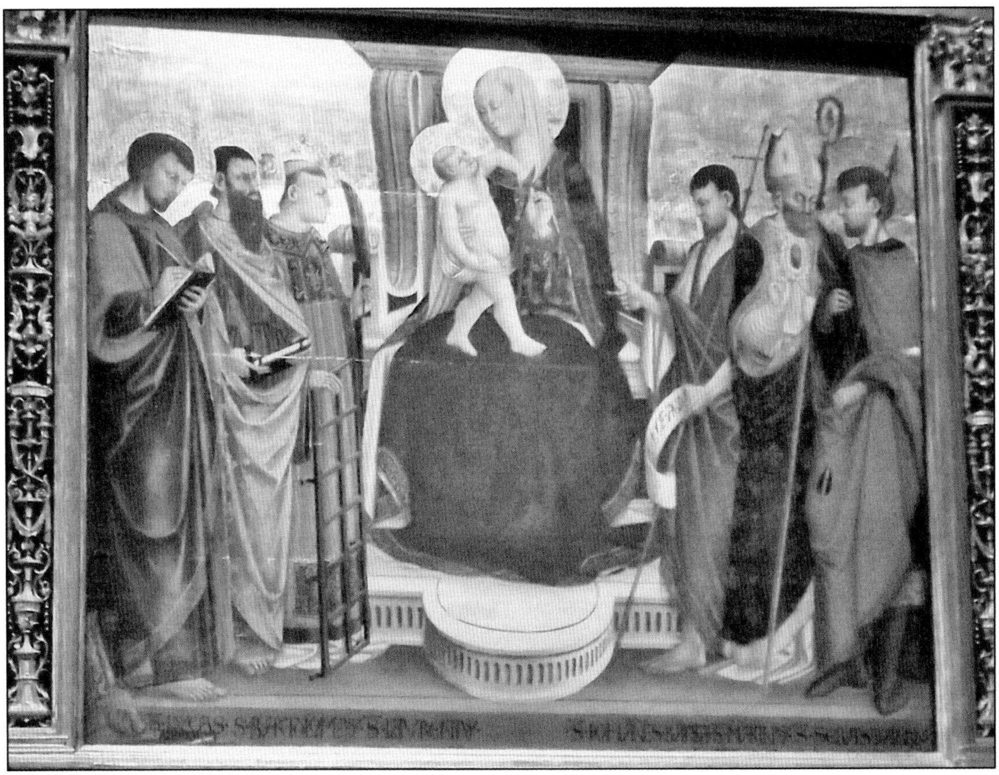

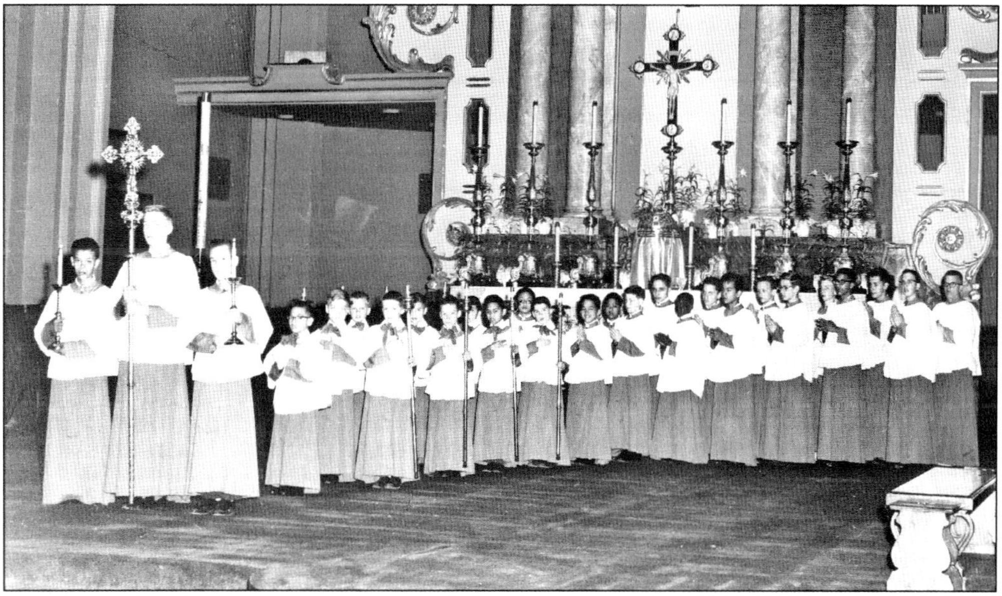

Through the years, St. James has been a place for spirituality, liturgy, music, and education, but the church has also been a place that stands for human rights and dignity. Bishop Gerald Shaughnessy, the fourth bishop of Seattle (1933–1950) guided parishioners through World War II and vigorously advocated against the internment of Japanese Americans during the war. (Courtesy of Archdiocese of Seattle.)

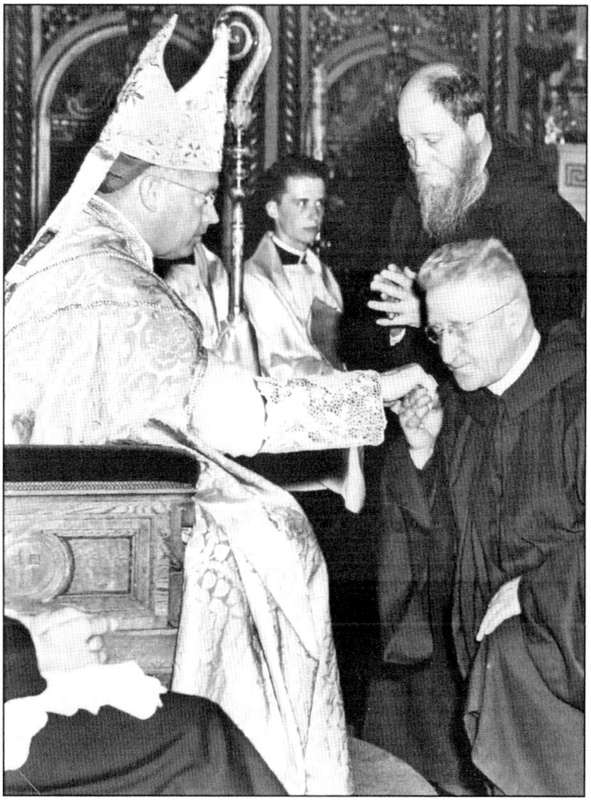

Thomas Connolly, the fifth bishop of Seattle (1950–1975), helped guide the church through the turbulent 1960s. He bravely supported the civil rights movement and labor and poverty issues. In February 1968, Seattle's Catholic Interracial Council hosted the first Interfaith Civil Rights Banquet. Archbishop Connolly addressed more than 2,000 people and challenged city leaders to support legislation on initiatives for open housing. He also reiterated that the church was committed to racial justice for all. He was honored with an award that night for his work on behalf of minorities. When Dr. Martin Luther King Jr. was assassinated on April 4, 1968, there was unrest and riots in many cities; always a man of prayer and peace, Archbishop Connolly was on the front lines urging everyone to respect and remember Dr. King's principles of love and nonviolence. (Courtesy of Archdiocese of Seattle.)

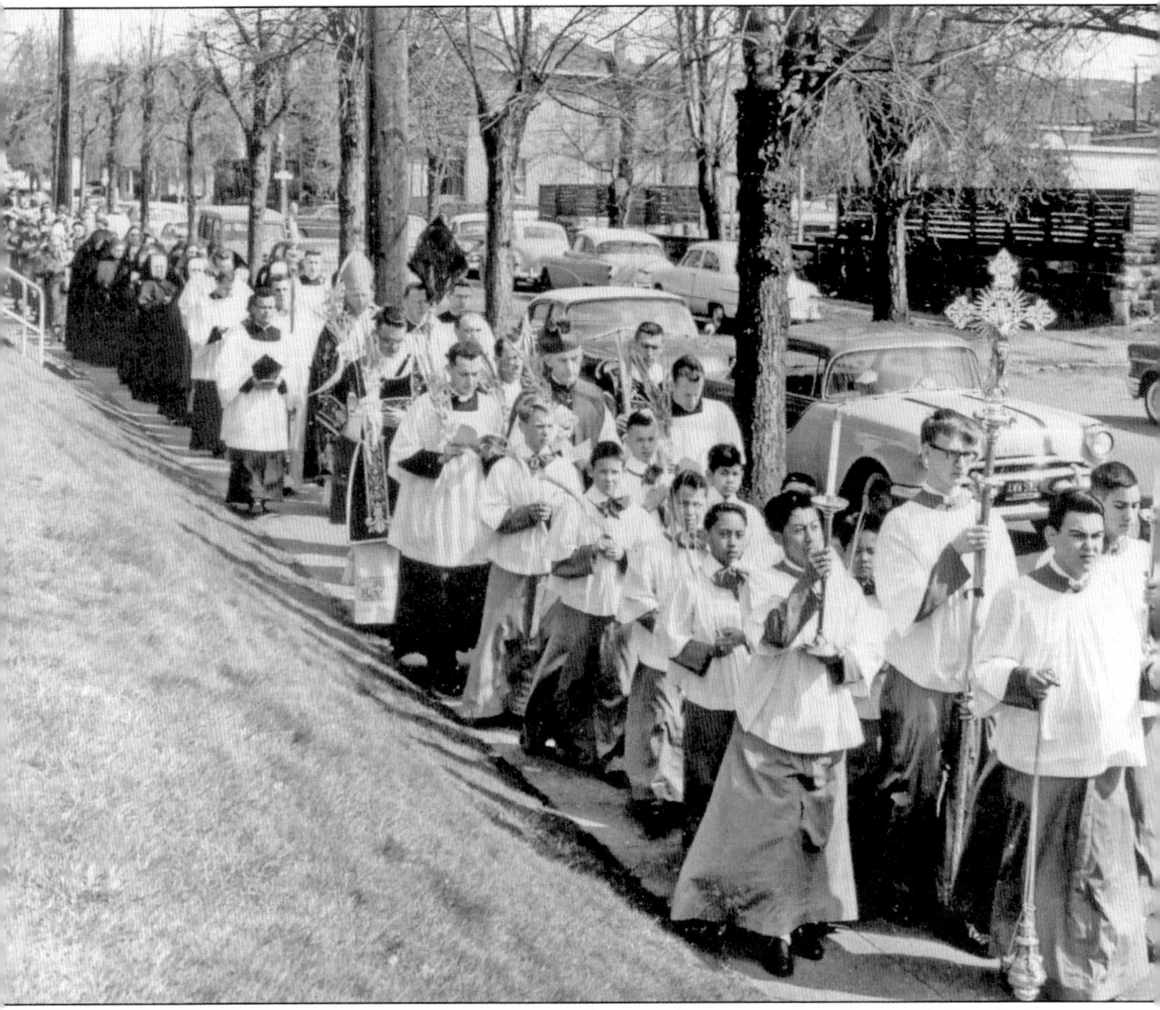

After the death of Dr. Martin Luther King, people prayed at various churches, including St. James, and more than 10,000 gathered to hold a memorial service on Palm Sunday, April 17. Archbishop Connolly gave the closing benediction asking for peace, understanding, and nonviolence. (Courtesy of Archdiocese of Seattle.)

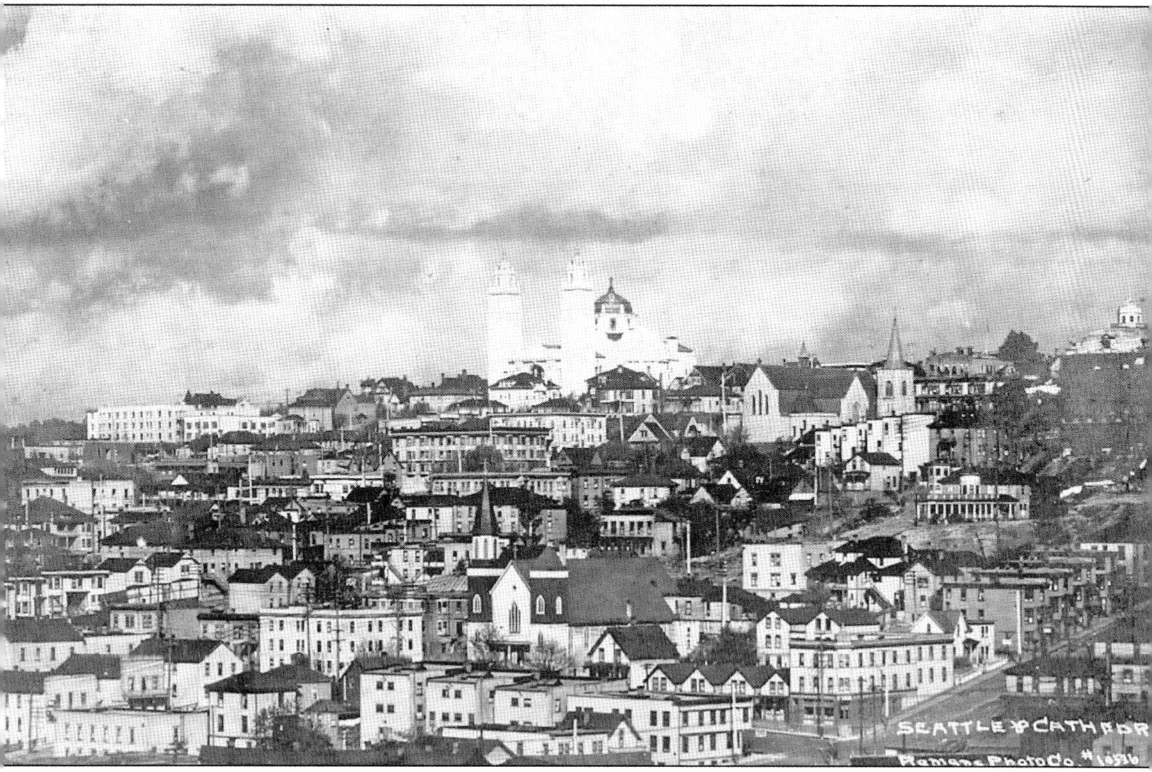

St. James Cathedral is seen in 1908. (Courtesy of Archdiocese of Seattle.)

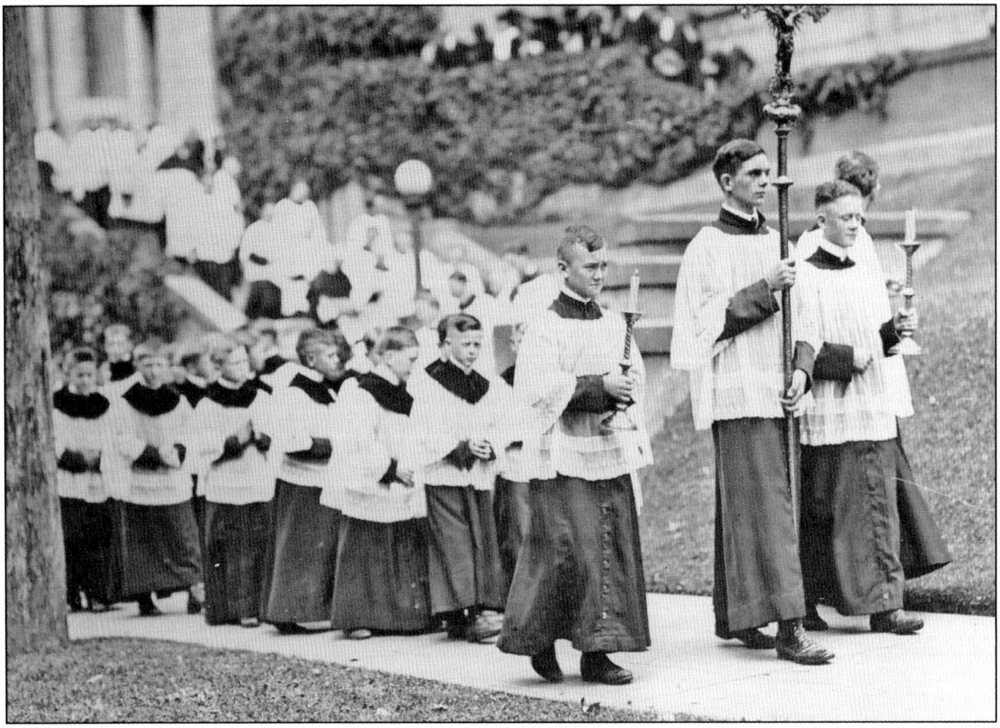

The procession above took place on Palm Sunday around 1920. Below, another procession enters St. James Cathedral at the installation of Archbishop Connolly in 1948. (Both, courtesy of Archdiocese of Seattle.)

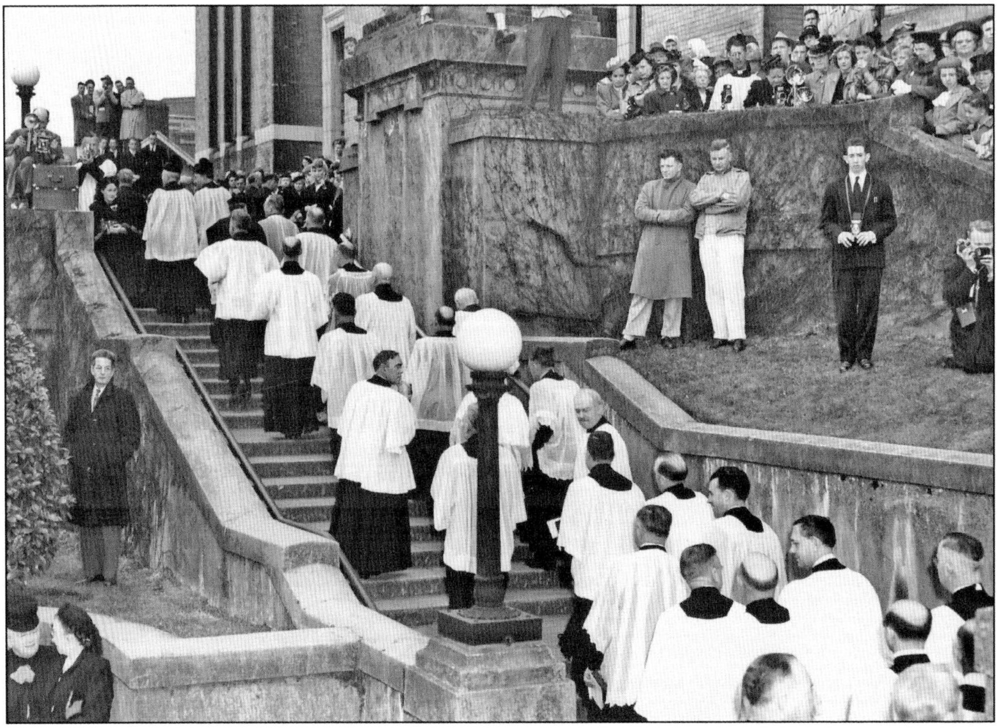

Two

Immaculate Conception Church

The Immaculate Conception Church was founded in 1891 and is the oldest standing Catholic church in Seattle.

The church was founded by 11 Jesuit priests, who were tasked with building the church, rectory, and a parochial school. The first church structure was built in 1893 at the corner of Ninth Avenue and Marion Street, now the location of Seattle University. The Jesuits were educators, so the church had a multipurpose design as a church and a school.

In 1904, the present church was built at Eighteenth Avenue and East Marion Street. It was completed in just six months and cost $65,000. The church was dedicated in December that year by Bishop Edward O'Dea, the bishop of Seattle. The beautiful structure has a grotto (a smaller replica of the famous grotto of Lourdes), ceiling murals, and carillon bells. Many of the church's artifacts are priceless and irreplaceable. The stained glass used in the windows is no longer available anywhere in the world. The wood communion rail, pulpit, and altar were carved by hand and painted by the Jesuit priests. There are also 22 statues that date to 1890–1920. The highest point of the dome reaches 150 feet. Behind the altars were living quarters for the Jesuits until the present rectory was built in 1912. The church could seat 950, the city's largest auditorium at the time. In addition to its historic landmark designation, the church was also designated a Seattle landmark on January 10, 1977, because of its historic architectural design and how it exemplifies the ever-changing heritage of the city. The old church was repurposed as a school for secondary and college students and was named Seattle College.

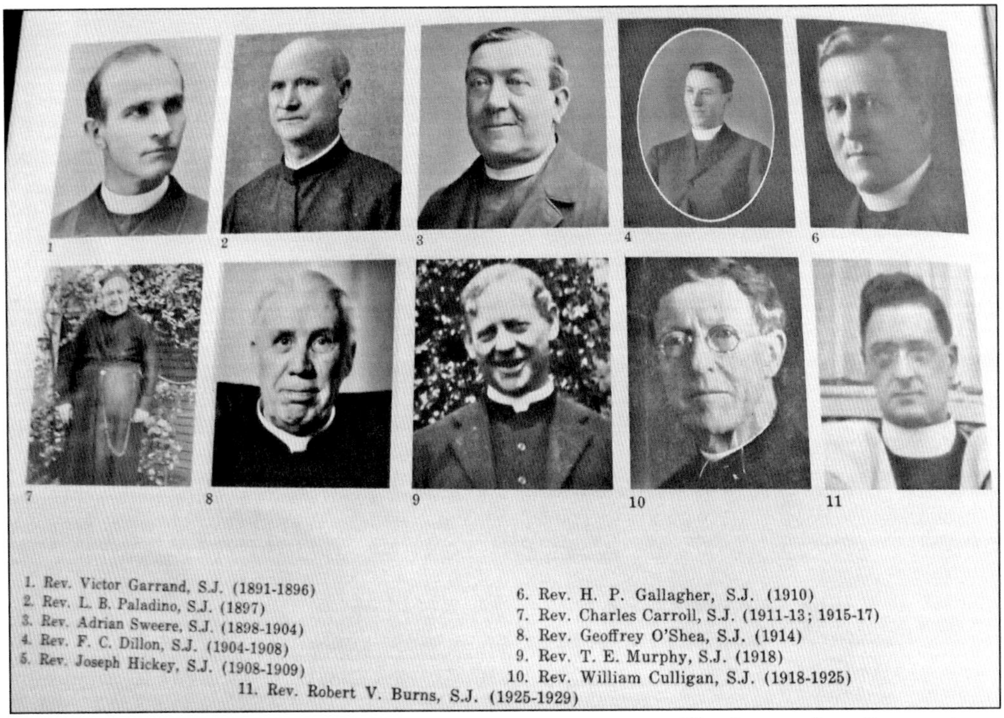

The Immaculate Conception Church was founded in 1891 by 11 Jesuit priests, who ran the church until 1929 on the grounds of what is now Seattle University. The church was Seattle's third parish, with Sacred Heart and Our Lady of Good Help preceding it. (Courtesy of Immaculate Conception Church.)

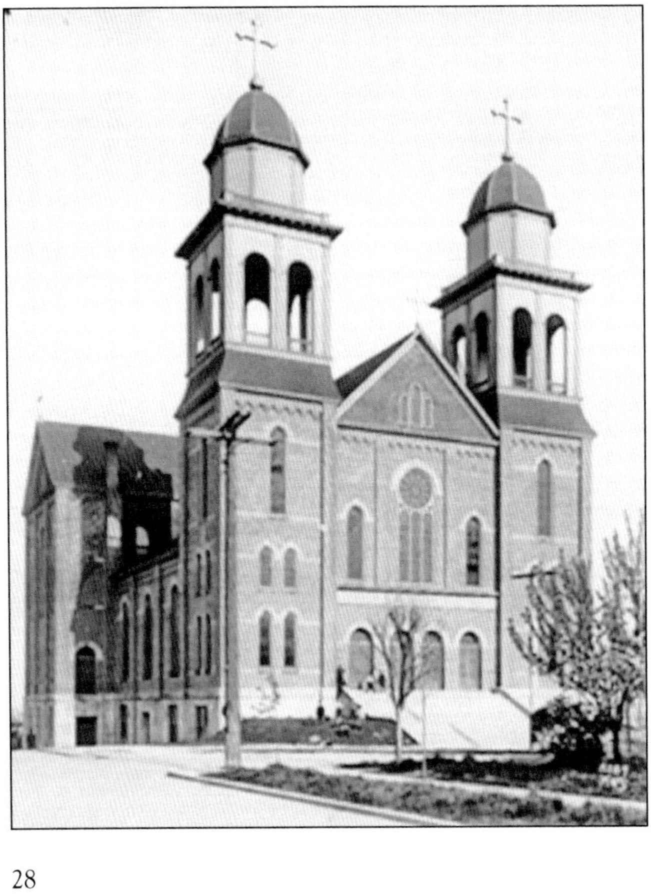

The Immaculate Conception Church was declared a national historic landmark in 1974. The church's interior has retained much of its historic look dating to the 1890s. (Courtesy of Immaculate Conception Church.)

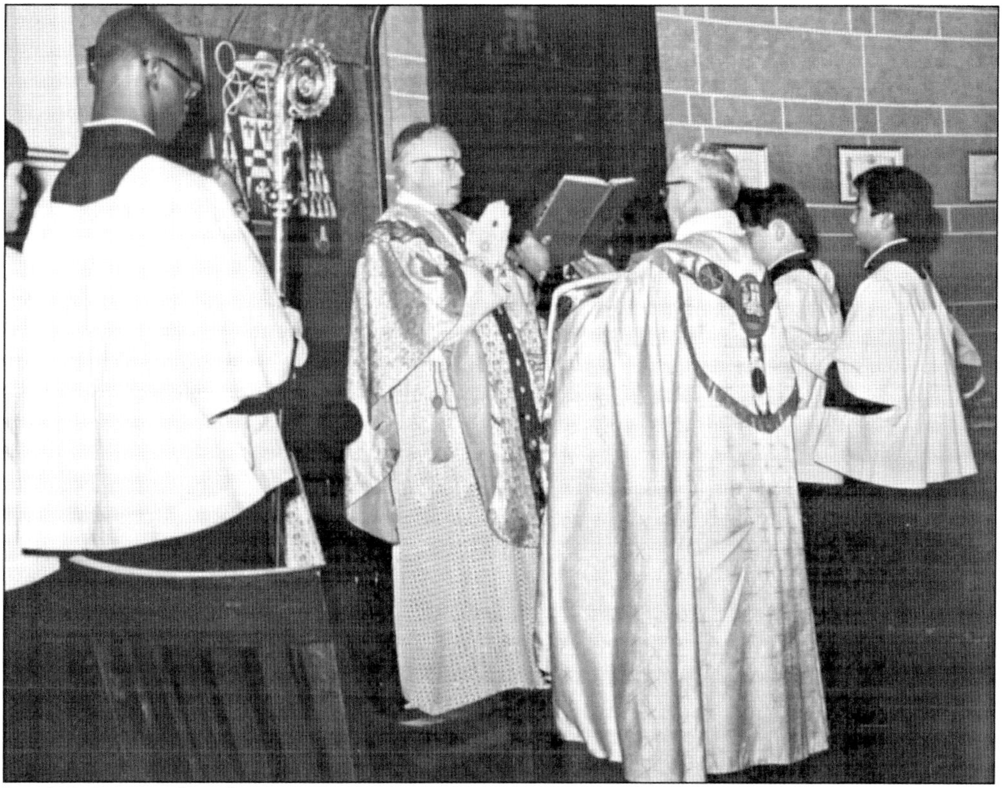

In 1918, Immaculate Conception was more than $165,000 in debt. One of the parishioners, a banker name Frank M. Sullivan, approached Pastor William Culligan about forming a "Dollar-A-Sunday" program where members used envelopes to contribute to the church. The envelope system spread throughout the diocese and the nation. Within a few years, the church's debt was paid off and there was enough money to reestablish the high school, repair the roof, and purchase a new home for the sisters, thanks mostly to the envelope system. (Courtesy of Immaculate Conception Church.)

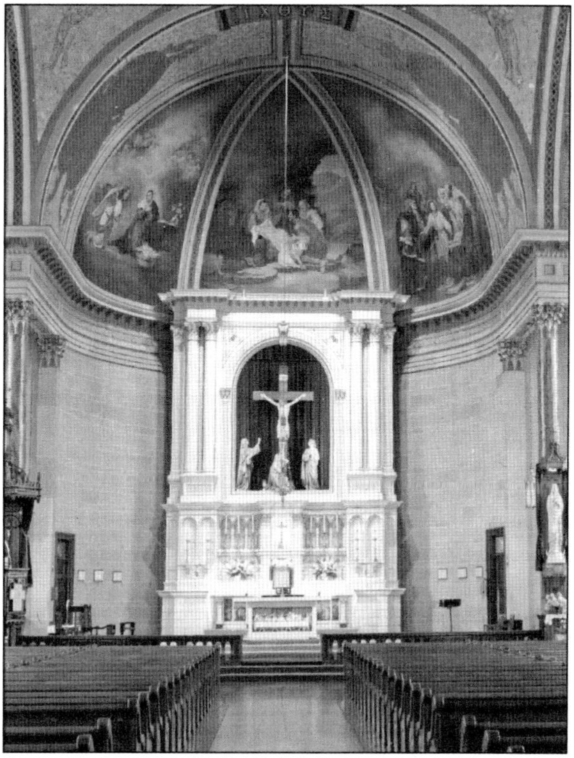

The church's grotto consists of ceiling murals, carillon bells, and irreplaceable stained glass windows. Jesuit priests hand-carved the communion rail, pulpit, and altar. The highest point of the dome reaches 150 feet. (Courtesy of Immaculate Conception Church.)

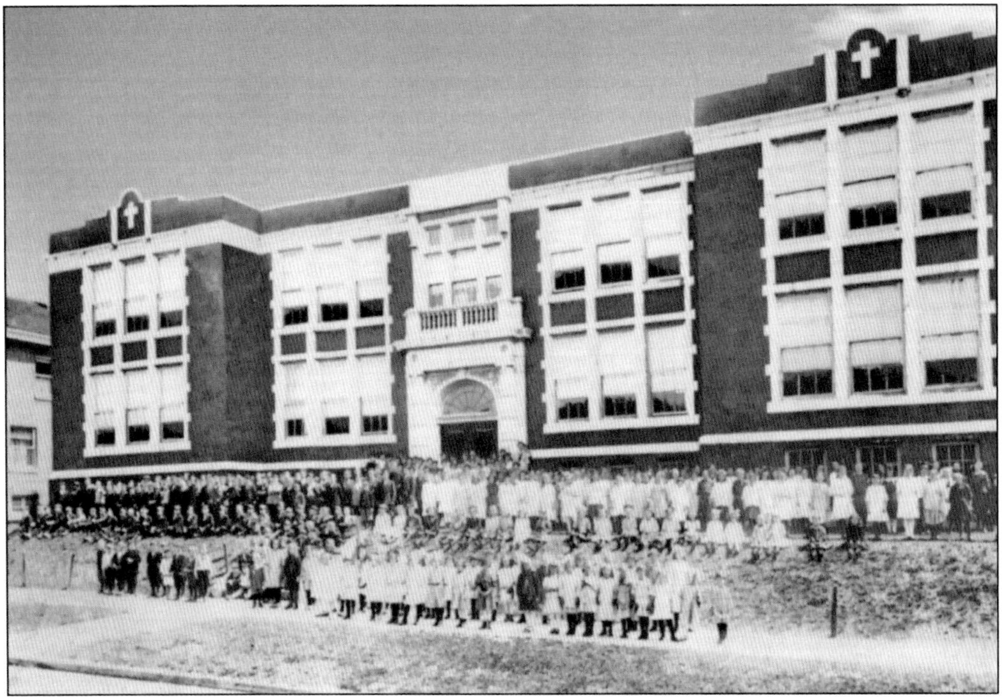

The Immaculate Conception Parish established the first parochial school in Seattle. The Sisters of the Holy Name were instrumental in establishing and operating the parochial schools. They opened a school for girls in 1880 and a school for boys in 1890. (Courtesy of Immaculate Conception Church.)

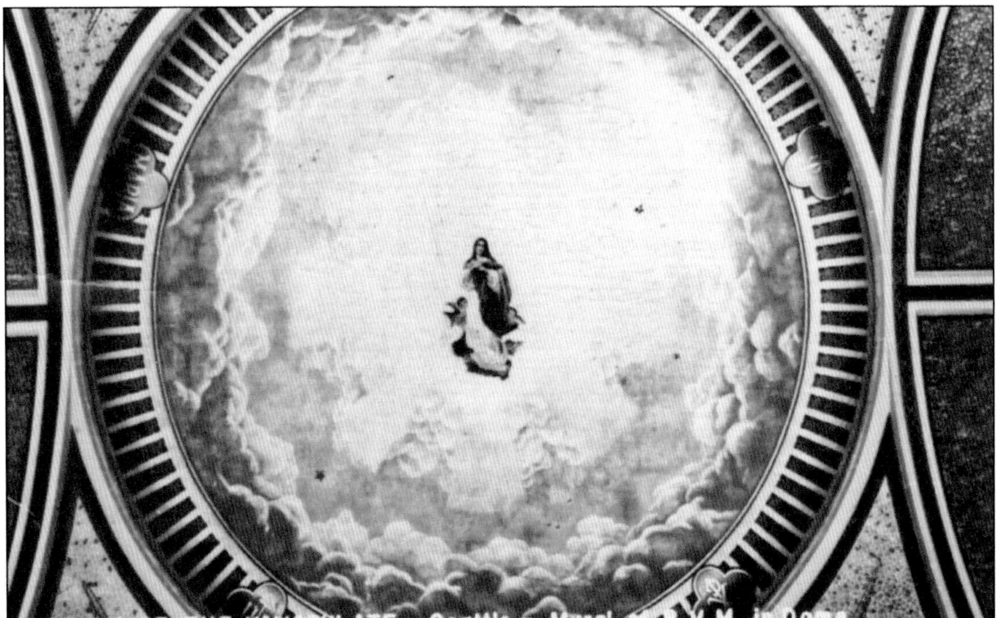

When the Immaculate Conception Church was established in 1891, the Sisters of the Holy Name remained to teach at the parish's parochial school, changing the name to the Immaculate Conception School. (Courtesy of Immaculate Conception Church.)

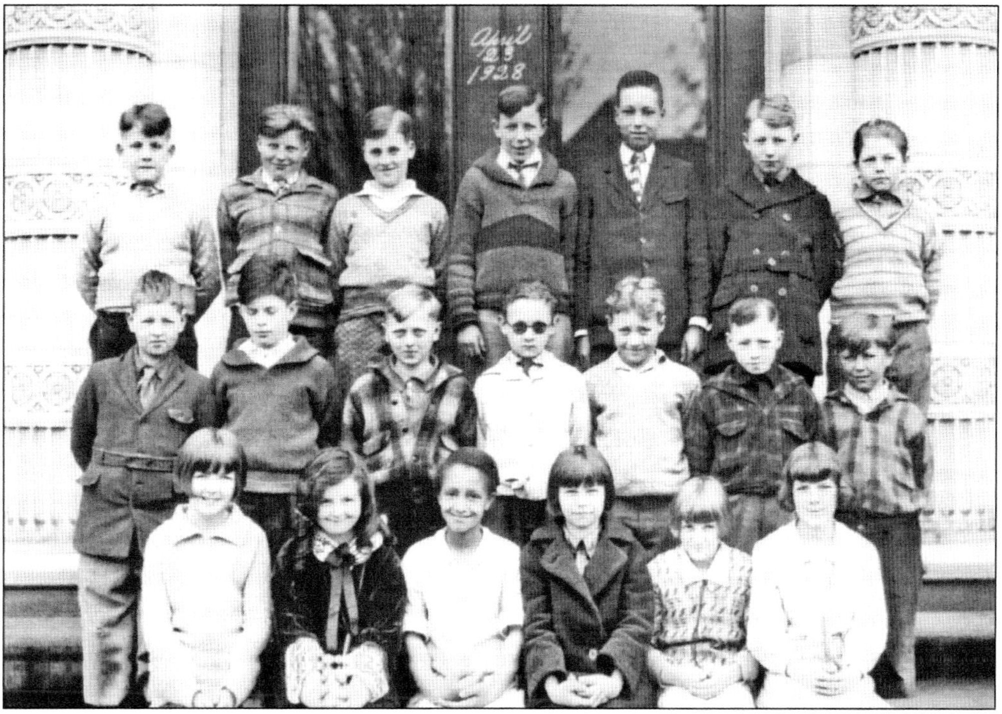

In 1895, a new school was built at Broadway and Marion Street. Since the Jesuits were teachers and educators, the new location was planned as both a church and a school. The school was a two-tiered system: the Broadway and Marion location (now Seattle College) was used to teach high school boys, and a different location, known as the WCTU (Women's Christian Temperance Union) Building, was used by the nuns to teach lower-grade boys and girls. (Courtesy of Immaculate Conception Church.)

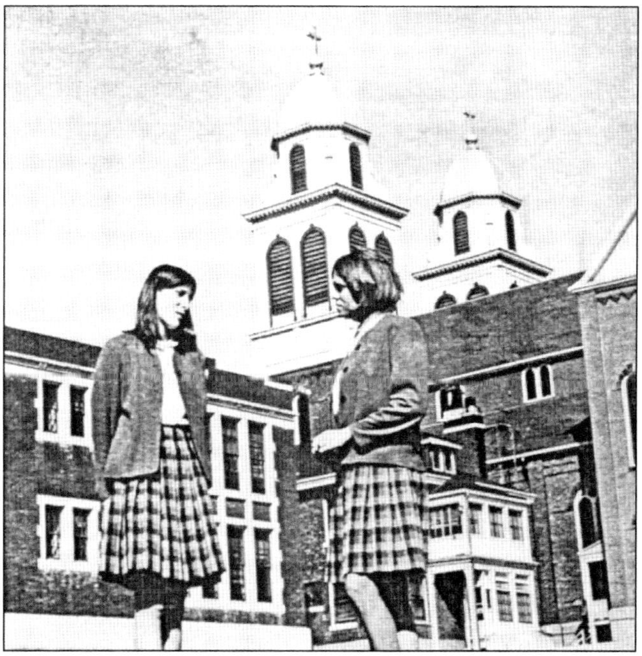

Enrollment for the lower-grade classes increased exponentially and eventually outgrew the WCTU space. In 1902, St. Rose Academy was opened on land that the nuns purchased. The school became independent of the parish. There was no parish school for grade schoolers from 1902 to 1906. However, the Jesuit priests were dedicated to teaching all students and wanted to reopen the parish school. On March 26, 1906, two sisters from St. Rose agreed to operate an elementary school in the basement of the Immaculate Conception Parish basement consisting of 65 boys and girls. (Courtesy of Immaculate Conception Church.)

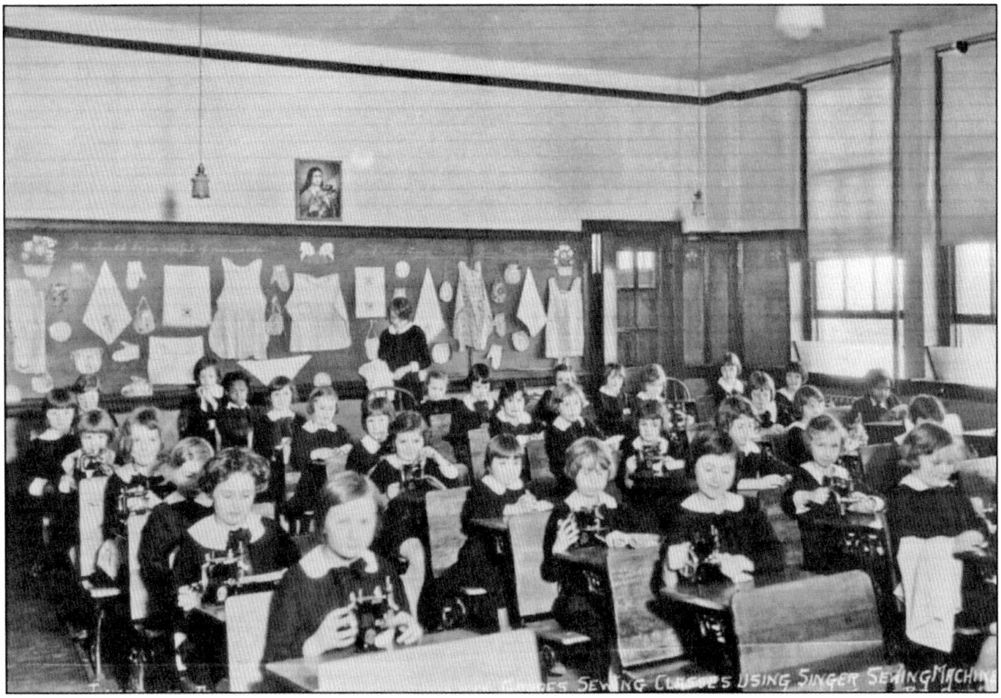

Eventually all the grammar school children were transferred from St. Rose to the parish school, and St. Rose Academy was closed in 1911. (Courtesy of Immaculate Conception Church.)

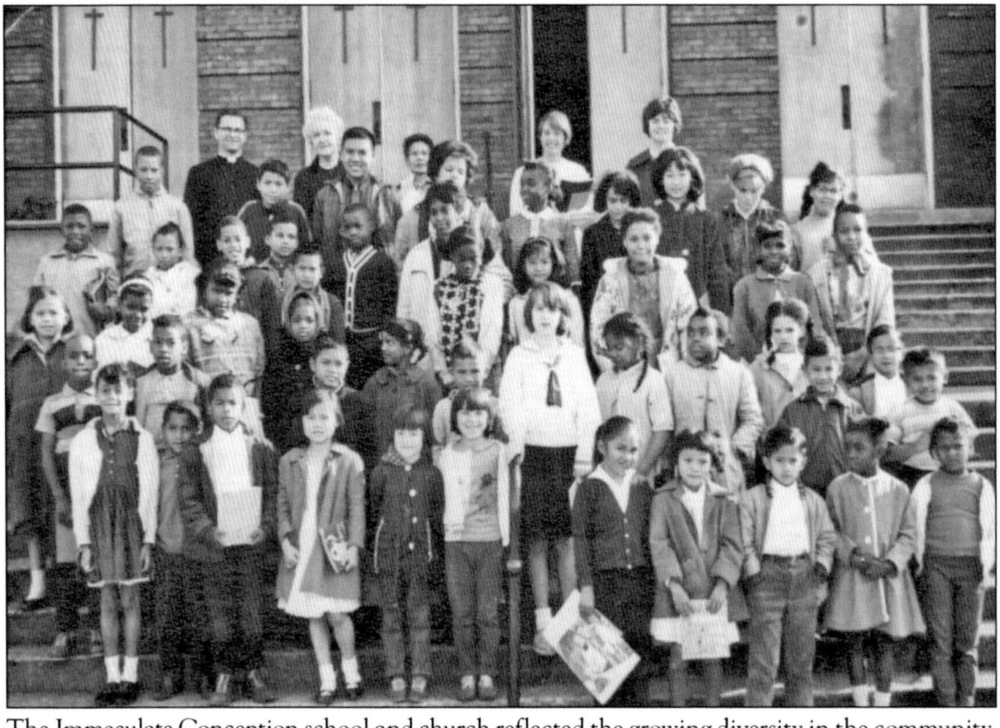

The Immaculate Conception school and church reflected the growing diversity in the community. (Courtesy of Immaculate Conception Church.)

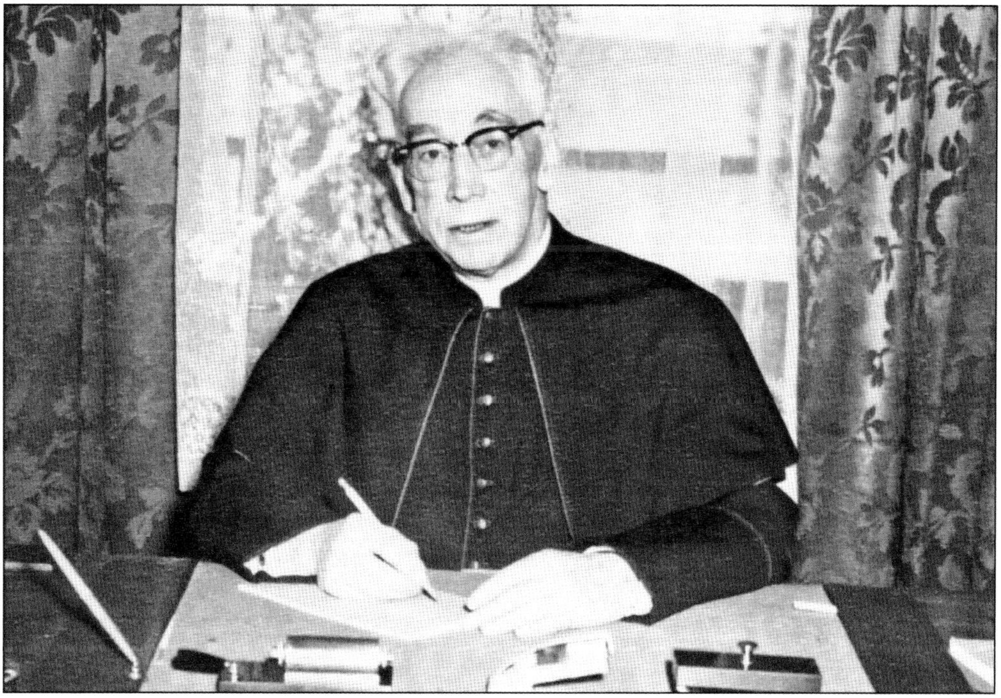

In 1929, the Jesuit priests asked the Archdiocese of Seattle to take over the pastorship of the Immaculate Conception Church. The priests were busy operating two other parishes, a high school, and a college. In response, on September 22, 1929, Monsignor Theodore Ryan became pastor of the Immaculate Conception Church, where he would remain for 31 years until his death in 1960. Monsignor Ryan was born in Seattle on August 11, 1890, and was the first Seattle native to be ordained to the diocesan priesthood. He was a student at the Sacred Heart School and Seattle College. He attended the Grand Seminary in Montreal (Bishop O'Dea's alma mater), where he was ordained on December 19, 1914. (Courtesy of Immaculate Conception Church.)

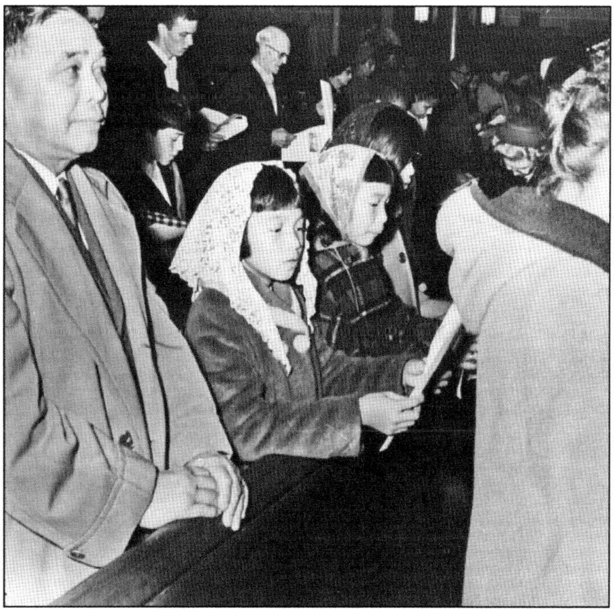

During his tenure, Monsignor Ryan guided the church through the Great Depression and a dramatic change in the church's racial and economic make-up. That diversity was nurtured and welcomed. Monsignor Ryan continued to meet the needs of his parishioners by advocating for better race relations and fair labor laws and served as an arbitrator on several committees. The congregation moved from predominately white to a more diverse congregation of African Americans, Japanese, Filipinos, and Native Americans. Monsignor Ryan became ill immediately after mass on January 18, 1960, and died five days later. (Courtesy of Immaculate Conception Church.)

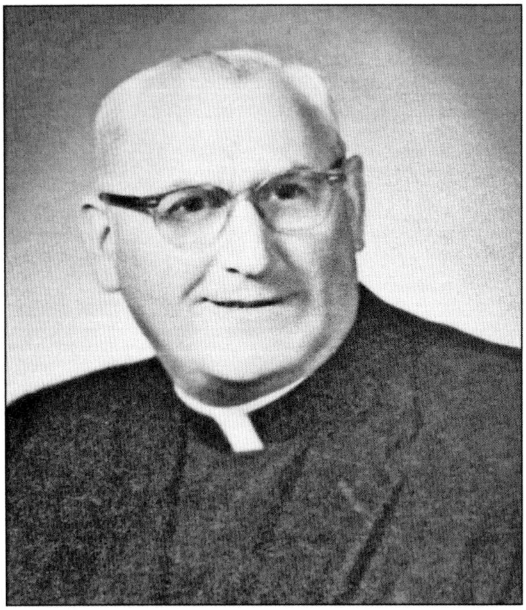

Over the next 50 years, many new pastors served at the Immaculate Conception. Fr. Edmund Long served from 1960 to 1967. (Courtesy of Immaculate Church.)

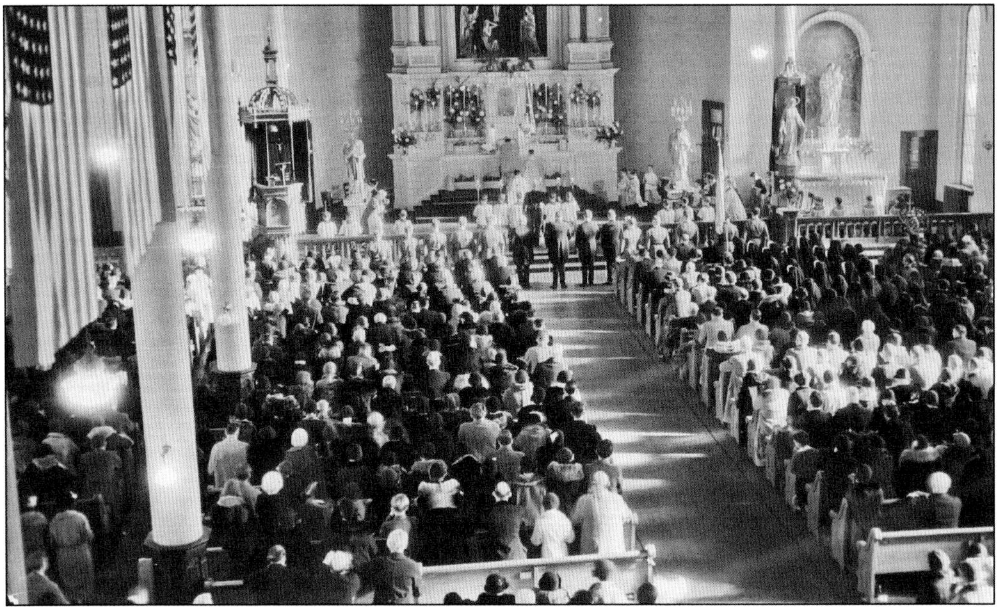

During the 1960s, minorities, women, the poor, young people, and the working class were challenging the status quo. Under the leadership of Pastor D. Harvey McIntyre, Immaculate Conception became known as "the Civil Rights Parish." Pastor McIntyre advocated not only for minorities but also for the poor, children, the terminally ill, the disabled, and anyone on the outskirts of society. He fought for equal access to quality education for all students. Pastor McIntyre was born in Vancouver, British Columbia, studied at St. Edward's Seminary in 1951, and continued in his studies at St. Thomas Seminary. He was ordained in 1959 and earned his canon law degree in 1963 from Catholic University, after which he took over as pastor and administrator of Immaculate Conception. He served for 10 years on the Seattle Human Rights Commission and was the director of Project Equality, an affirmative action program of the Archdiocese of Seattle. (Courtesy of Immaculate Conception Church.)

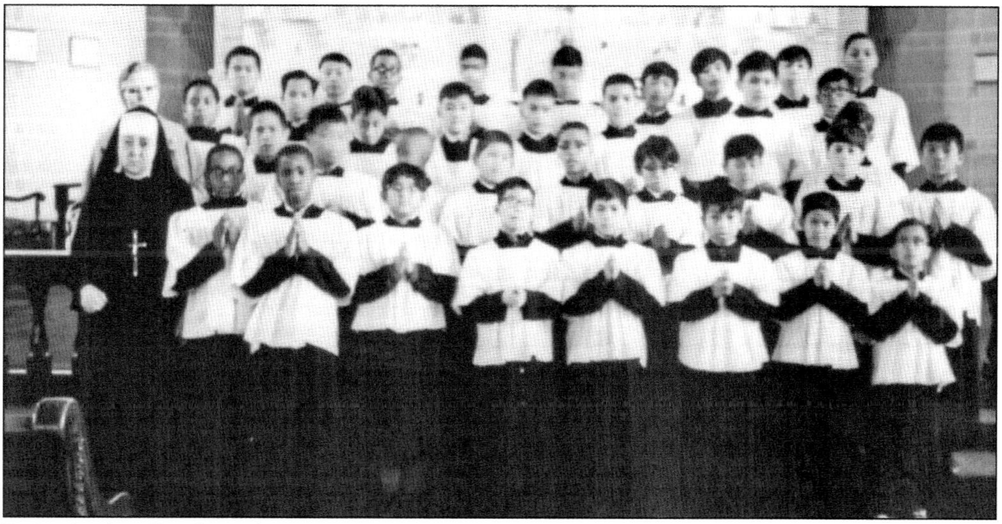

Fr. Michael Holland was the pastor from 1973 to 1977, when the church's population began to decline. Fr. John Cornelius served from 1978 to 1997 and was the first black pastor in the Archdiocese of Seattle. In 1982, a fire caused severe damage to the church. According to the *Seattle Times*, the church's basement was destroyed, and the main part of the church's interior was damaged by smoke. Other pastors over the years included Fr. Armando Guzman, Fr. William Herrick, Fr. Emmanuel Iweh, Fr. Fabian MacDonald (who served for 10 years), and Fr. Victor Olvida. The present pastor is Fr. Maurice Mamba. (Courtesy of Immaculate Conception Church.)

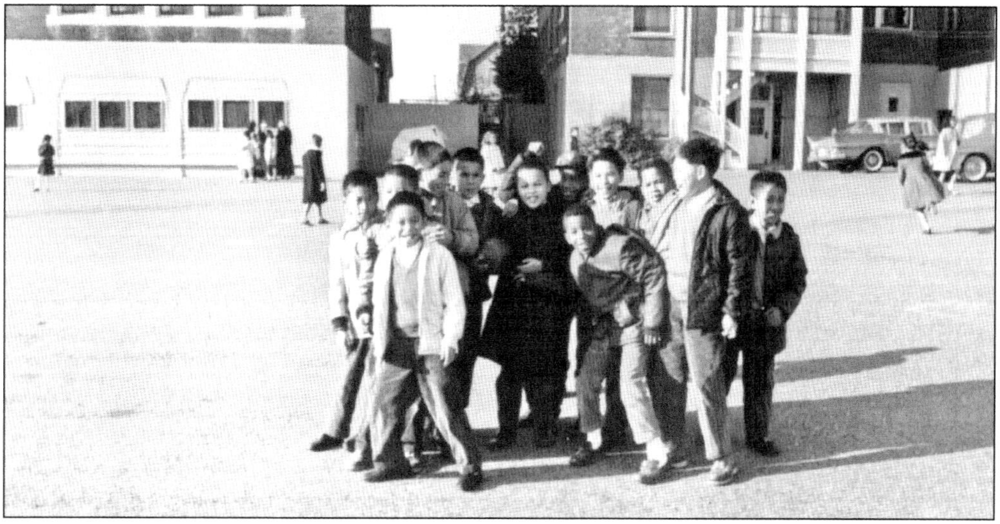

In 1912, the Sisters of the Immaculate Conception took residence at the first official convent, at Eighteenth Avenue and Columbia Street. While they taught at the parish school, the nuns lived at the Holy Name Academy. When the school was moved to the St. Rose Academy in 1901, the location became a residence and school. The parish school closed for a time but reopened in 1906, and the nuns who taught at the reopened school had to commute again. The following year, after the sisters took residence at Eighteenth Avenue and Columbia Street, a larger house was rented for the nuns across from the school. The growing student population needed more teachers. Soon the staff outgrew that location, and in 1919, a permanent residence was purchased at Sixteenth Avenue and East Columbia Street. The building remains home today to 19 sisters. (Courtesy of Immaculate Conception Church.)

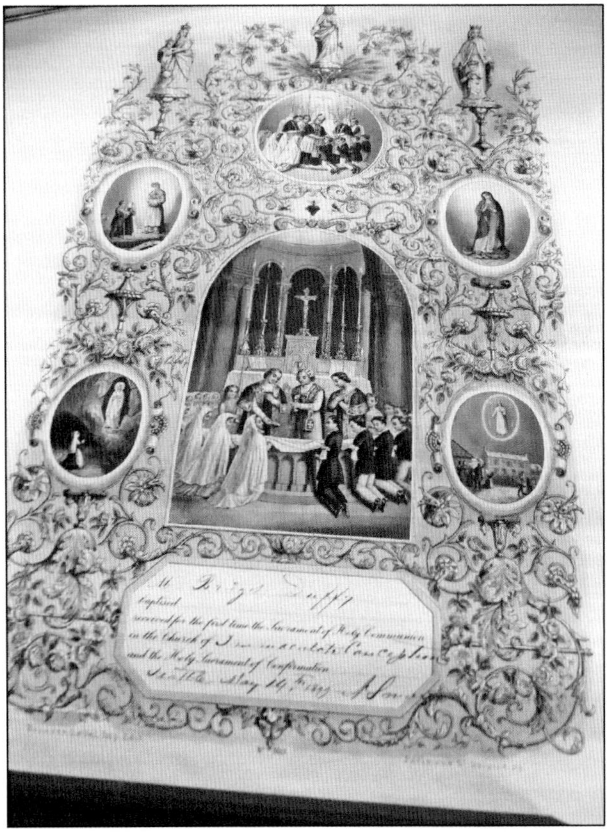

This original communion certificate from 1897 was donated to the church's archives. (Courtesy of Immaculate Conception Church.)

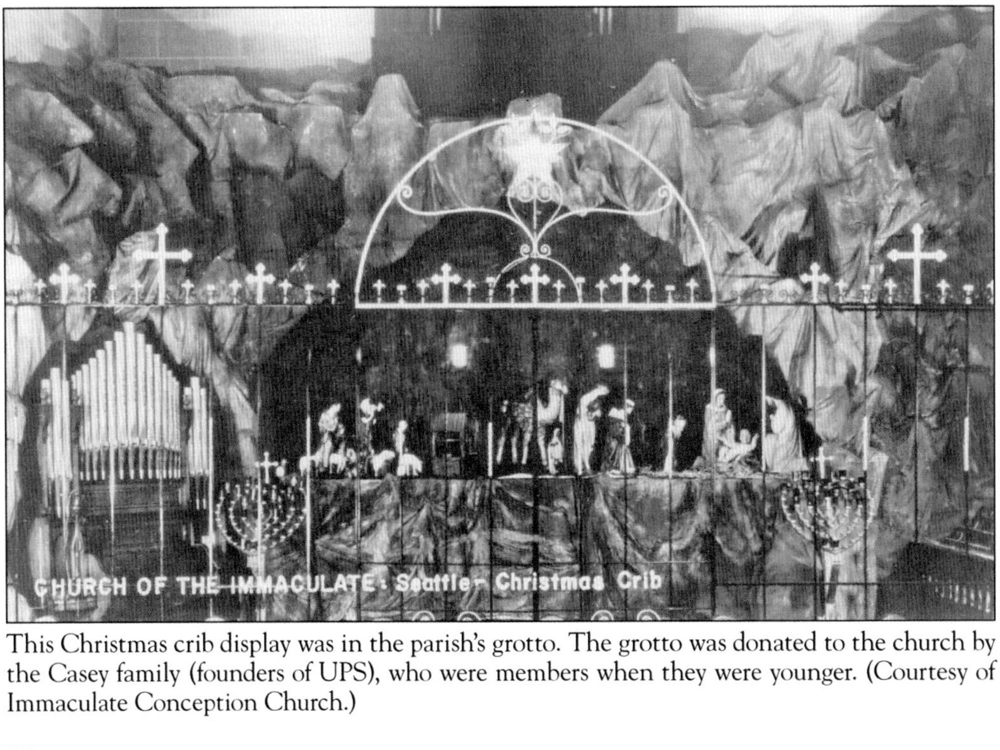

This Christmas crib display was in the parish's grotto. The grotto was donated to the church by the Casey family (founders of UPS), who were members when they were younger. (Courtesy of Immaculate Conception Church.)

Three

Trinity Parish Episcopal Church

Trinity Parish is Seattle's first Episcopal parish. It was the fourth church organized by what is now the Episcopal Diocese of Olympia. The very first service, on July 14, 1855, was officiated by Rev. John McCarty. However, the parish did not actually move forward until 1866. Building a church here at that time could have been considered risky, because in 1865, Seattle could best be described as a pioneer town with a population of only 500 to 1,000 people. Trinity Parish constructed its first permanent building in 1870 at Third Avenue and Jefferson Street. The parish didn't have a pastor for several years, but a series of temporary pastors led the congregation.

In 1878, Trinity received its first rector, Rev. George Herbert Watson, who immediately got to work. Reverend Watson served the parish for 18 years until he died in 1896 at the age of 50. Reverend Watson's legacy of outreach and inclusiveness remains a cornerstone of the church's core values. Those values have been embraced and expanded upon by all subsequent pastors.

One of the church's missions has always been outreach, and within the first 10 years, Trinity established five mission churches along with Grace Hospital, one of the first hospitals in Seattle. The 40-bed, two-story facility opened in 1887 at the corner of Eighth Avenue and James Street. The hospital closed in 1894, and the building was torn down in 1905.

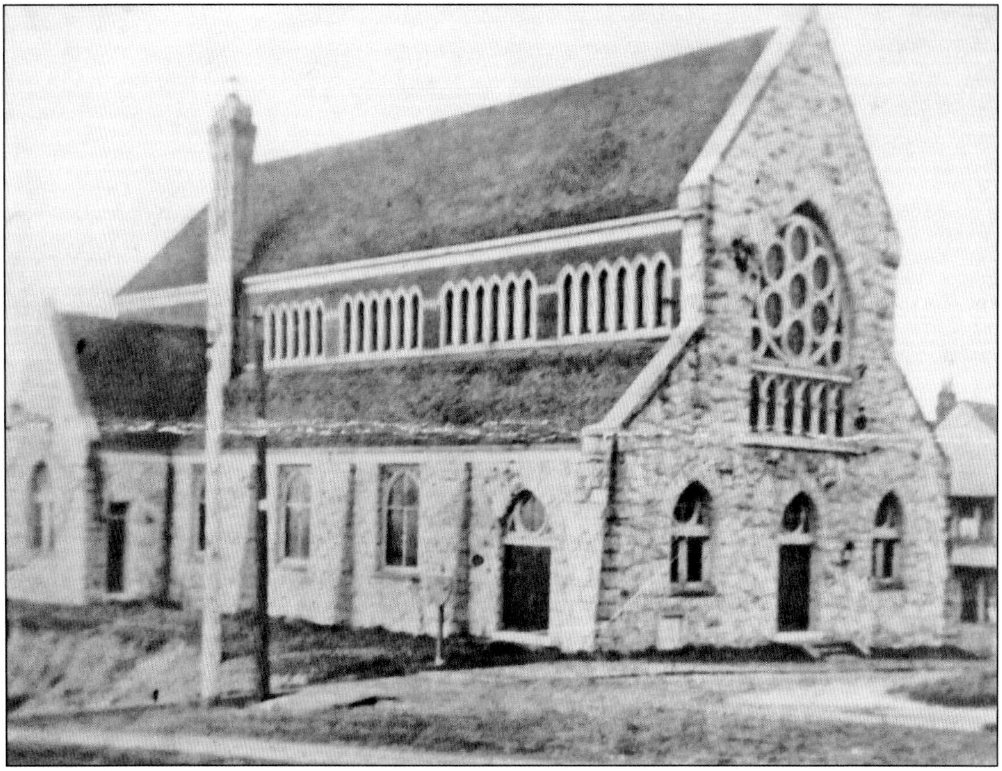

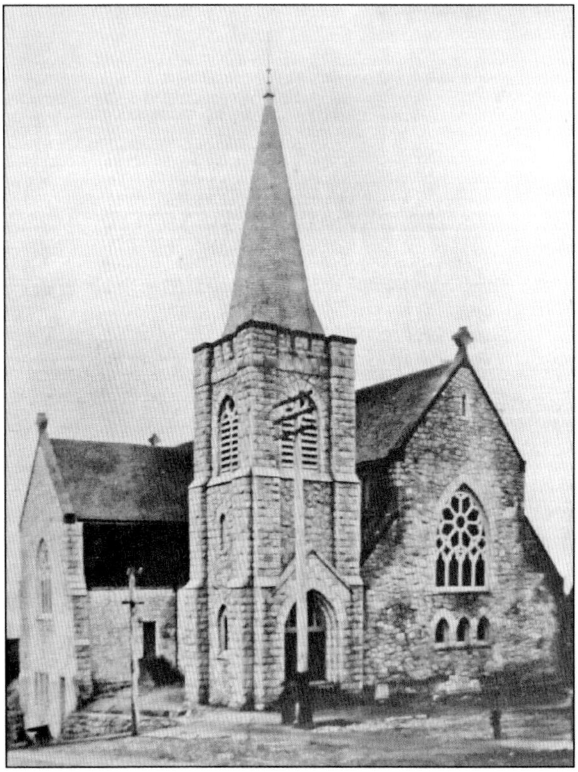

Tragedy struck Seattle in 1889; the year of the Great Seattle Fire. On June 6, the downtown area was engulfed by a raging fire that destroyed the entire central business district. The fire started at a woodworking shop while an employee was heating glue over a gasoline fire. The glue boiled over, and fire spread to the wood floors and quickly grew out of control. Efforts to stop the fire were fruitless. When the fire reached Third Avenue, Trinity Parish was standing directly in its path. The wood-frame church burned quickly. (Courtesy of Trinity Parish archives.)

The church and parishioners were undaunted by the destruction and quickly rebuilt. In 1892, a new church was erected at Eighth Avenue and James Street, the church's present location. (Courtesy of Trinity Parish archives.)

In 1897, Trinity welcomed its second rector, Rev. Herbert Henry Gowan. He was born in 1864 and served Trinity as rector until 1914. Reverend Gowan was a forward-thinking visionary and a voracious reader who was reported to read a book a day. He also spoke several languages, including Arabic, Chinese, English, Hebrew, and Japanese. (Courtesy of Trinity Parish archives.)

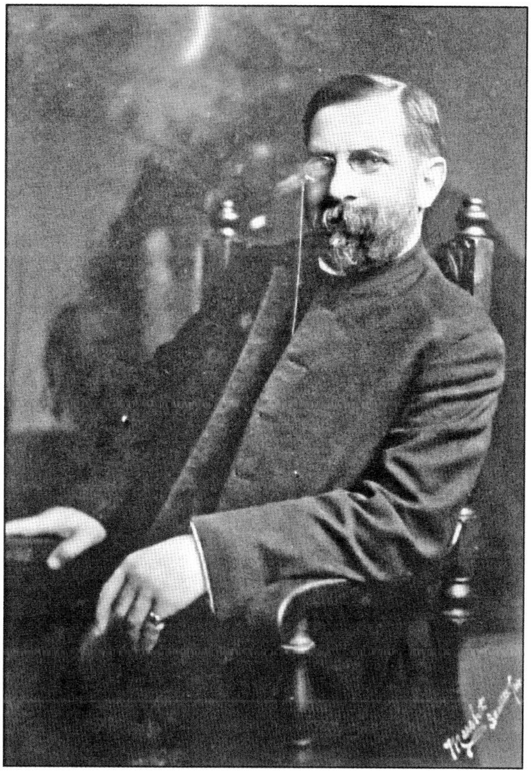

Reverend Gowan left Trinity Parish in 1914 to work at the University of Washington. The Department of Asian Languages and Literature is housed in Gowan Hall, named in his honor. He died in 1960. (Courtesy of Trinity Parish archives.)

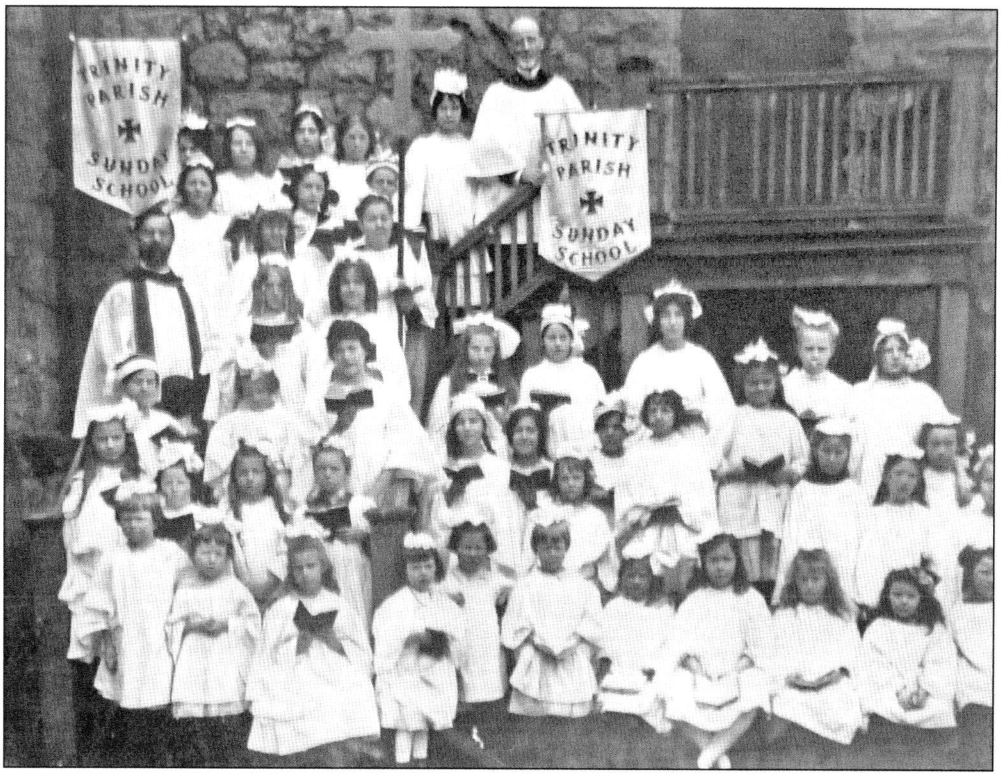

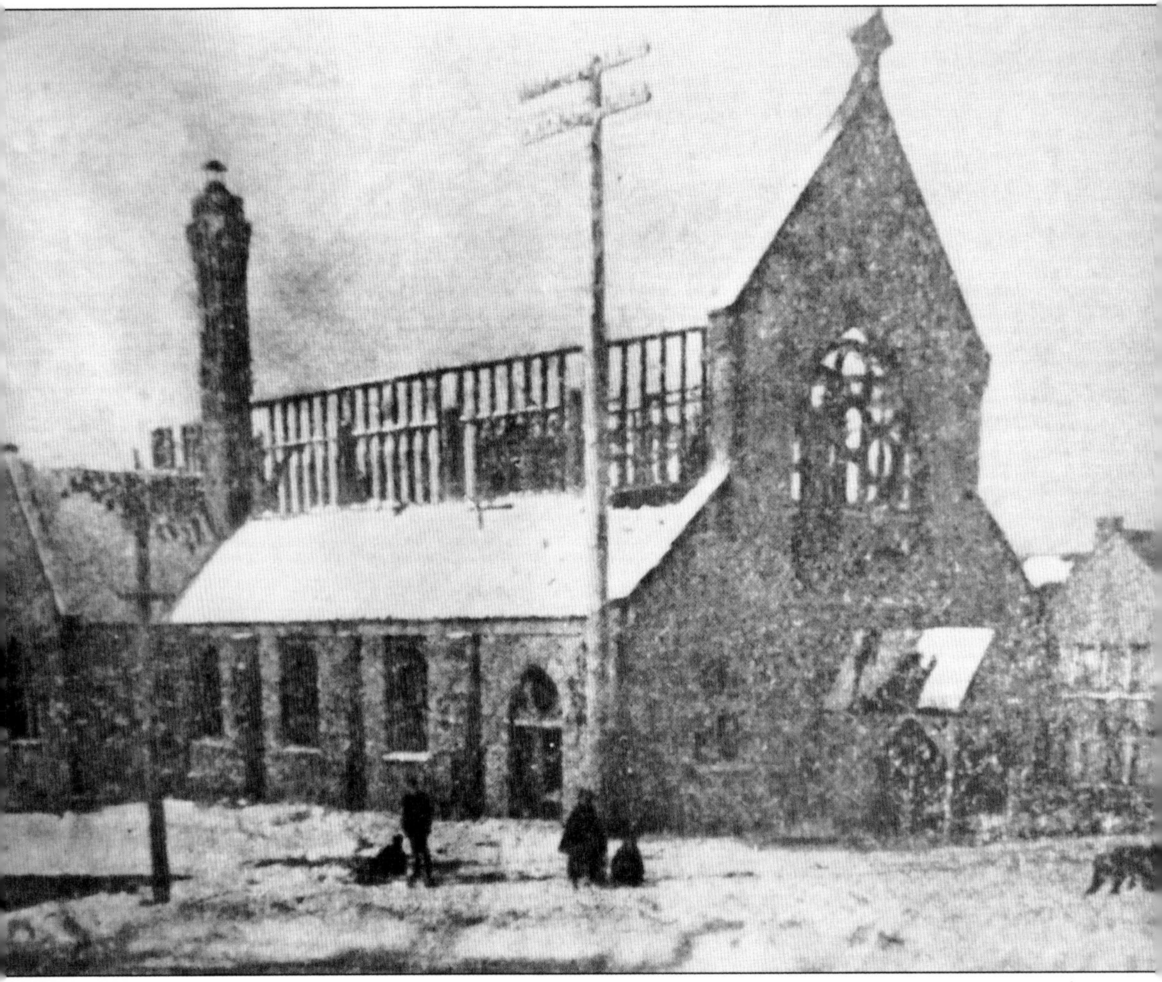

In 1902, Trinity Parish was struck again by a calamitous fire that gutted the church; only the walls were left standing. Under the strong leadership of Reverend Gowan, the congregation again rallied and rebuilt in its present state in the tradition of English stone churches. It expanded its space, added German stained-glass windows and an Italian marble altar, and reopened. In 1930, the church further remodeled by adding a kitchen, a gym, a parish hall, and classrooms through a generous donation by the Cox family. In 1903, Rector Gowan launched a mission (now St. Peter's Parish) to serve Seattle's growing Japanese American community. (Courtesy of Trinity Parish archives.)

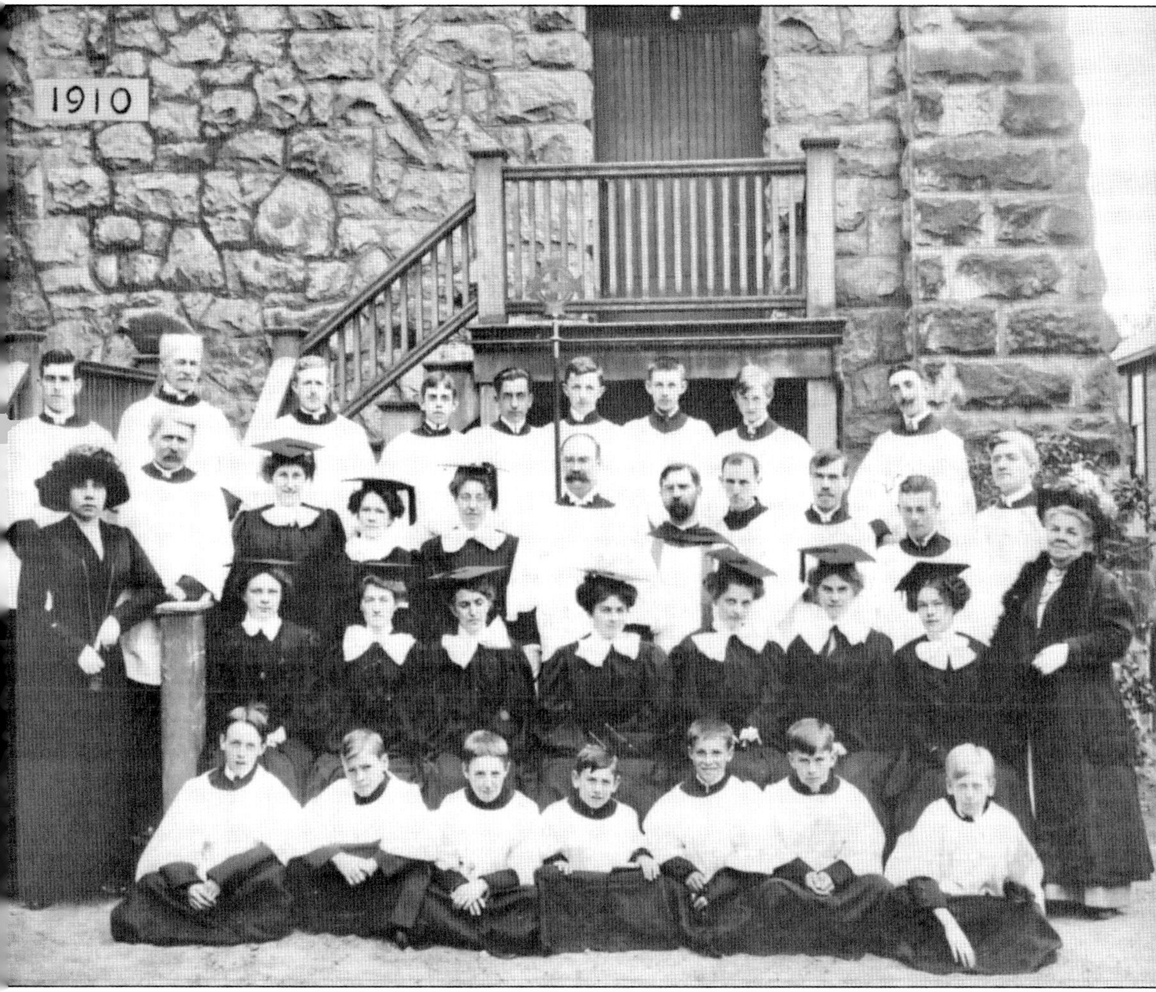

A Sunday school class is pictured in front of the church in 1910. (Courtesy of Trinity Parish archives.)

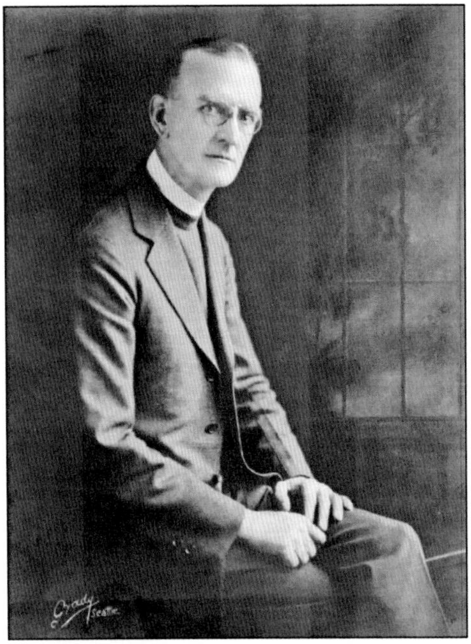

Canon William H. Bliss became the church's third pastor in 1914 and remained until his death in 1924. Canon Bliss was a social advocate who guided the church through the First World War. In 1922, he became chairman of the diocese's social service commission and advocated for a minimum wage law for women. He also established the White Cross Society to fight drug addiction. Canon Bliss received national praise for his efforts. Fr. Stanley Mook succeeded Bliss and guided the church through the Great Depression. He continued the urban ministries, but a dispute with how he handled church funds resulted in the church asking for his resignation. He sued, and a settlement was reached when he agreed to be reassigned to Vancouver. In 1934, Fr. Lewis Bailey replaced him as the church's rector. (Courtesy of Trinity Parish archives.)

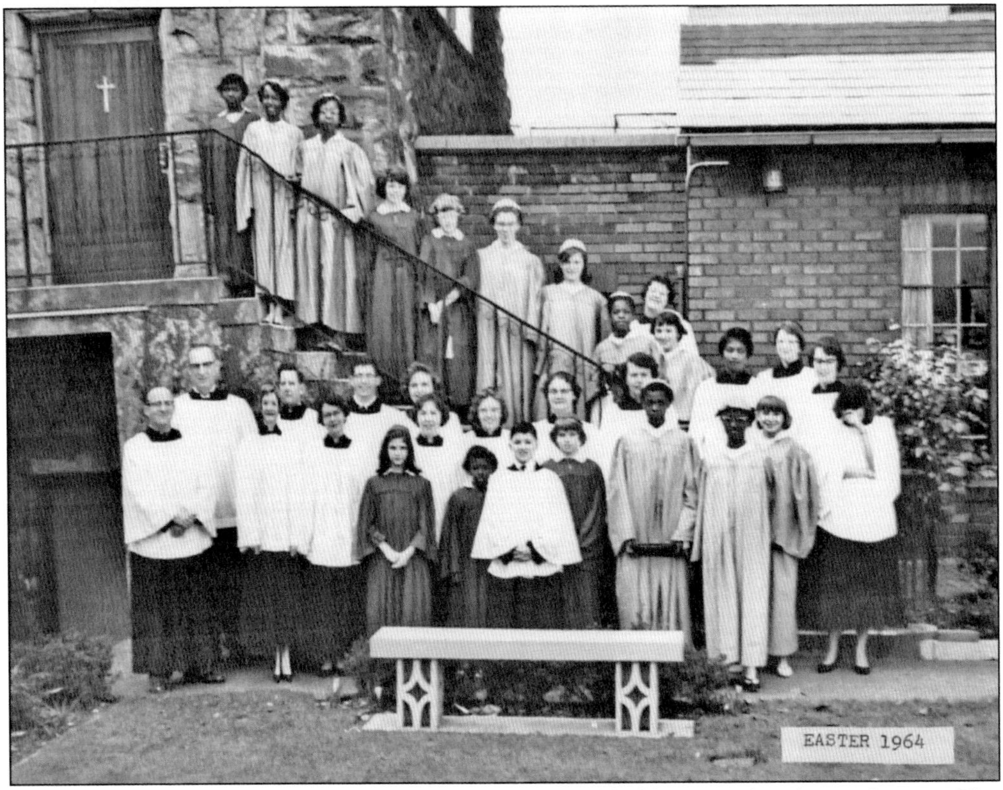

During the 1960s, Trinity's congregation waned considerably, like most churches in the area. The next few rectors, John Craine (1944–1950), John Wyatt (1950–1957), and Paul Langpaas (1957–1982), continued in their ministries and grew the congregation through outreach. Throughout the years, Trinity has remained true to its roots as a mission church. (Courtesy of Trinity Parish archives.)

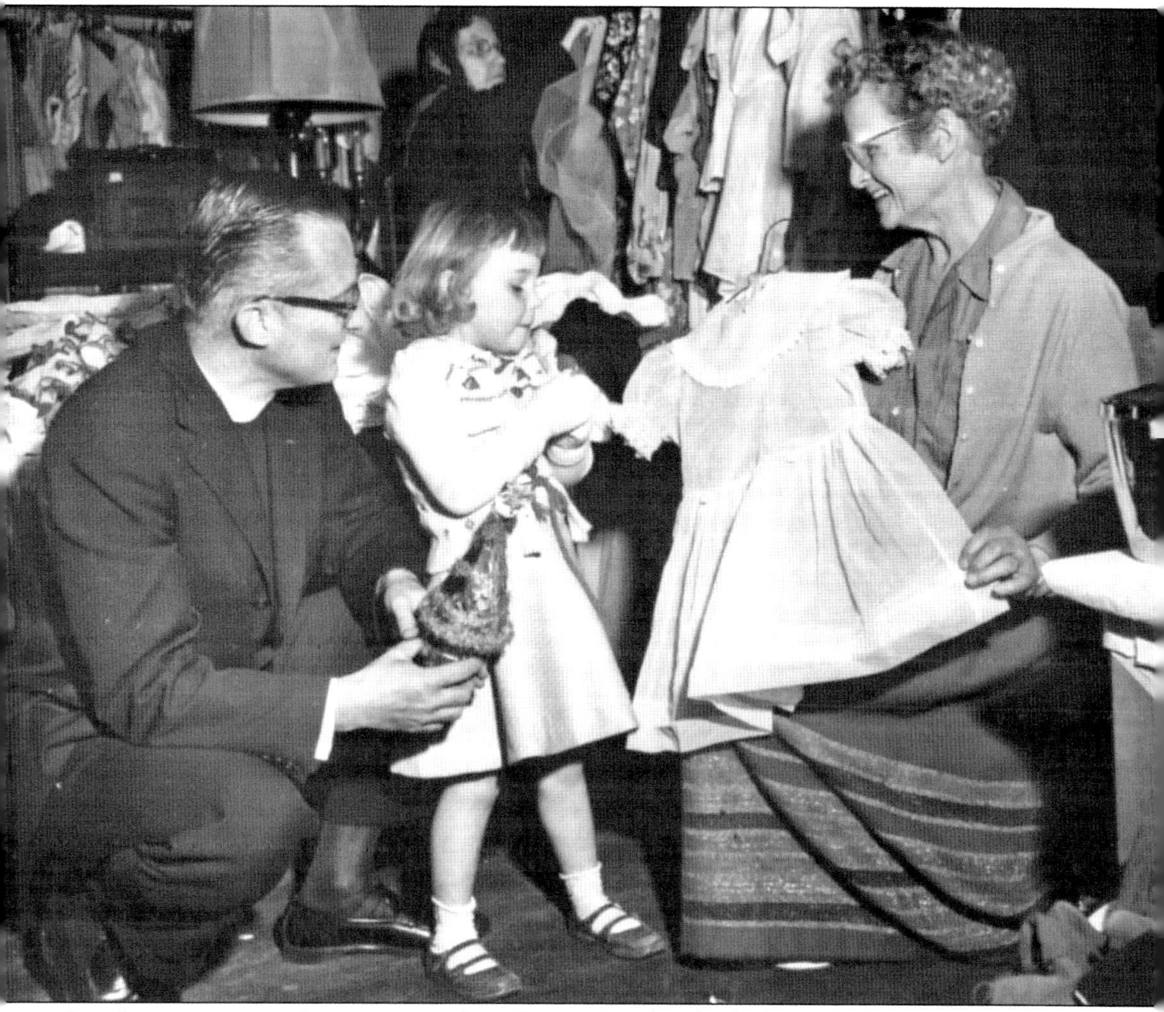

Social service outreach programs such as Trinity Parish's thrift shop, which was established during the Depression, have greatly helped those in the community who need help. (Courtesy of Trinity Parish archives.)

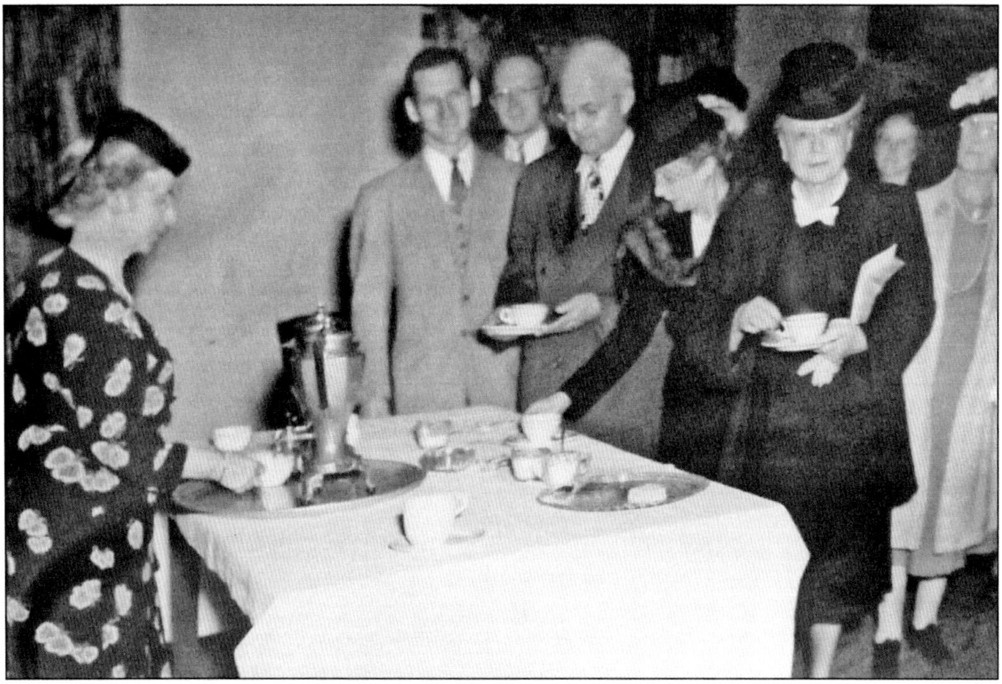

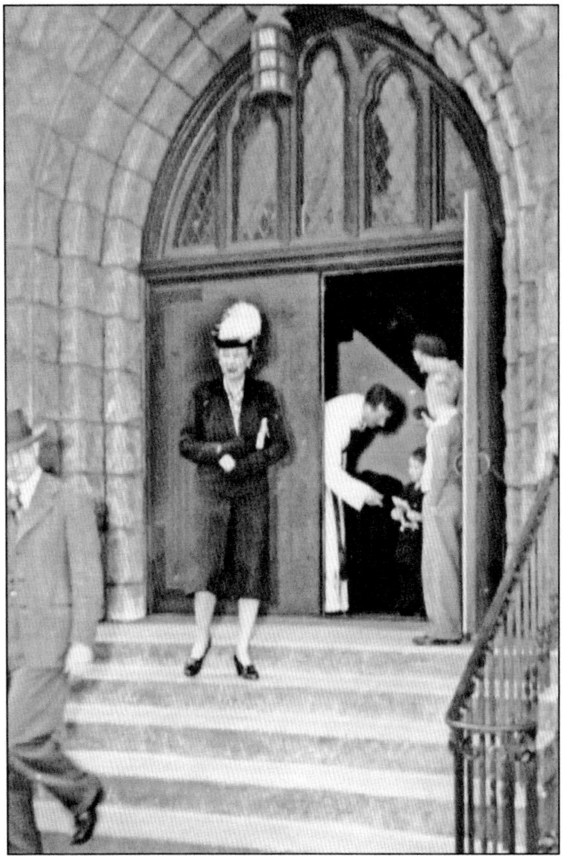

Trinity Parish had an active congregation that met frequently for church socials, as in this c. 1940 photograph. (Courtesy of Trinity Parish archives.)

Parishioners arrive for church service around 1940. (Courtesy of Trinity Parish archives.)

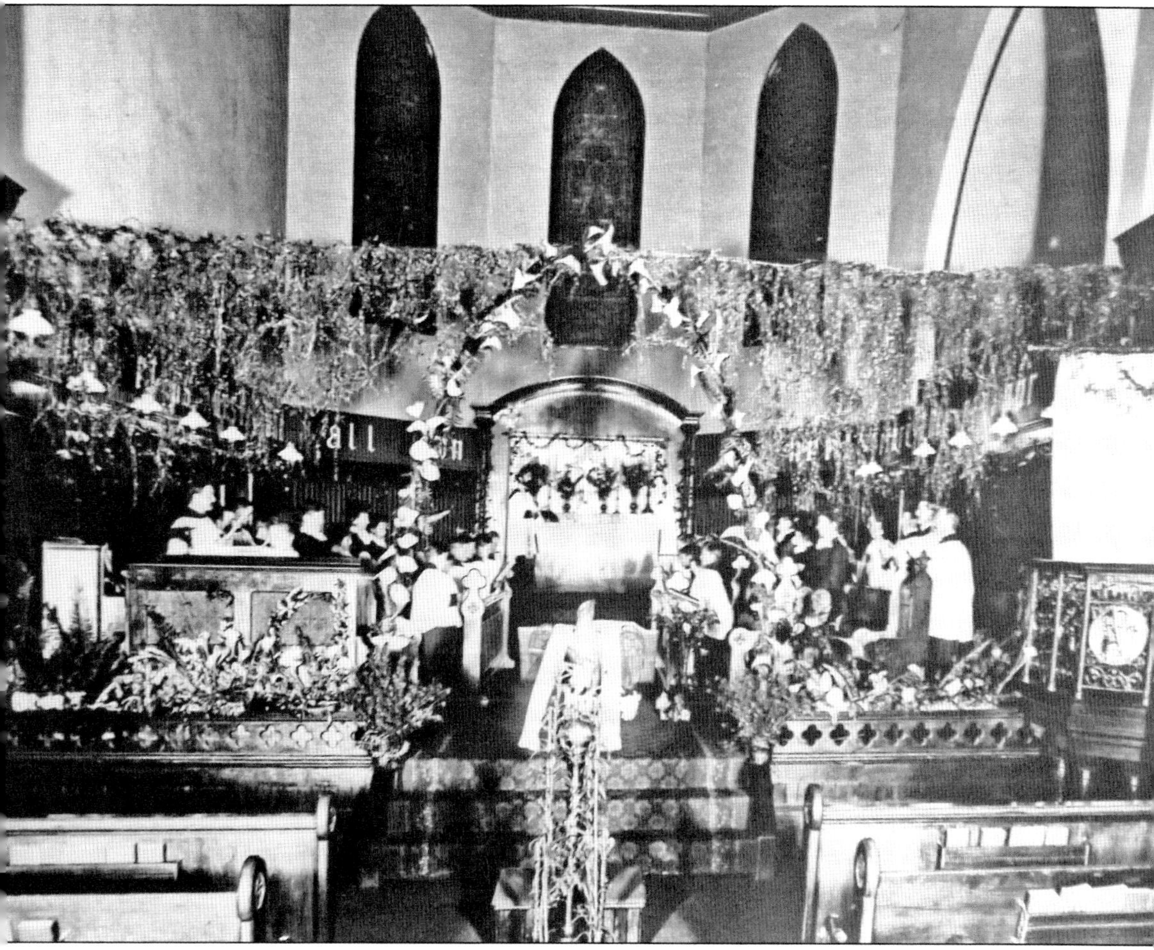

An Easter celebration at Trinity is seen around 1935. (Courtesy of Trinity Parish archives.)

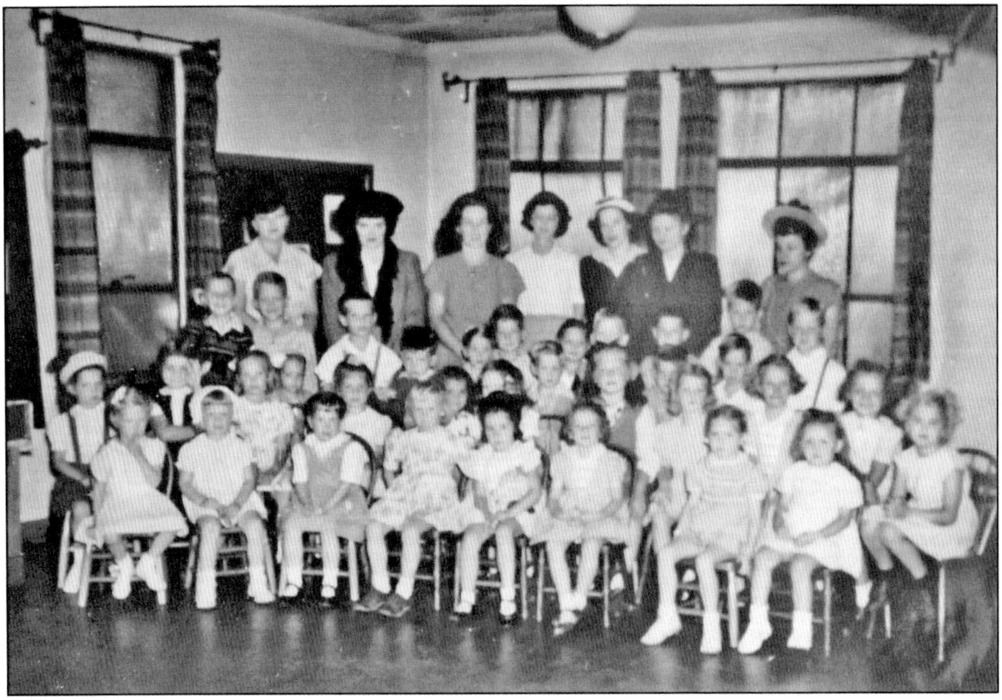

Young kids are pictured in Sunday school around 1960. (Courtesy of Trinity Parish archives.)

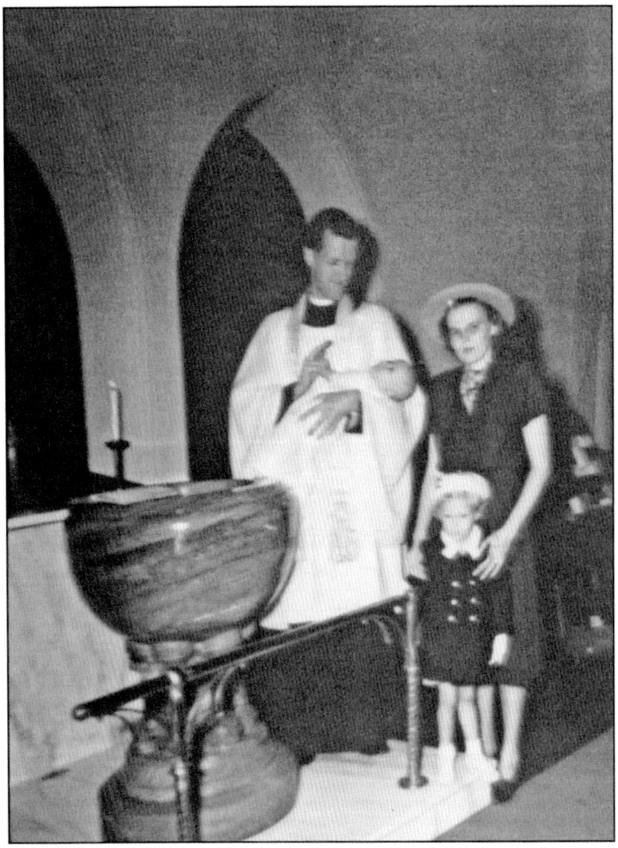

Around 1948, a baby is baptized by Rev. John Craine, rector from 1944 to 1950. (Courtesy of Trinity Parish archives.)

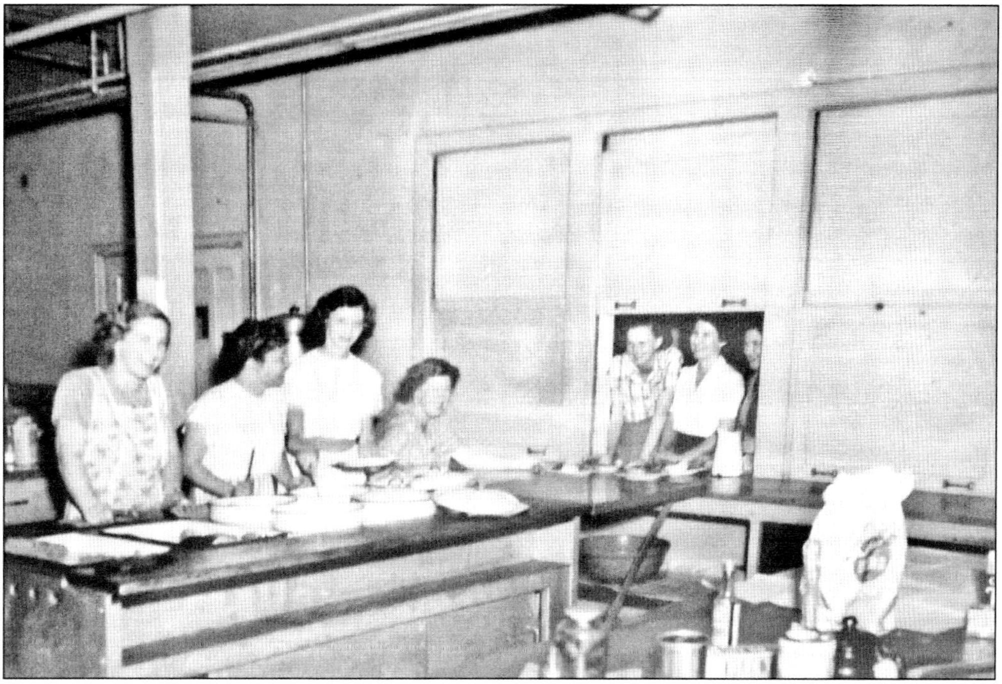

Trinity is the headquarters for the foodbank program Northwest Harvest. The program was established in 1967, when the Ecumenical Metropolitan Ministry was organized specifically to deal with the growing problem of the poor. Access to nutritious food was found to be a problem, and Northwest Harvest was formed as a temporary solution. However, the need became greater and ongoing, and the program became a permanent fixture. Northwest Harvest started out as a local Seattle foodbank and expanded to a statewide food relief program. (Courtesy of Trinity Parish archives.)

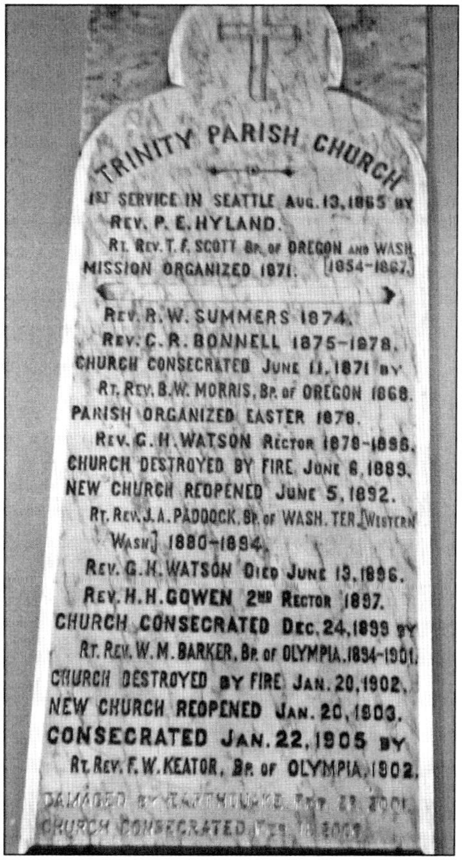

Despite its many challenges over the years—wars, the Great Depression, racial and equality strife during the 1960s, and population change—the church has continued through it all. (Courtesy of Trinity Parish archives.)

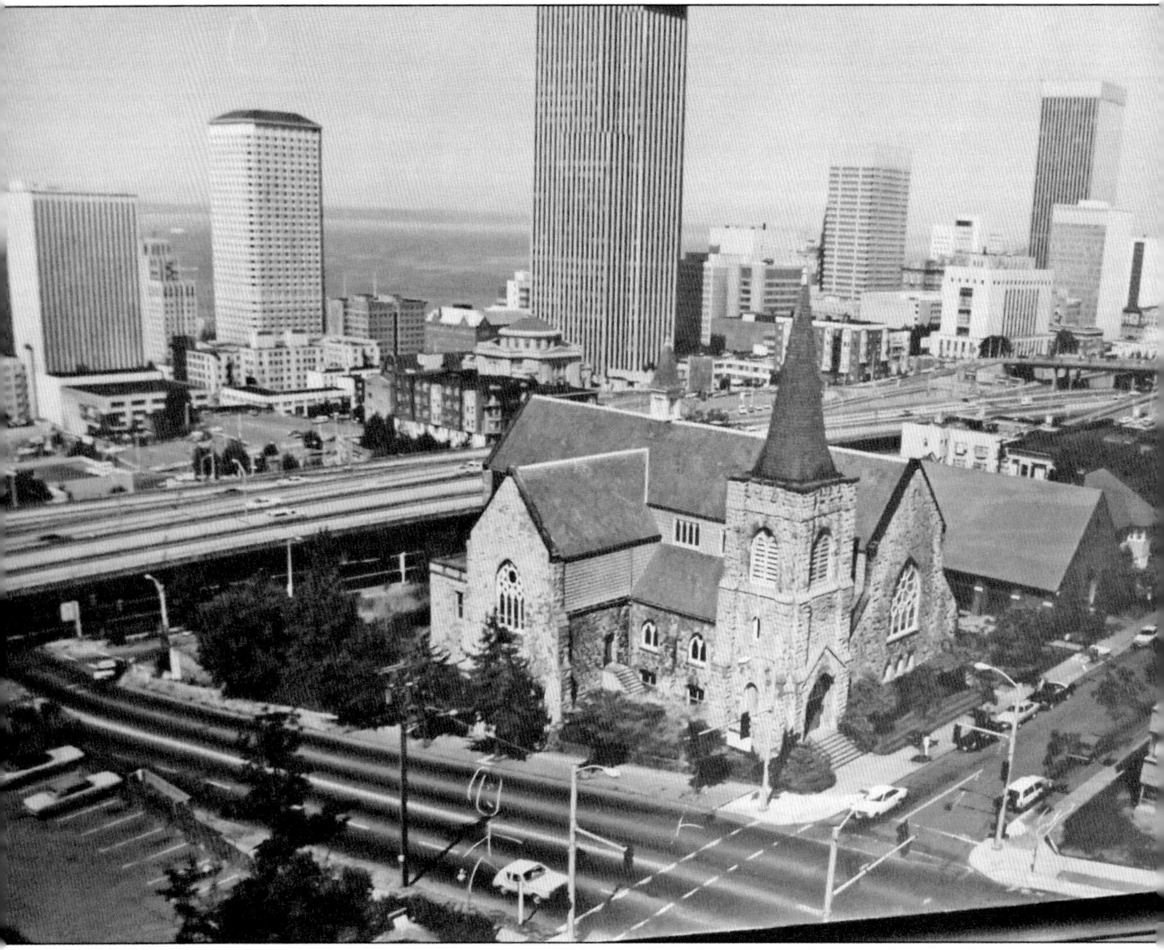

Once again, the parish's very existence was threatened in 2001 when the structure was severely damaged by the Nisqually earthquake. The church was declared uninhabitable, and to repair it would cost millions of dollars. Undaunted, the church set about raising the funds; parishioners donated more than $2 million, and additional funds came from a FEMA grant ($2.2 million), and other supporters and donations. All told, the parish raised $7 million, and the church was rebuilt and opened again for Christmas Eve celebrations in 2005. Modern rectors such as Fr. Allan Parker and current rector Paul Collins have guided the church, and Trinity Parish is still standing as Seattle's oldest church. It was designated a national historic landmark in 1976. The church and the city surrounding it are seen here around the 1970s. (Courtesy of Trinity Parish archives.)

Four

Temple de Hirsch Sinai

During the late 1890s, Seattle was rapidly growing from a pioneering mining and lumber town into a major city. By 1899, the growing city had attracted many Jewish citizens who had no place to worship. Members of the Jewish community rented Marion Hall, at Ninth Avenue and Yesler Way, for all temple-related events including holy days. However, Marion Hall was not adequate and was not a permanent sanctuary. The Jewish population was rapidly growing, and there was a pressing need for a permanent synagogue.

On May 29, 1899, seven men met with the idea to build a temple based on Reform Jewish principles and thought. They named the temple after the Jewish philanthropist Baron Maurice de Hirsch, and Temple de Hirsch was born.

The founding officers included Leo Kohn, president; Emanuel Rosenberg, vice president; Sol Friedenthal, secretary; Max Bornstein, treasurer; Simon Degginger, trustee; I.E. Moses, trustee; and I. Korn, trustee.

Seventy families contributed $2,400, and construction began in 1901 at Boylston Avenue and Marion Street. The cornerstone was laid, and it was decided that the basement would be built first, with a second-floor sanctuary to be built later; more than 1,000 people attended the ceremony.

The first service was held on Rosh Hashanah in 1901; Rabbi Theodore Joseph of Lancaster, Pennsylvania, was elected as the temple's first spiritual leader. Even though the temple wasn't complete, many functions were conducted in the completed basement. There was a study room where children could study for their bar and bat mitzvahs and a Sunday school for religious study. However, before the temple could be completed, the congregation had grown so rapidly that instead of remodeling or expanding to accommodate the growth, the leaders decided that a new temple should be built.

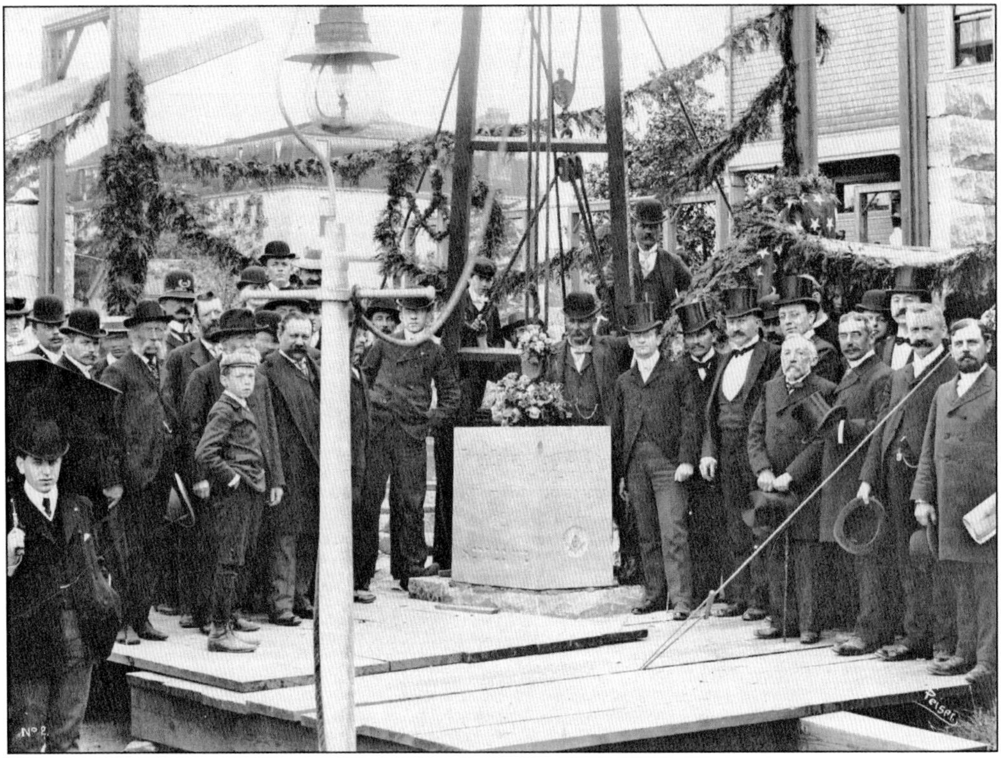

The cornerstone for Temple de Hirsch on Boylston Avenue is laid in this 1901 ceremony. (Courtesy of University of Washington Special Collections UW29948.)

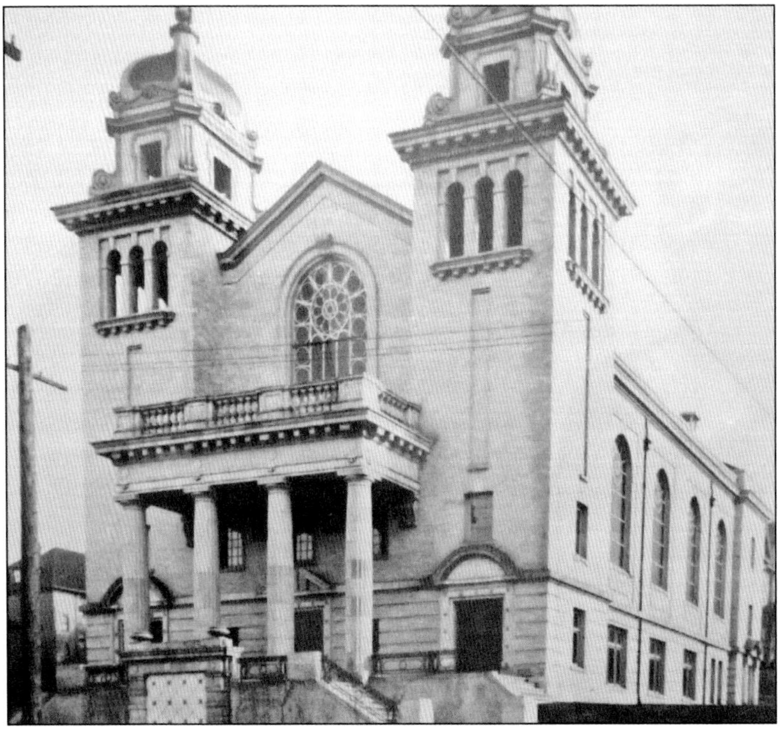

In 1907, a new temple was constructed at Fifteenth Avenue and Union Street, and in 1908, the dedication ceremony was presided over by Rabbi Samuel Koch. (Courtesy of Temple de Hirsch Sinai.)

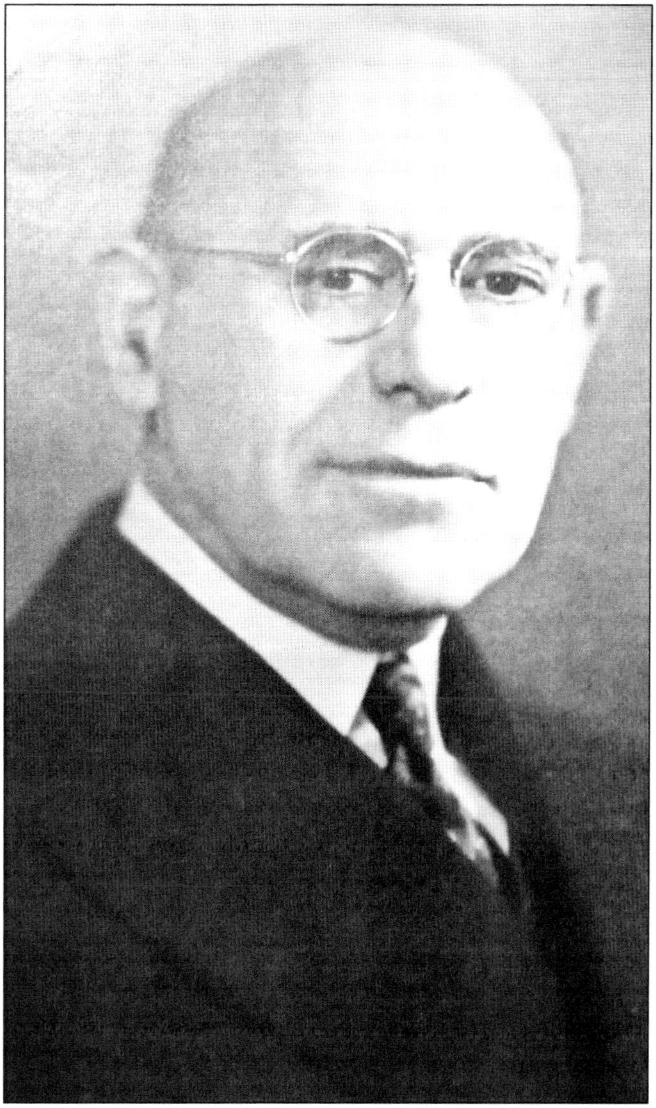

Rabbi Koch succeeded Rabbi Joseph in 1906 and would remain the temple's rabbi for more than 35 years. Under his leadership, the congregation grew at a rapid pace. Rabbi Samuel Koch was born in Denver, Colorado, in 1874. He was ordained at the Hebrew Union College in Cincinnati, Ohio. After moving to Seattle, he received a master of arts degree from the University of Washington. Rabbi Koch immediately became a local and national spiritual leader and social advocate. In 1908, he was invited to deliver the invocation at the Democratic National Convention in Denver. He frequently served on committees with members of other religions to increase awareness, tolerance, and peace. In 1914, Rabbi Koch was on the board of many social welfare organizations. He worked closely with Seattle mayor George Cotterill to unite all the social services agencies (around 50) into one central organization, then known as the Community Chest and now known as the United Way. He also worked to create a children's hospital that is today known as Children's Hospital and Regional Medical Center. He was one of the founders of the local chapter of the National Conference of Christians and Jews. He was also a leader in the Masonic organization; a member of the Seattle Library Board and of the Ministerial Association; and served as president of B'nai B'rith. (Courtesy of Temple de Hirsch Sinai.)

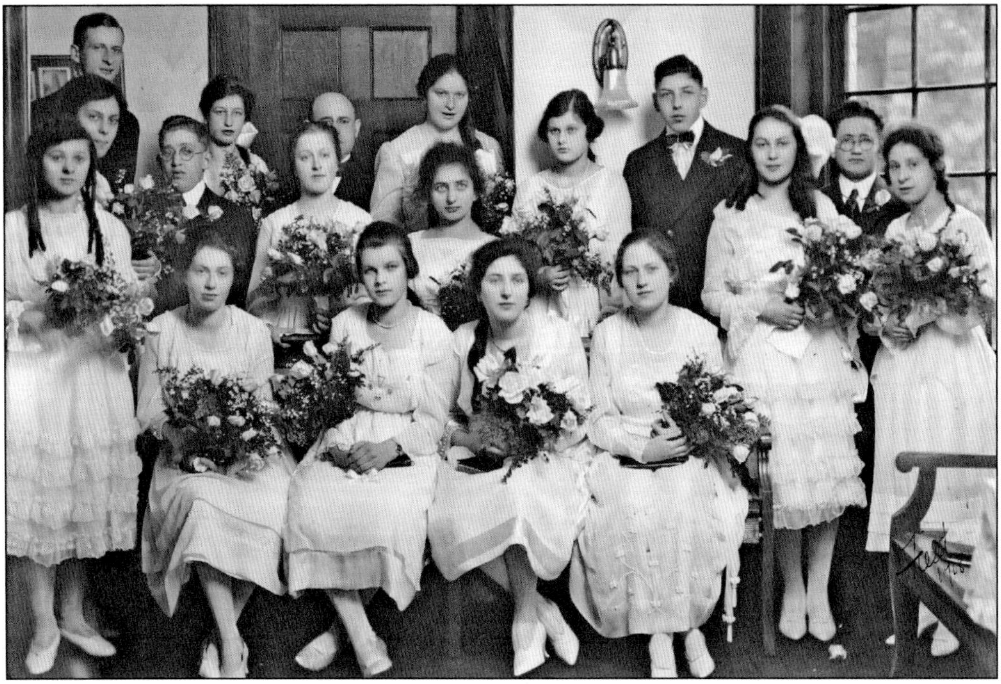

In 1909, Rabbi Koch established the church's newsletter, *Temple Tidings*, which started as a weekly newsletter, then became a monthly publication, and is still in production today as a bimonthly newsletter. He was devoted to the religious school, which was formed in 1906. Under his leadership, the temple school drew children from all over the city, and Rabbi Koch welcomed them regardless of their background or if they were members of the temple. In 1910, the temple library was established by the women's auxiliary. The library consists of materials on Judaism, history, culture, and the Holocaust. (Courtesy of University of Washington Special Collections UW1417.)

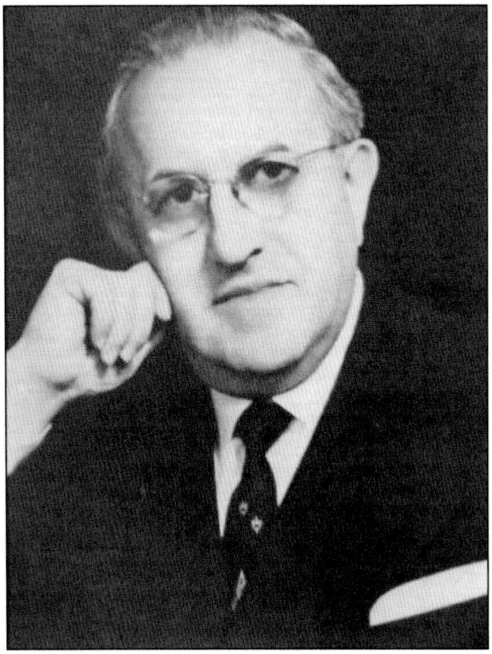

Rabbi Koch was a music lover and felt that music should be an integral part of worship. In 1930, he attended a wedding and met an interesting and talented musician, cantor, and educator by the name of Samuel E. Goldfarb, who was born on June 18, 1891, on the Lower East Side of New York City. Perhaps his most famous song is "The Dreidel Song," which has become a staple during Hanukkah. (Courtesy of Temple de Hirsch Sinai.)

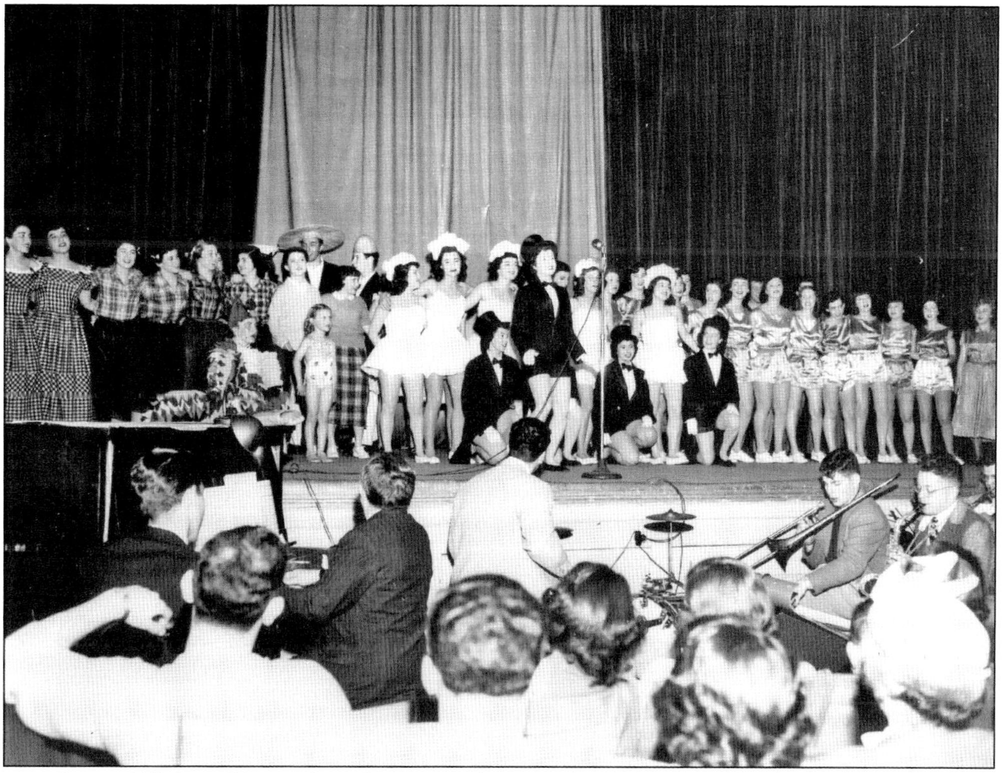

In 1930, Goldfarb and his wife, Sylvia, moved to Washington where they met Rabbi Koch at a wedding. Rabbi Koch was so impressed with Goldfarb that Goldfarb became Temple de Hirsch's music director that same year, a position he would hold for more than three decades. Temple de Hirsch's music program soared under the directorship of Goldfarb. (Courtesy of University of Washington Special Collections UW37781.)

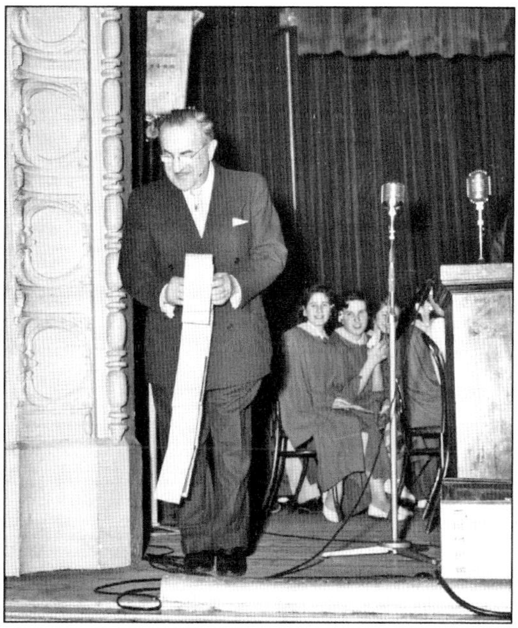

Goldfarb made a huge impact on the church music scene. His rousing and touching performances became nationally known and were one of Temple de Hirsch's claims to fame. He directed choirs, played the organ, composed and arranged music, coached singers, and wrote and directed Hanukkah shows. The choirs were coached from early on, starting with the junior choir and progressing to intermediate and senior choirs. It is said that Jimi Hendrix played one of his first professional performances in the temple basement. Goldfarb's work outside of his temple duties included directing the Halevy Singers and the Sephardic Men's Choir. Goldfarb retired in 1968, leaving a nationally known music program at Temple de Hirsch. He died in 1978 on Mercer Island. (Courtesy of University of Washington Special Collections UW37782.)

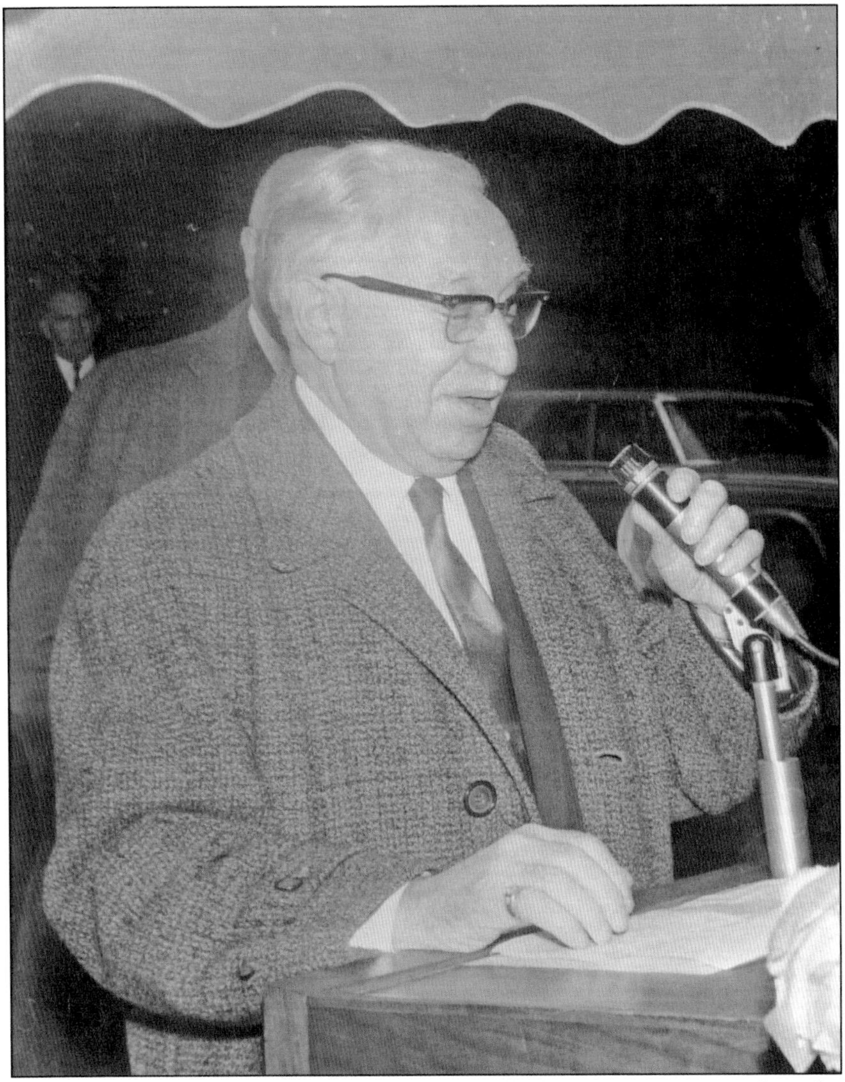

The Jewish faith has a tradition called Pikua'ne Fesh, which means coming to the aid of others through acts of loving kindness. One person who truly lived up to that concept was Rabbi Raphael H. Levine, who succeeded Rabbi Koch in 1942 and served as Temple de Hirsch's chief rabbi and rabbi emeritus for 42 years. The teacher, humanitarian, author, and artist was born in Vilna, Lithuania (at that time part of the Russian Empire), around August 1901. He was the youngest of 12 children. When he was a child, his family moved to the United States, settling in Duluth, Minnesota. One of his brothers had moved there after being released from jail after an unjust arrest—Jewish families were often harassed. He originally wanted to be an attorney and graduated from the University of Minnesota Law School in 1926. While in law school, he worked evenings and weekends teaching at the local synagogue and was named president of the local menorah society. He connected so deeply with his spirituality that he decided to follow his calling and enrolled in the Hebrew Union College, graduating in 1932. The country was in the midst of the Great Depression, and jobs, even for rabbis, were not plentiful, so he accepted an assignment at a synagogue in Liverpool, England. While there, he started having weekly dinners bringing together Christians and Jews to bring about more understanding between the two religions. (Courtesy of University of Washington Special Collections UW37783.)

In 1942, Rabbi Levine joined Temple de Hirsch. He was most of all a humanitarian who worked hard to improve the world. He served as a board member of the Rotary Club, United Good Neighbors, Community Psychiatric Clinic, the Washington Society of Crippled Children, the Governors' Committees on the Study of Problems of Mental Health, and the State Committee on Crime and Delinquency. Rabbi Levine became nationally known for his ecumenical work. He constantly reached out to help eliminate or ease racial and religious tensions. (Courtesy of Temple de Hirsch Sinai.)

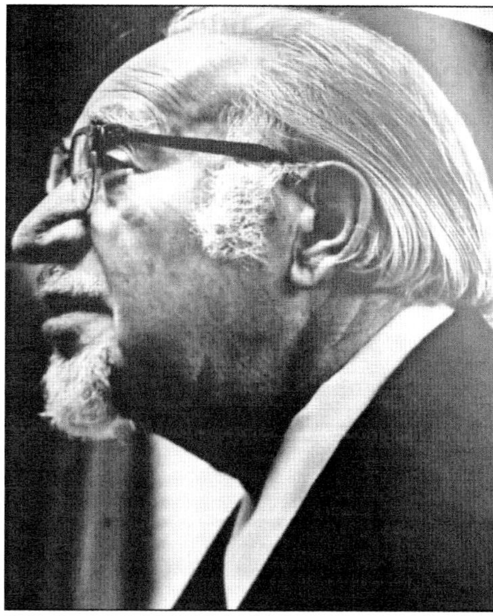

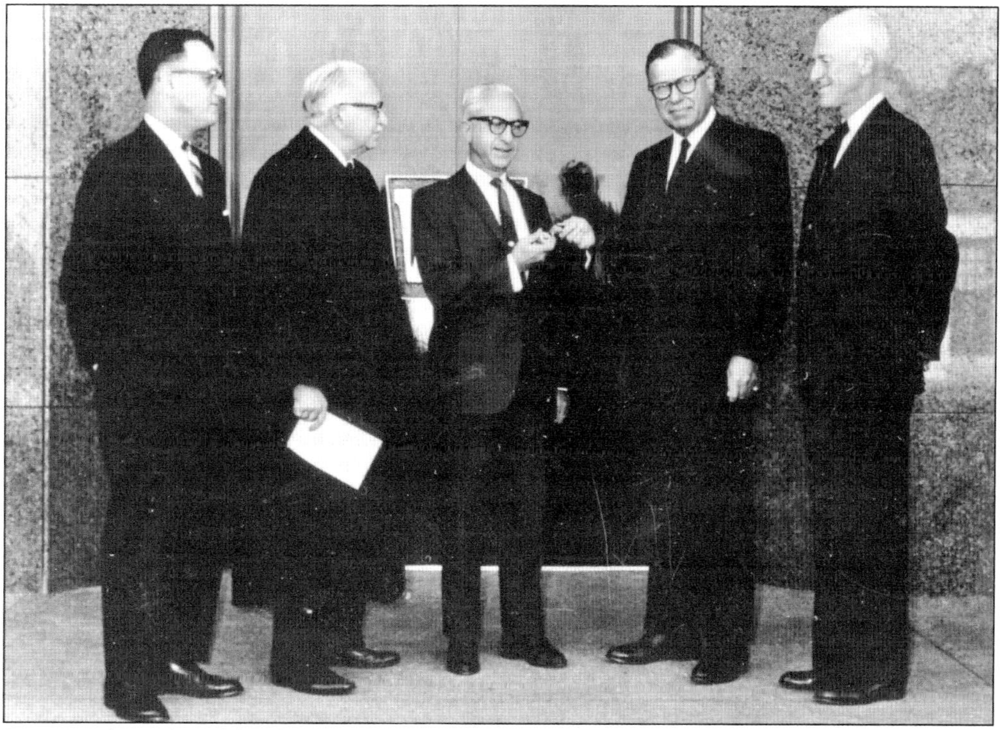

In 1960, the political landscape changed for the country. Sen. John F. Kennedy had won the nomination for the Democratic Party and would be the first Catholic president. The Kennedy nomination had unleashed religious prejudice, and the anti-Catholic hate was palpable. Rabbi Levine wanted to combat those sentiments and approached KOMO television about developing a program bringing a panel of religious leaders together. The show, titled *The Challenge*, debuted in 1960 and aired for 14 years. Rabbi Levine (second from left) and others are pictured at the dedication ceremony for the new Temple de Hirsch in 1960. (Courtesy of University of Washington Special Collections UW1310.)

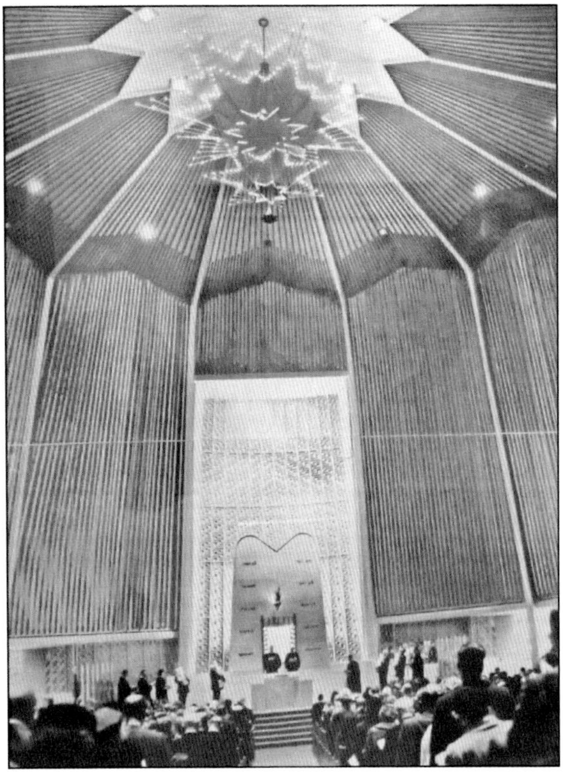

Rabbi Levine didn't shy away from the civil rights movement. On November 8, 1961, Dr. Martin Luther King Jr. arrived for his only visit to Seattle during the movement. Dr. King was scheduled to speak at a local church, but once the news reported that King was speaking, the church cancelled King's lecture. Rabbi Levine graciously offered Temple de Hirsch to the iconic civil rights leader, and his speech was received enthusiastically. In 1963, Rabbi Levine helped to write ordinances that helped to overturn discriminatory housing practices. (Courtesy of Temple de Hirsch Sinai.)

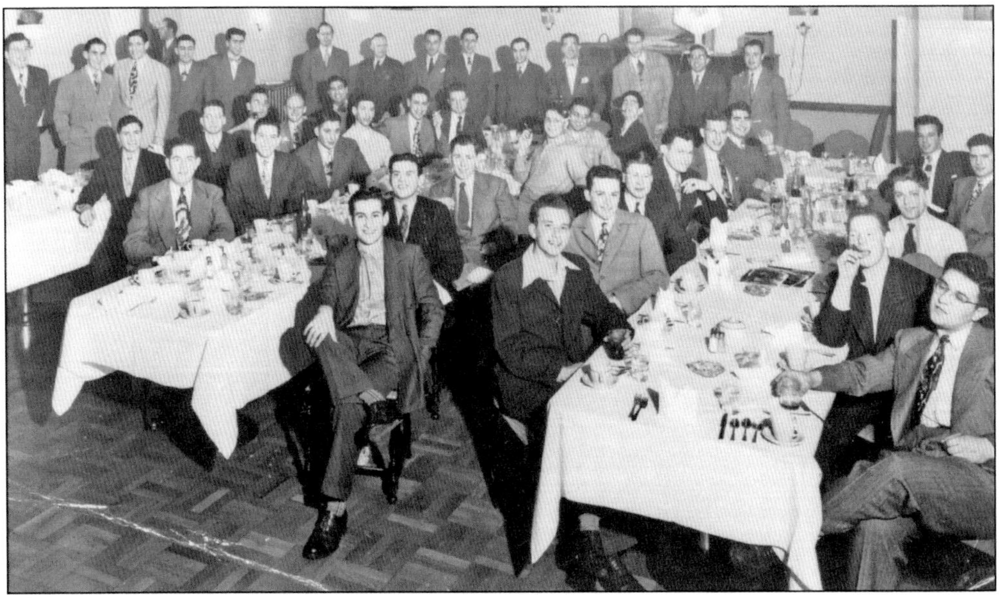

Rabbi Levine semi-retired from Temple de Hirsch in 1969 and became rabbi emeritus; his television show continued until 1974. In October 1984, he was a passenger in a car that was involved in a head-on collision on the floating bridge. He later slipped into a coma and died on November 4 of head injuries. Rabbi Levine was often criticized for combining politics and religion, but he said that equality was a moral issue he couldn't ignore. (Courtesy of University of Washington Special Collections UW2280.)

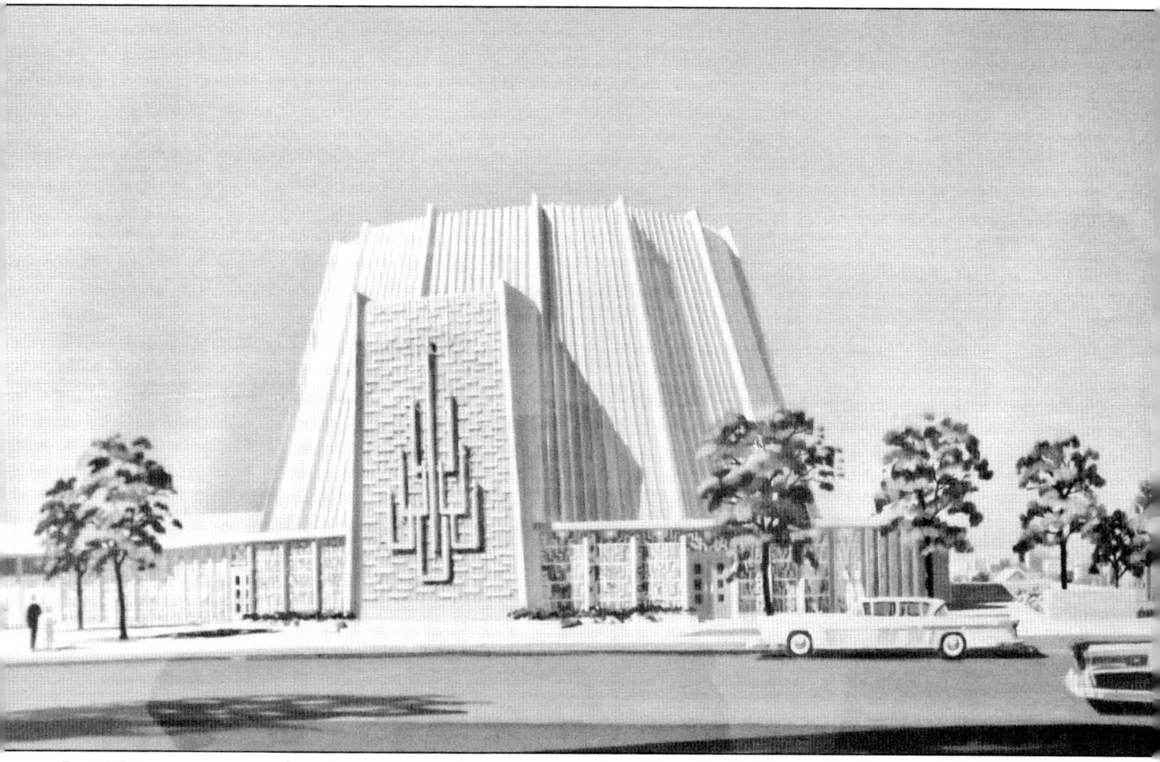

In 1960, to accommodate its ever-growing congregation, Temple de Hirsch built a new synagogue at 1511 East Pike Street in a building designed by B. Marcus Priteca. The old building was declared a historic landmark in 1983. The building was eventually demolished in 1993. In 1971, Temple de Hirsch merged with Temple Sinai, the Reform congregation in Bellevue. From then on, the temple would be known as Temple de Hirsch Sinai. In 1970, Earl Starr took over as rabbi; he retired in 2001. (Courtesy of Temple de Hirsch Sinai.)

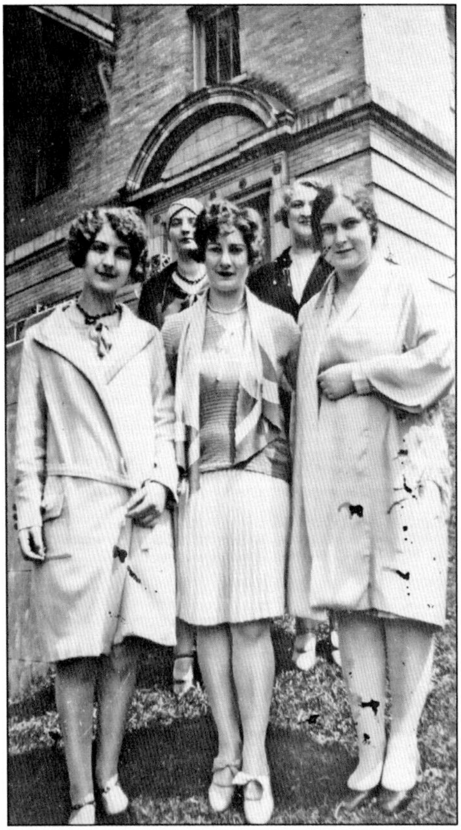

This confirmation class is graduating on Shavuot in 1929, the 30th anniversary of Temple de Hirsch. (Courtesy of University of Washington Special Collections UW1116.)

A Workmen's Circle dinner meeting hosts Jewish servicemen at Temple de Hirsh in 1943, during World War II. (Courtesy of University of Washington Special Collections UW37784.)

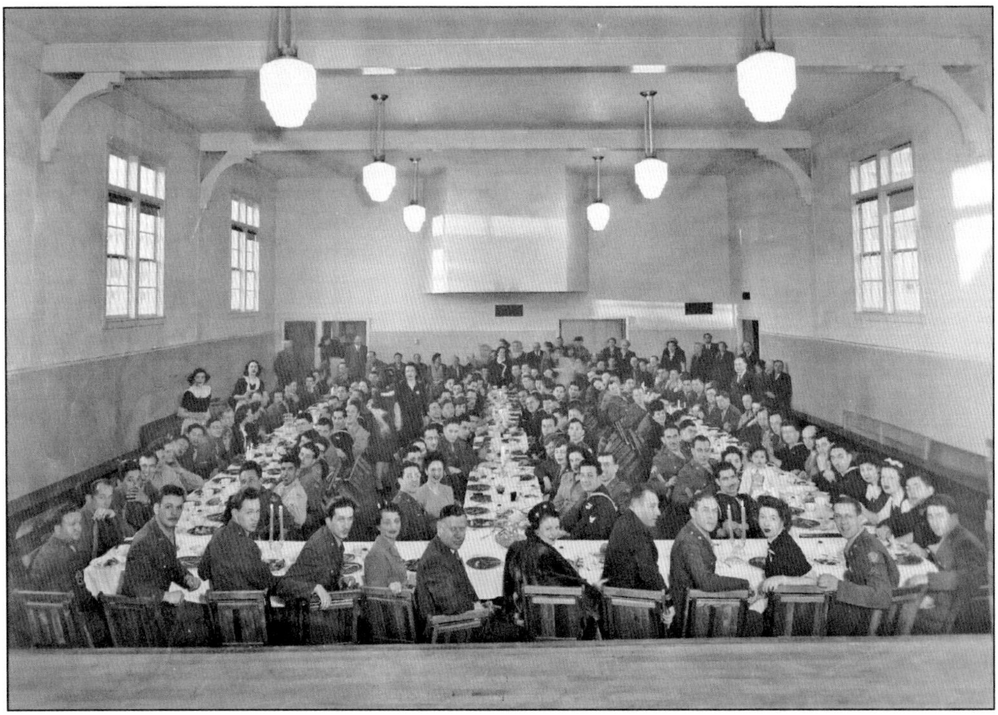

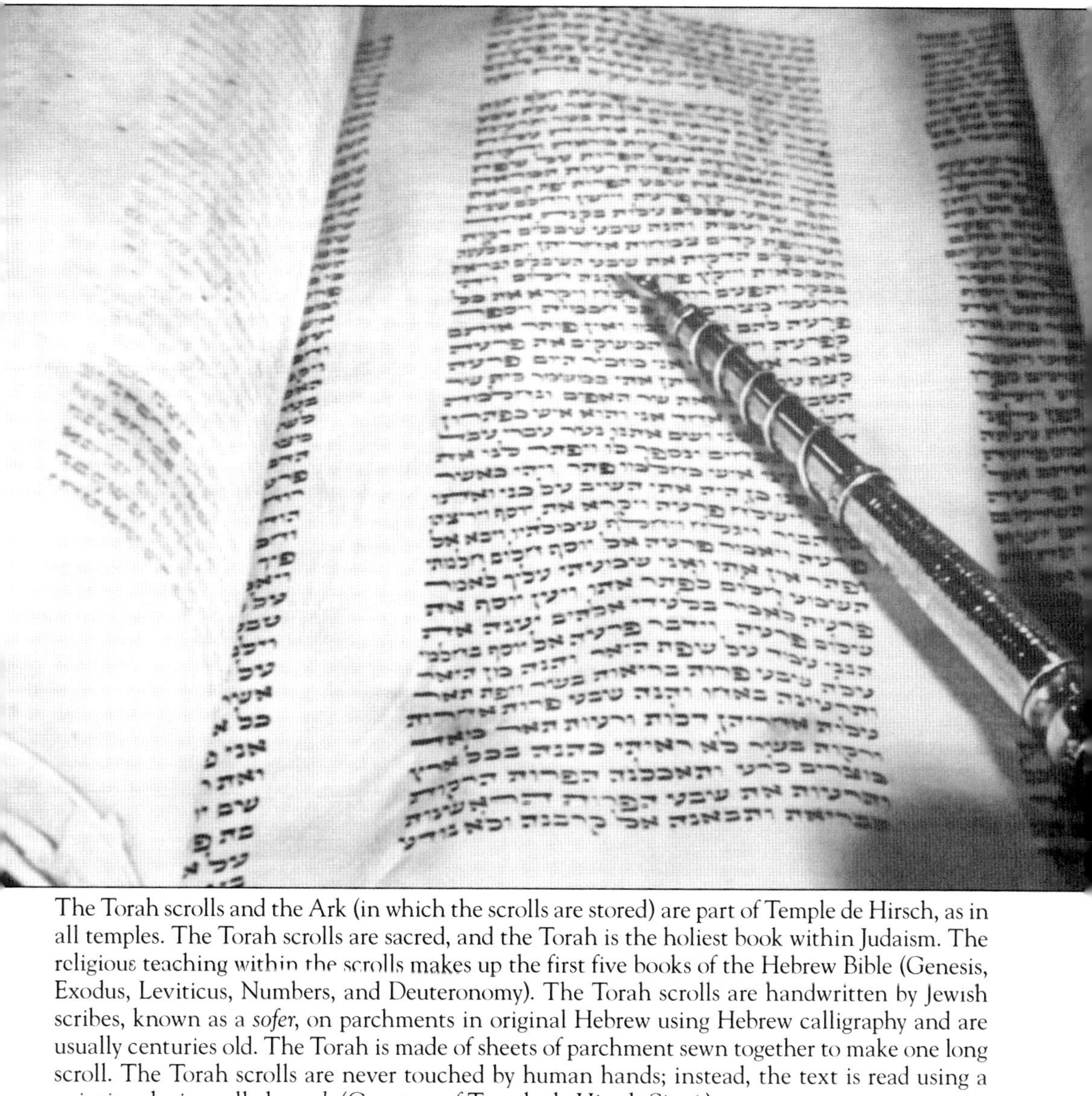

The Torah scrolls and the Ark (in which the scrolls are stored) are part of Temple de Hirsch, as in all temples. The Torah scrolls are sacred, and the Torah is the holiest book within Judaism. The religious teaching within the scrolls makes up the first five books of the Hebrew Bible (Genesis, Exodus, Leviticus, Numbers, and Deuteronomy). The Torah scrolls are handwritten by Jewish scribes, known as a *sofer*, on parchments in original Hebrew using Hebrew calligraphy and are usually centuries old. The Torah is made of sheets of parchment sewn together to make one long scroll. The Torah scrolls are never touched by human hands; instead, the text is read using a pointing device called a *yad*. (Courtesy of Temple de Hirsch Sinai.)

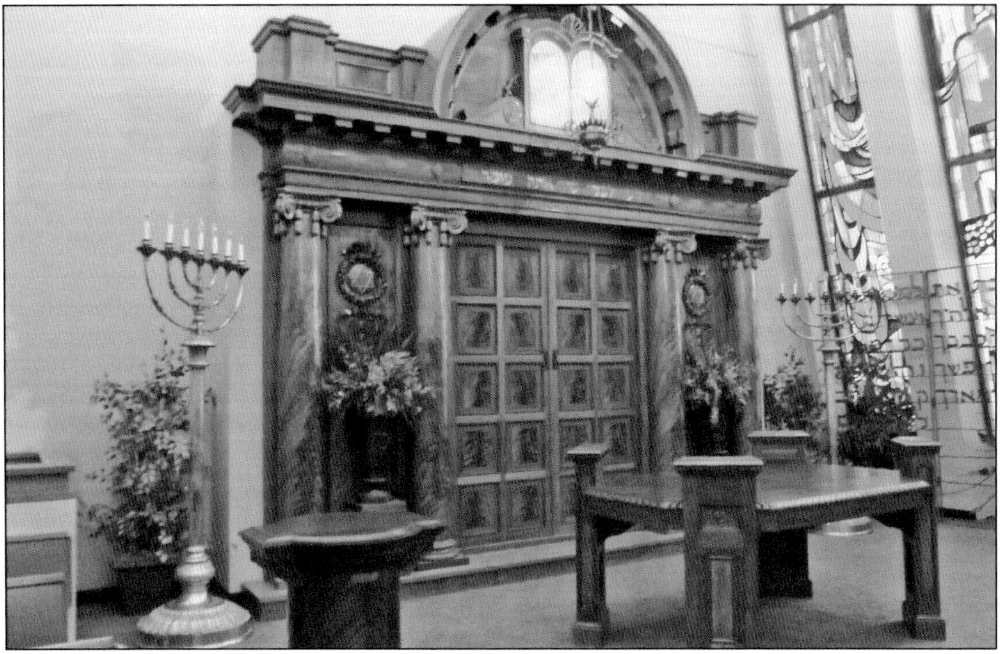

The scrolls are stored in a cabinet-like structure known as the Ark or the Holy Ark, which is usually in front of the sanctuary and placed on the eastern wall so that when the congregation is facing the Ark, it is facing the holy city of Jerusalem. The Holy Ark is opened only during special prayers and when removing the scrolls during services. The scrolls at Temple de Hirsch were secured by David Kaufman, whose daughter, Sara, was the first Jewish child born in Seattle. (Courtesy of Temple de Hirsch Sinai.)

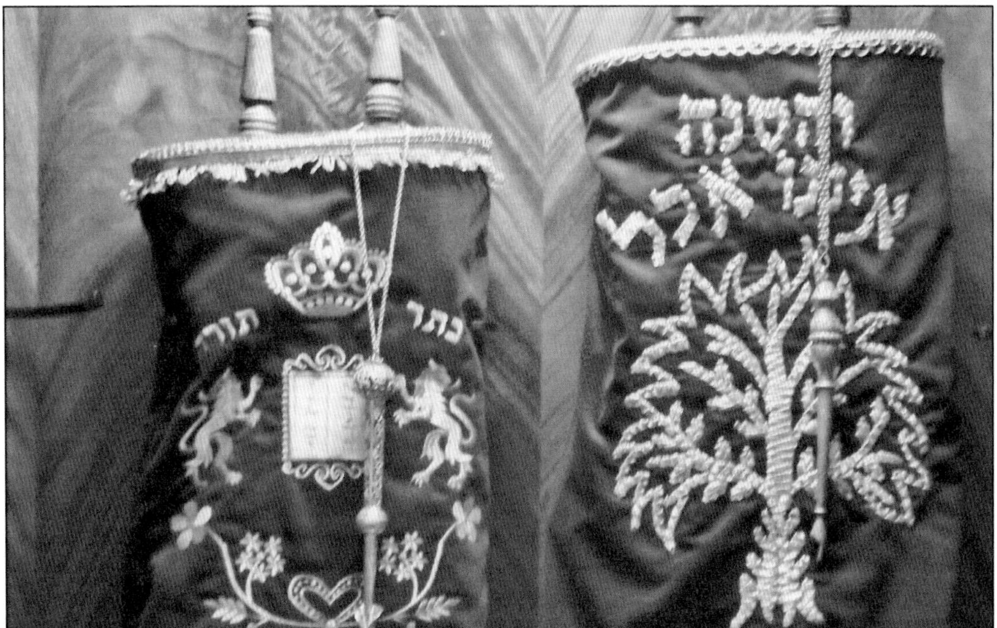

The scroll is usually rolled by two shafts attached to its sides and is covered by a fine fabric. (Courtesy of Temple de Hirsch Sinai.)

Five

Seattle Betsuin Buddhist Temple

The Seattle Betsuin Buddhist Temple (also known as the Seattle Buddhist Church) dates to November 15, 1901, when Rev. Kakuryo Nishijima performed the first Buddhist service in the Pacific Northwest. The Seattle Betsuin Buddhist Temple is affiliated with the Buddhist Churches of American (BCA) and is based on the Jodo Shinshu tradition.

Jodo Shinshu, also known as Shin Buddhism, dates to 1224 and was founded by a Japanese Buddhist monk named Shinran. It is the most widely practiced branch of Buddhism in Japan.

Many Japanese had immigrated to Seattle as early as 1882. By the early 1900s, more than 250 Japanese were working in King County. Many Japanese came to Seattle to work on the railroad or in lumber, jobs that were available because many white residents went to seek their fortune during the gold rush. Anti-Japanese sentiment began to take over and Japanese immigrants faced discrimination on many levels. Laws were passed to openly discriminate against Asians in general and people of Japanese heritage in particular. The legislation was meant to strip Japanese immigrants of any rights, including becoming citizens or owning land.

However, the Japanese immigrants persevered and wanted to practice their religion. Many began to meet in various noodle shops to worship. But with more and more Japanese immigrating to Seattle, a permanent house of worship was needed.

After establishing Buddhist missions in California, especially in San Francisco, the North American Buddhist Mission wanted to expand and establish Buddhist missions in the Pacific Northwest. In the summer of 1900, the mission sent an unofficial minister to test the waters. During the fall of 1900, Rev. Shodo Hatano and Tatsujiro Akiyoshi traveled to Seattle, collecting signatures and gauging interest in establishing a Buddhist temple. The results were very positive, and 57 businessmen asked that Seattle be the fourth mission in America and the first outside of California.

On November 1, 1901, Kakuryo Nishijima came to Seattle to start a Young Men's Buddhist Association (YMBA). He met with prominent people and founders to establish a series of bylaws for the new temple, which included sponsoring Sunday Buddhist sermons, creating and maintaining a Sunday school for young children, and sponsoring special observances such as marriages and funerals.

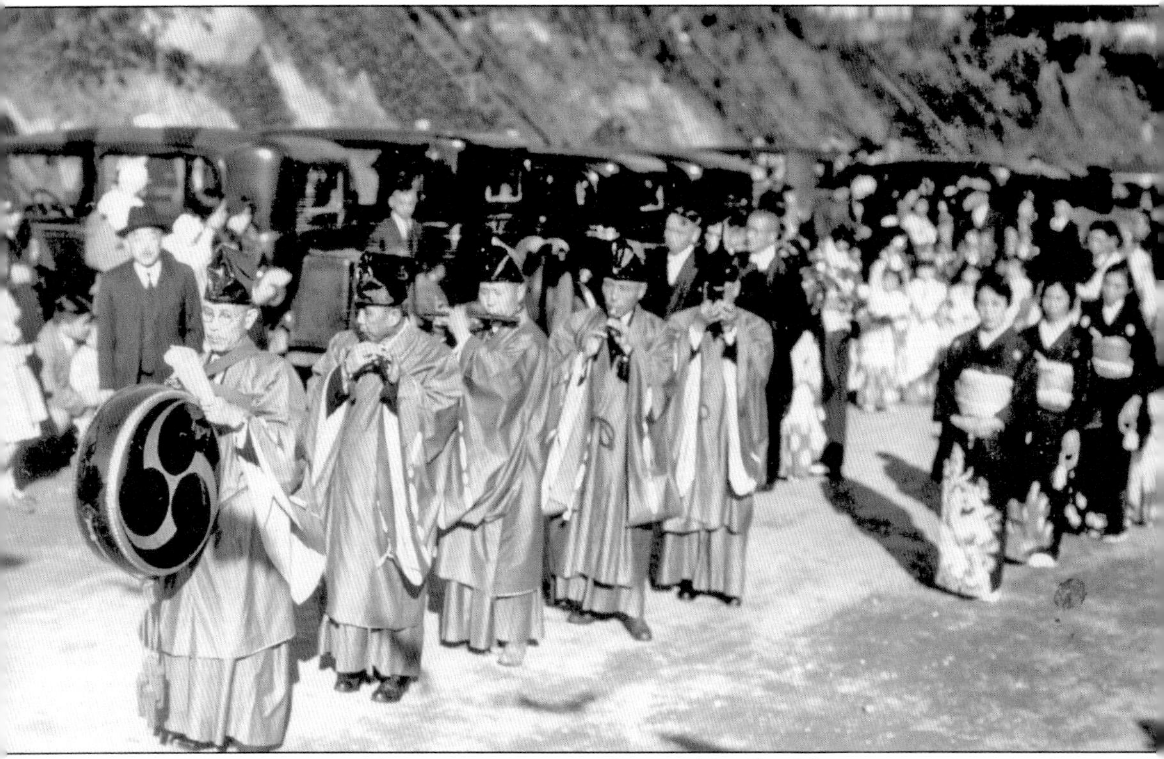

Rev. Gendo Nakai arrived from Japan in 1902 as the temple's official first minister. In 1902, there were nearly 3,000 Japanese living in the Seattle area; most were railroad and sawmill workers. The blocks south of Yesler Way became known as China Town. Reverend Nakai stayed from 1902 to 1907; in 1903, he organized a committee of prominent businessmen to discuss purchasing land to build a temple. Reverend Nakai, along with Tatsujiro Akiyoshi, one of the founders of the YMBA, fought back hard against crime organizations. In 1906, Akiyoshi became secretary of the anti-crime Human Society and partnered with others in the religious community (Baptists, Presbyterians, Methodists, and Catholics) to try to rid the city of criminal activities. (Courtesy of Seattle Buddhist Temple Archives Collection.)

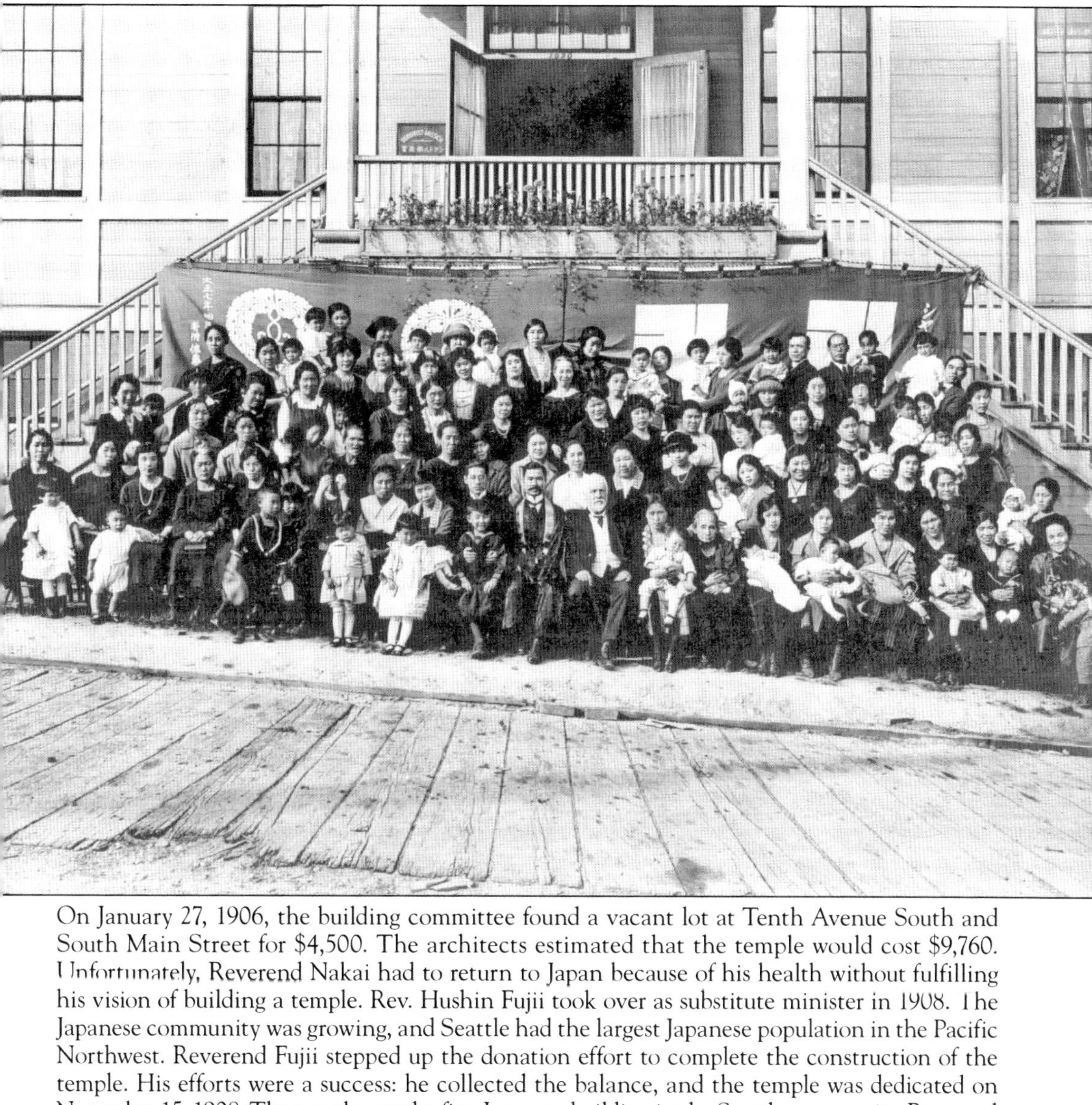

On January 27, 1906, the building committee found a vacant lot at Tenth Avenue South and South Main Street for $4,500. The architects estimated that the temple would cost $9,760. Unfortunately, Reverend Nakai had to return to Japan because of his health without fulfilling his vision of building a temple. Rev. Hushin Fujii took over as substitute minister in 1908. The Japanese community was growing, and Seattle had the largest Japanese population in the Pacific Northwest. Reverend Fujii stepped up the donation effort to complete the construction of the temple. His efforts were a success: he collected the balance, and the temple was dedicated on November 15, 1908. The temple was the first Japanese building in the Seattle community. Reverend Fujii served for 14 years and announced that the official name of the church would be Seattle Temple Branch of the Hompa Hongwanji. Reverend Fujii is pictured in the front row. (Courtesy of Seattle Buddhist Temple Archives Collection.)

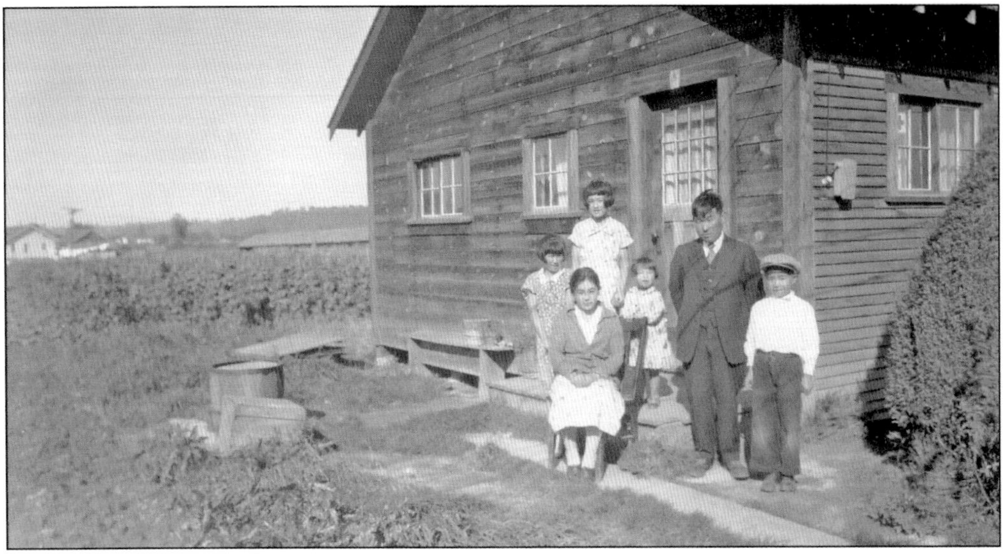

During the Great Depression, the temple had the unenviable task of guiding the congregation through the greatest financial downtown in history. The temple developed a culture club comprising successful leaders of the Japanese community and white businessmen; through the organization, Japanese immigrants and Nisei (second-generation) were given resources for finding jobs. The temple also expanded its welfare committee services to help more people in need who were hungry and homeless. The Japanese community was not immune to bank closures. Masajiro Furuya's Pacific Commercial Bank went bankrupt. Here, a Japanese family is pictured on a farm. (Courtesy of Seattle Buddhist Temple Archives Collection.)

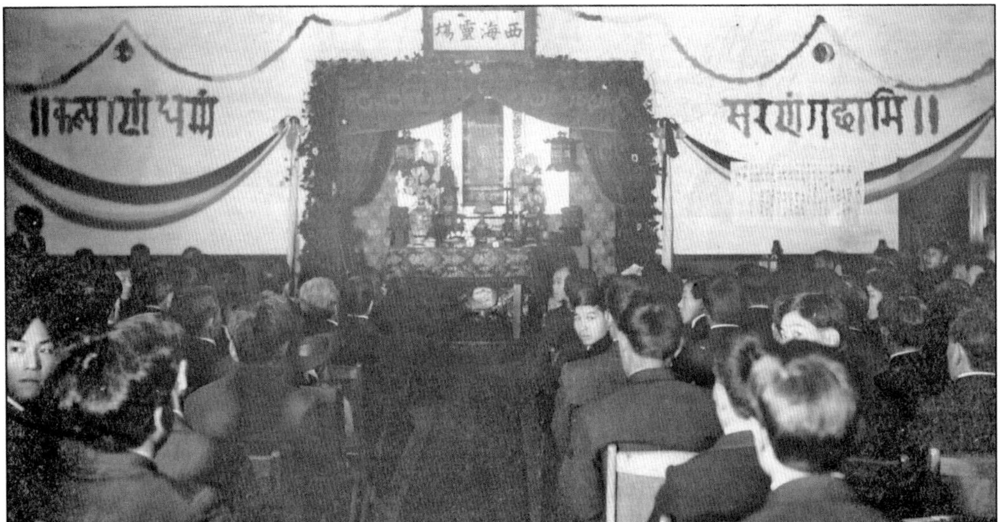

On December 7, 1941, the United States was sent into a state of shock when Japan executed surprise military air strikes against the American naval base at Pearl Harbor near Honolulu, Hawaii. More than 2,000 soldiers and sailors died in the devastating attack, and more than 1,000 more were wounded. Pres. Franklin D. Roosevelt asked Congress to declare war on Japan the day after the attack. After the declaration of war, more than 110,000 people of Japanese ancestry (two-thirds of them American citizens) were deported or imprisoned in internment camps, more than 10,000 from Seattle and King County. (Courtesy of Seattle Buddhist Temple Archives Collection.)

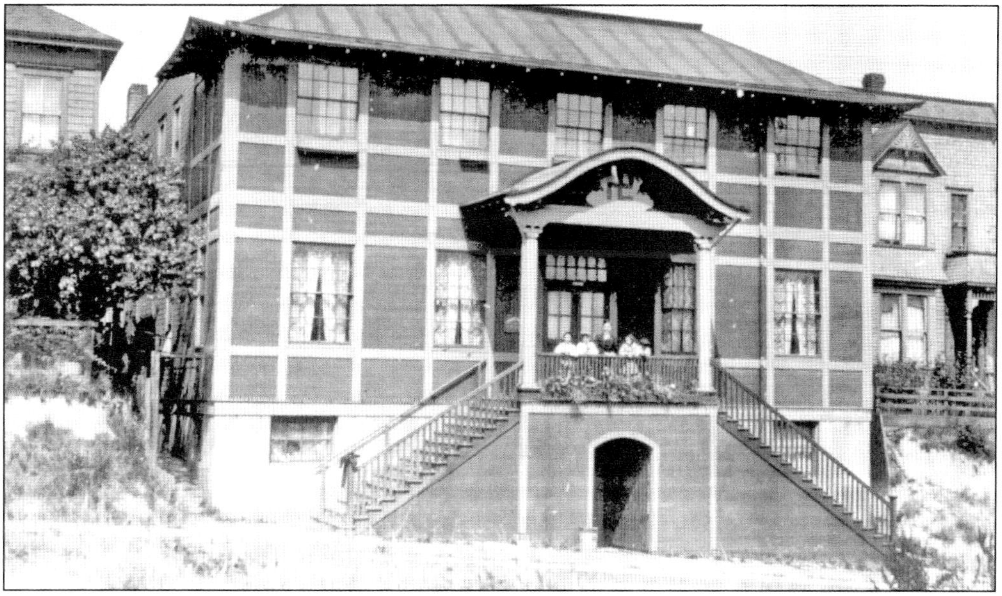

The consequences were swift and severe. On the night of December 7, the FBI, US Marshals, Seattle police, and sheriffs began arresting members of the Japanese community deemed dangerous, which included members of the Buddhist temple who were officers of the Japanese Chamber of Commerce. Life in Seattle began to change for people of Japanese descent. Many felt that all their hard work to build businesses and establish relationships with the broader Seattle community had disappeared. (Courtesy of Seattle Buddhist Temple Archives Collection.)

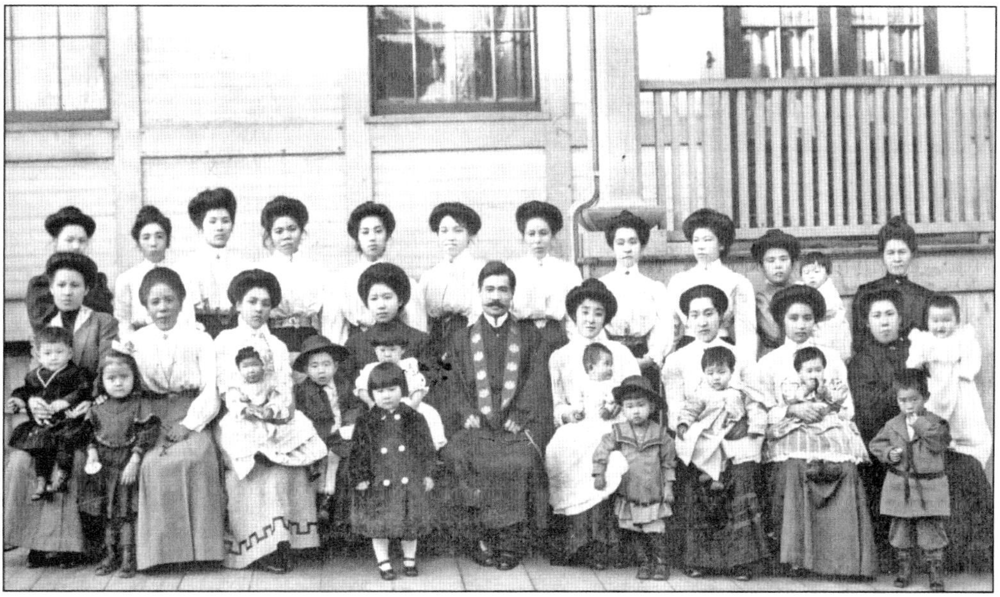

On December 23, 1941, the Japanese American Citizen League emergency council planned an Americanism Rally at Seattle Buddhist Temple, hoping to quell some of the anti-Japanese sentiment that had grown since the attack. However, beginning on August 10, 1942, many Seattle Japanese residents were moved to the Minidoka Relocation Center in Idaho. They were only allowed to take with them what they could carry, so many had to find places to store their belongings on short notice. (Courtesy of Seattle Buddhist Temple Archives Collection.)

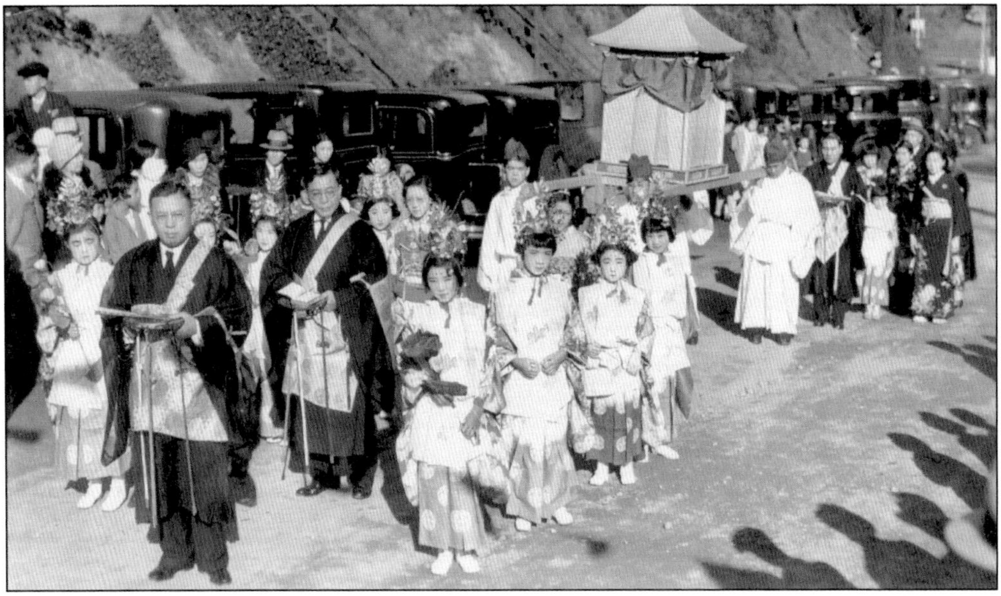

On February 21, 1942, the US government seized control of the church, and no one could enter, even to retrieve personal belongings. The temple was leased and used as the US Maritime Commission Office. (Courtesy of Seattle Buddhist Temple Archives Collection.)

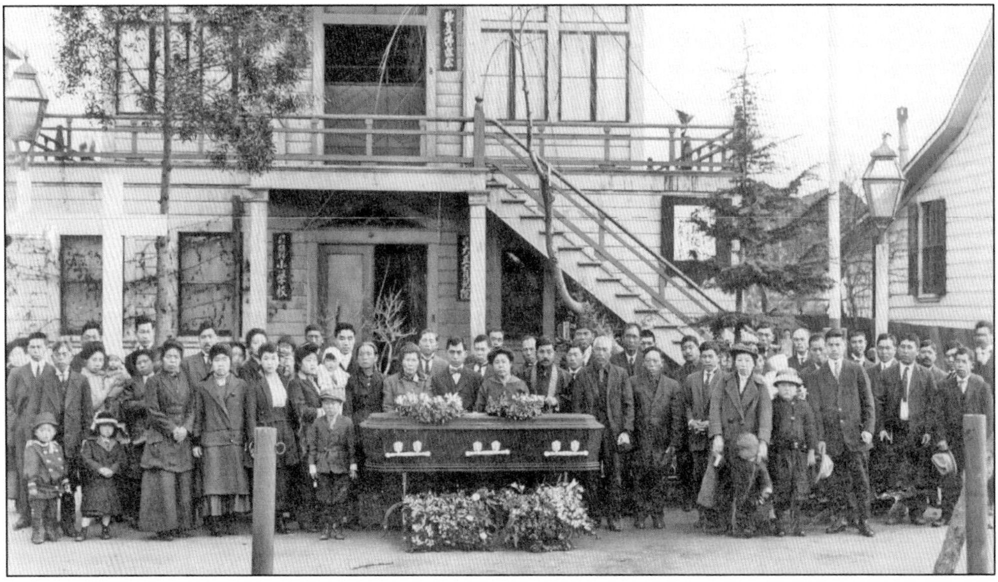

In August 1945, the United States dropped atomic bombs on the cities of Hiroshima and Nagasaki, Japan, and Japan surrendered. Japanese Americans could return from the internment camps beginning in January 1945, but many had lost their homes and businesses. Some, like barber Isamu Sakoda, reopened their businesses. Churches and compassionate citizens helped many retrieve their businesses and homes. The Seattle Betsuin Buddhist Temple had to start over. There was no minister. Reverend Ishikawa was interned until September 1945, and by that time, all 17 Seattle Buddhist board members were returned to Seattle. Rev. Gikan Nishinaga, the head minister of Tacoma, conducted the first service after the internment was over at Seattle Kendo Hall on September 23, 1945. (Courtesy of Seattle Buddhist Temple Archives Collection.)

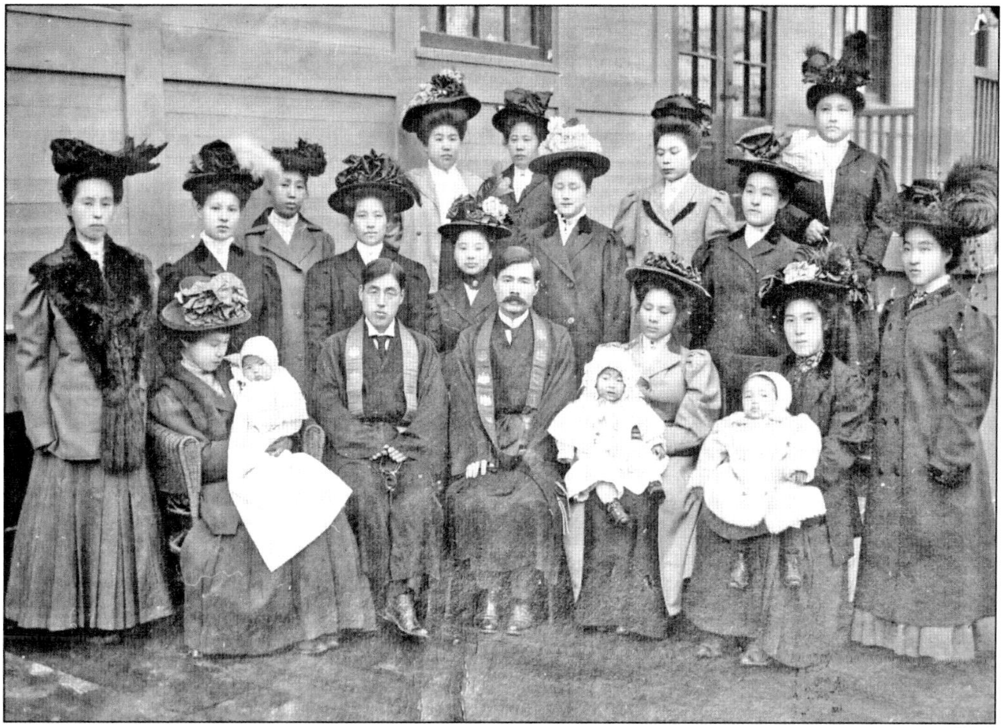

The newly formed Women's Buddhist Association is pictured in 1908 with Rev. Hoshin Fujii. (Courtesy of Seattle Buddhist Temple Archives Collection.)

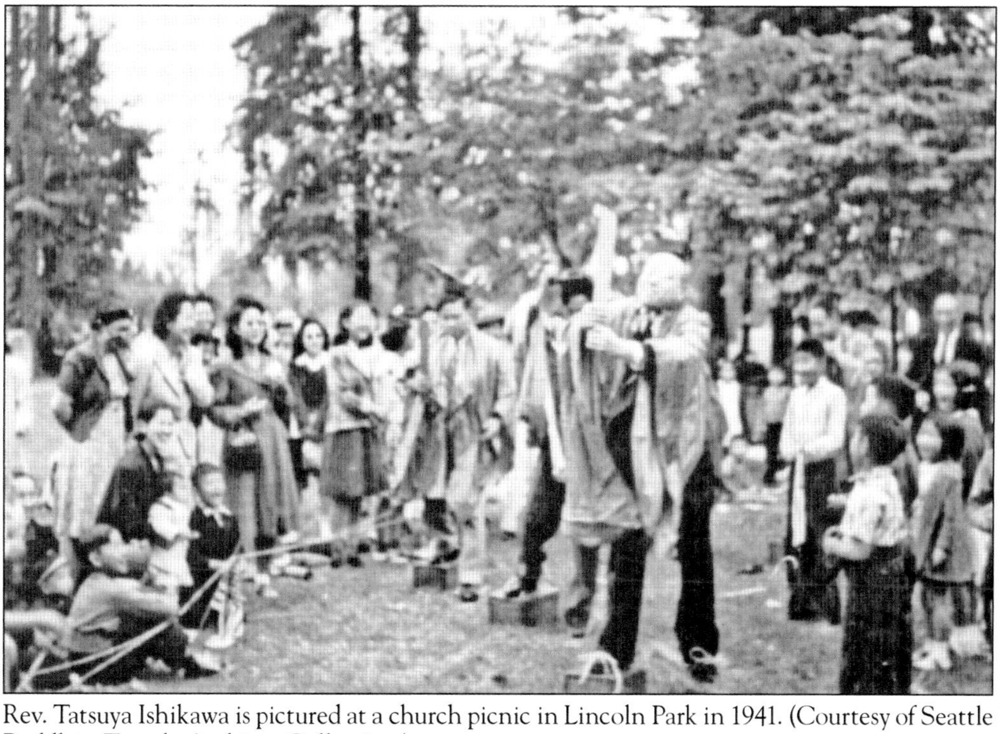

Rev. Tatsuya Ishikawa is pictured at a church picnic in Lincoln Park in 1941. (Courtesy of Seattle Buddhist Temple Archives Collection.)

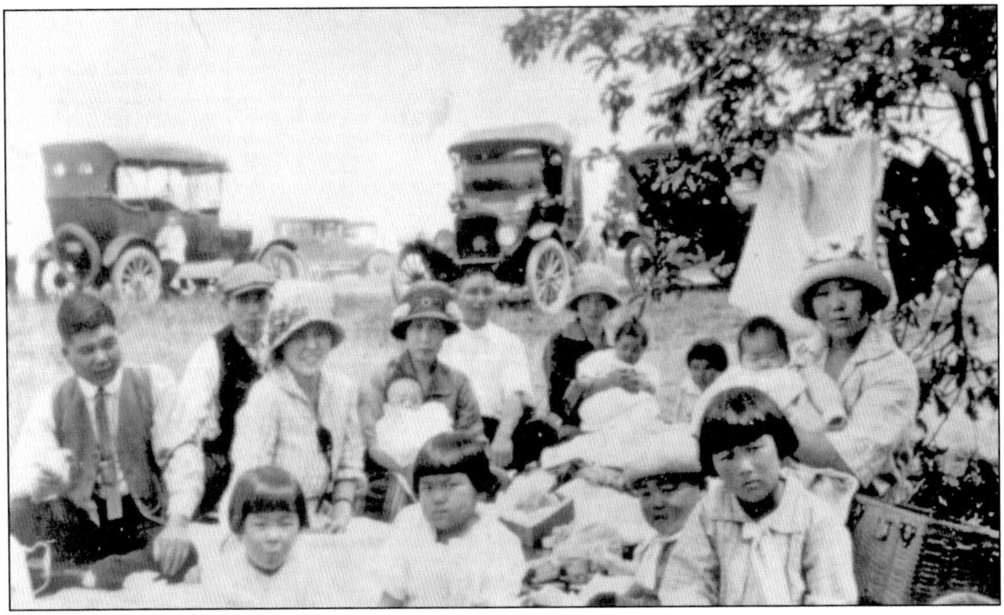

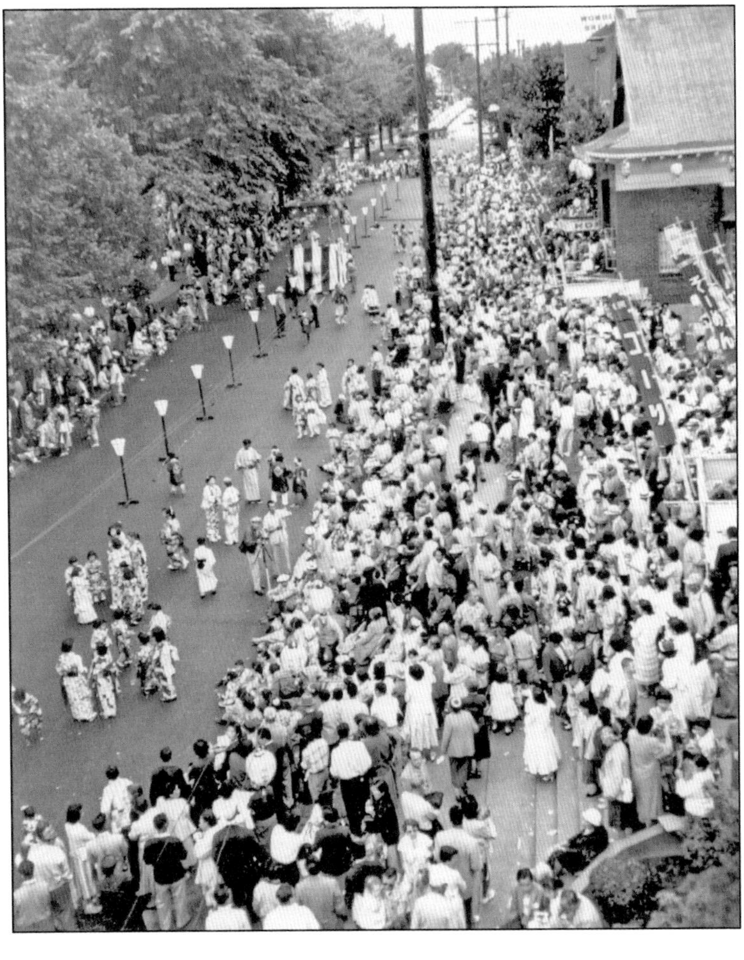

A church picnic is pictured around 1920. (Courtesy of Seattle Buddhist Temple Archives Collection.)

A Bon Odori Festival is pictured in 1935. Bon Odori is a summer festival to honor the spirits of ancestors. These dancers are dressed as the 47 Ronin. The story of the 47 Ronin has been made into many movies in Japan. (Courtesy of Seattle Buddhist Temple Archives Collection.)

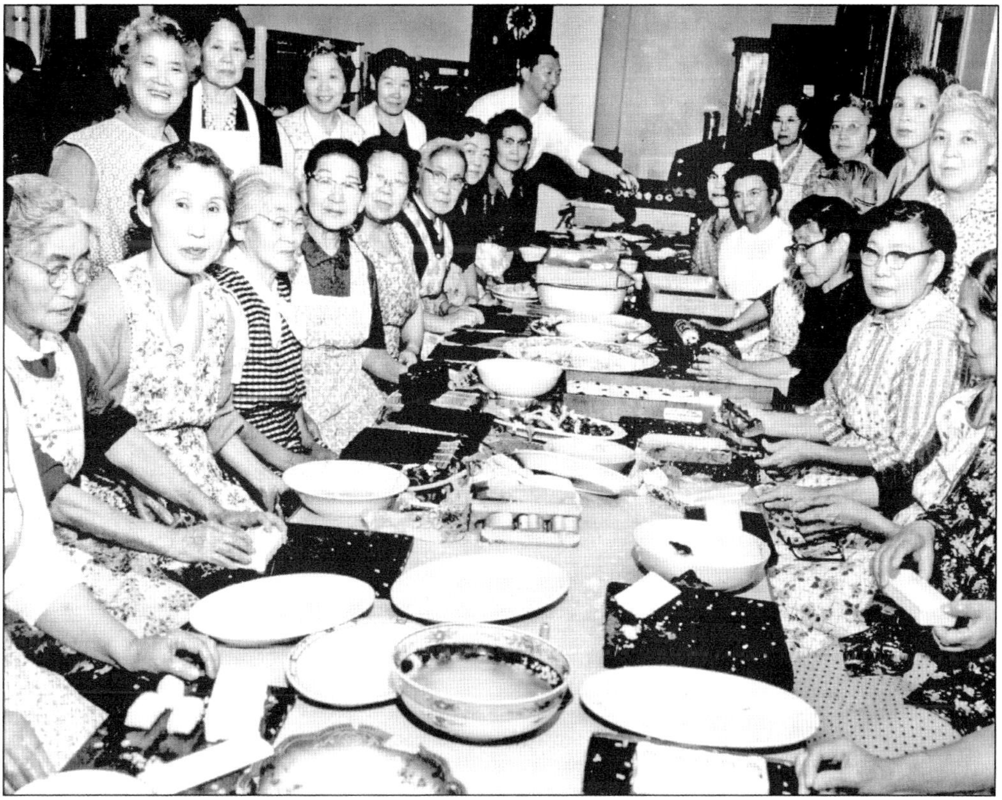

Issei are pictured making sushi. Issei are people who have emigrated from Japan. (Courtesy of Seattle Buddhist Temple Archives Collection.)

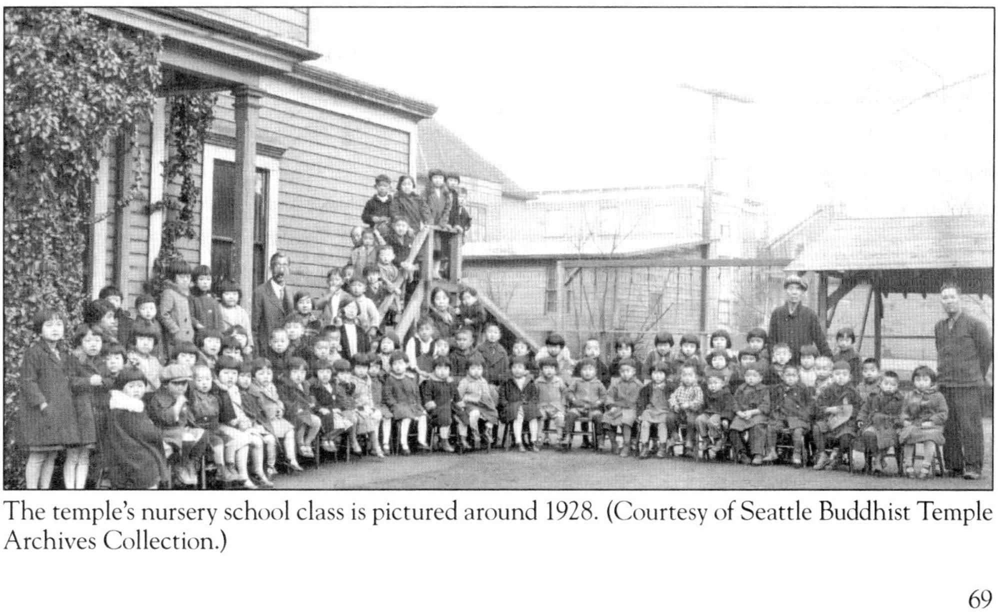

The temple's nursery school class is pictured around 1928. (Courtesy of Seattle Buddhist Temple Archives Collection.)

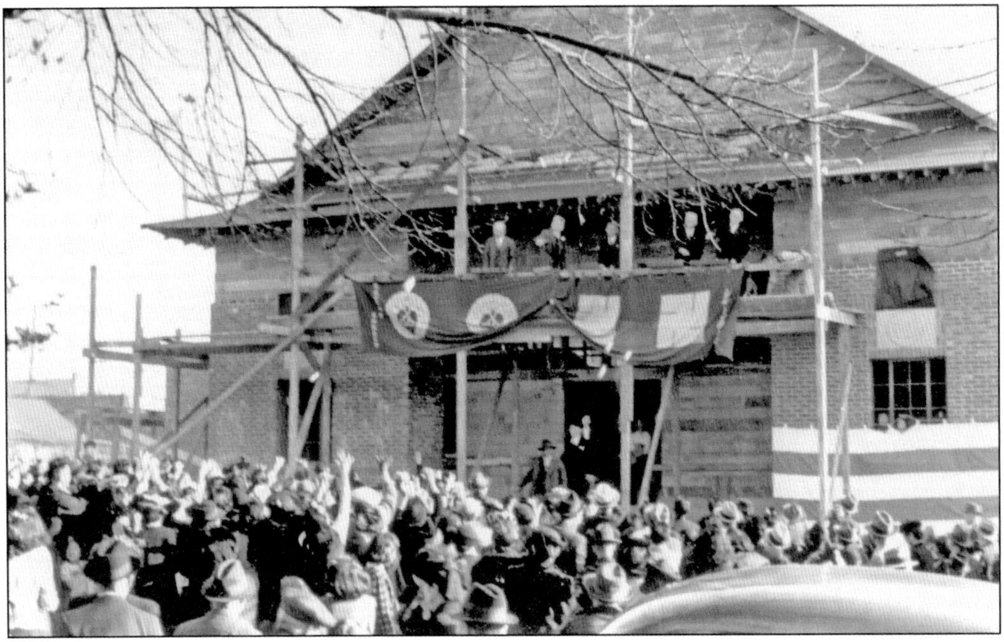

In 1941, a Muneage ceremony is held for the temple at 1425 South Main Street. A Muneage ceremony is a Japanese tradition in which offerings such as fruit, rice, and salt are thrown off a newly completed building to insure longevity. Here, rice cakes are thrown off the scaffold. (Courtesy of Seattle Buddhist Temple Archives Collection.)

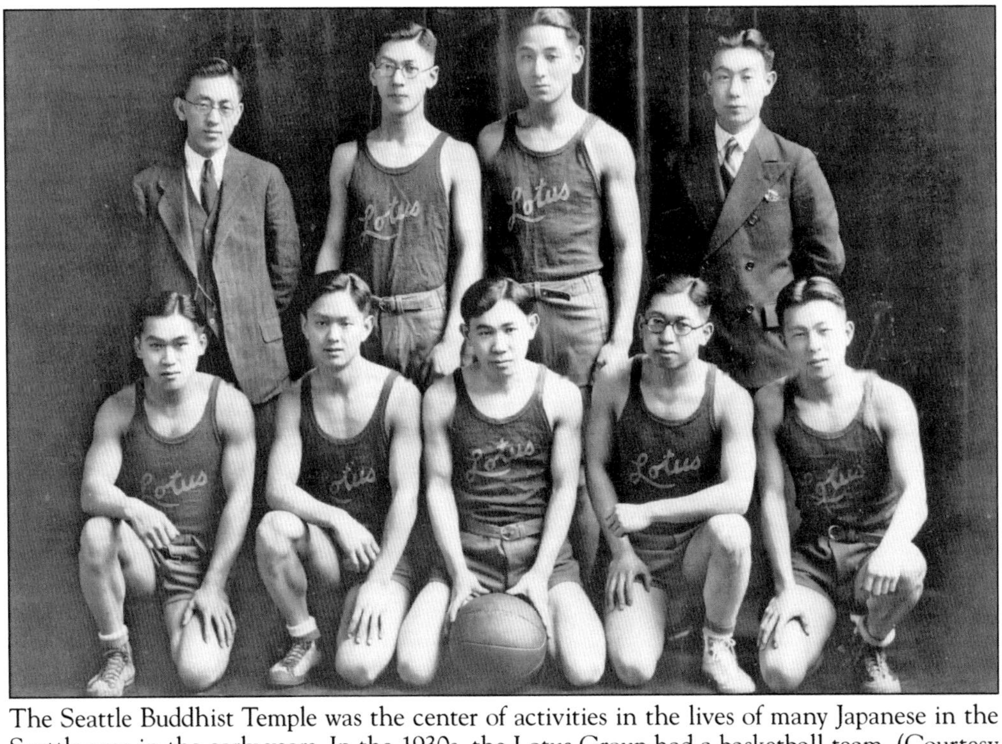

The Seattle Buddhist Temple was the center of activities in the lives of many Japanese in the Seattle area in the early years. In the 1930s, the Lotus Group had a basketball team. (Courtesy of Seattle Buddhist Temple Archives Collection.)

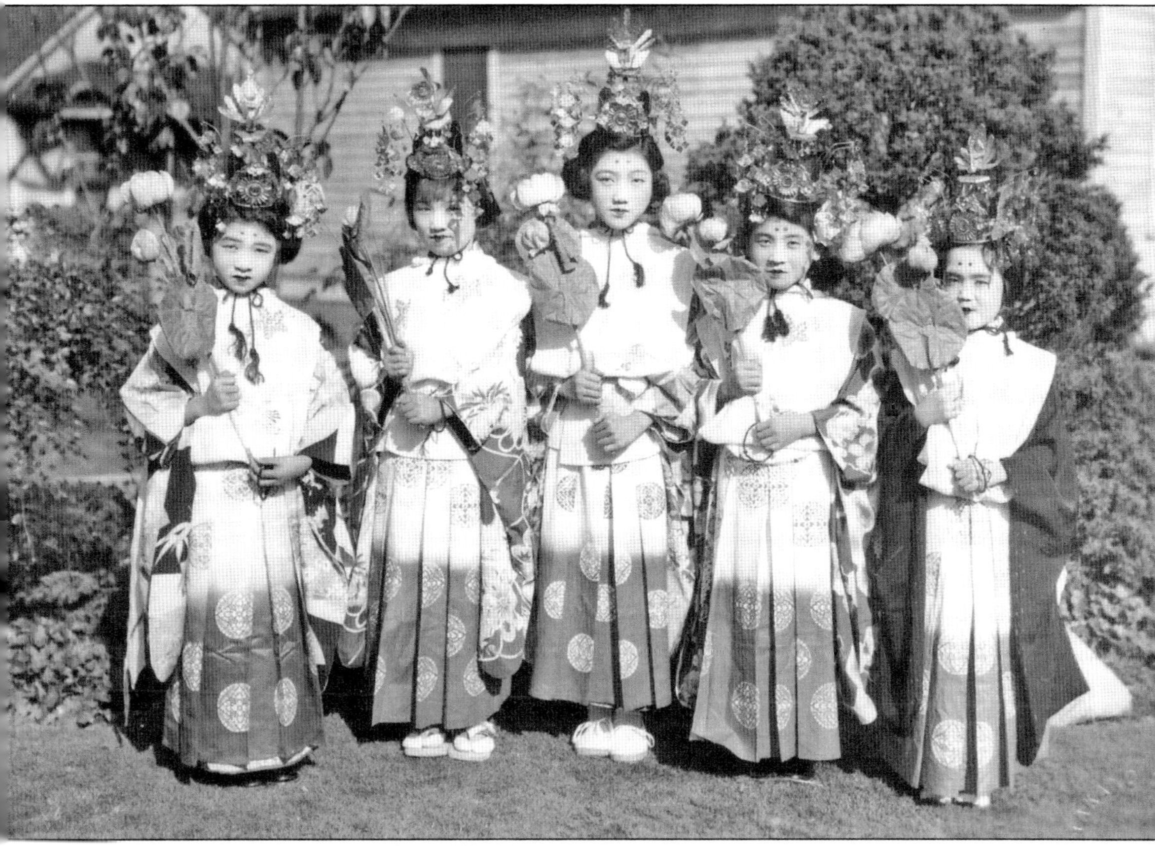

Five girls are pictured in 1941 in formal Buddhist wear as Chigo participants for a formal procession that occurs prior to a special occasion. Both boys and girls dressed in traditional Chigo costumes join in a procession with priests. The procession traces its roots to the time of Shakyamuni Buddha. (Courtesy of Seattle Buddhist Temple Archives Collection.)

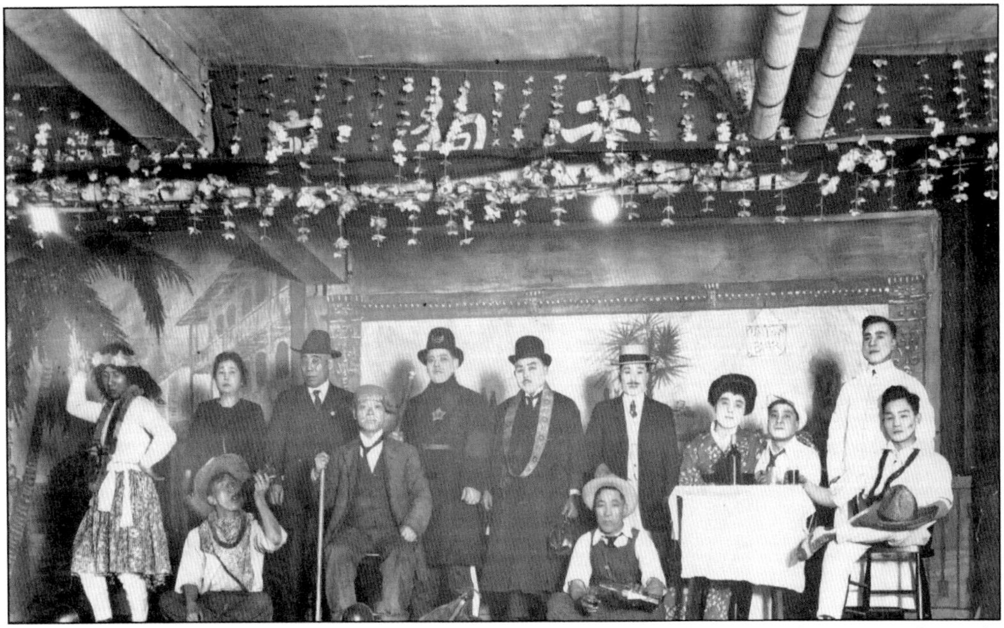

The Lotus Group puts on a program in the basement of the church in 1915. (Courtesy of Seattle Buddhist Temple Archives Collection.)

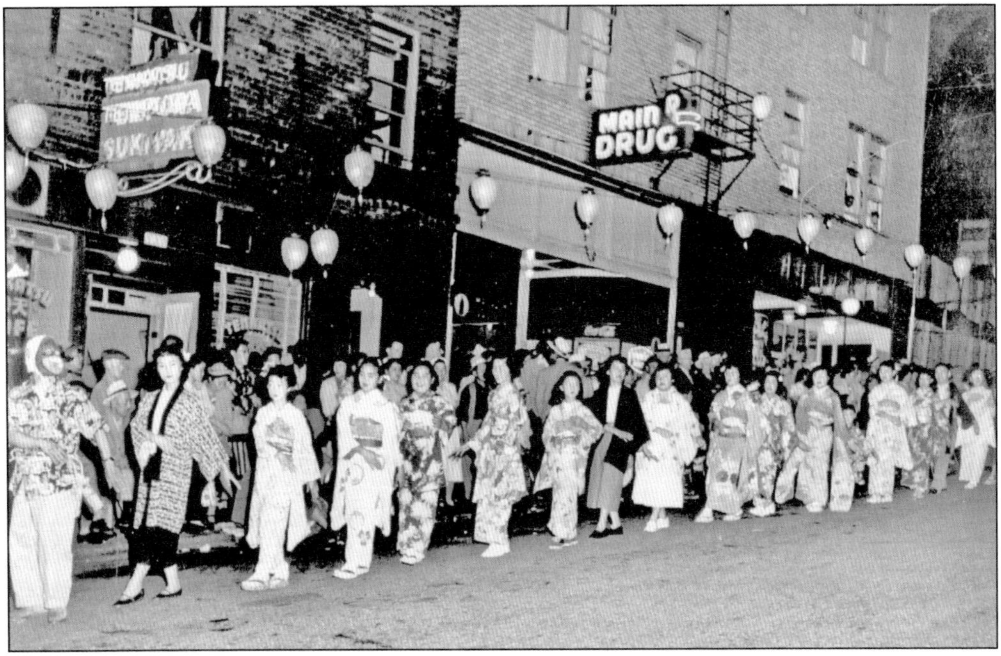

The Japanese community put their lives back together. The temple began to grow again. In 1945, a new auditorium was dedicated. In 1948, the church started a day nursery program and a Boy Scout troop. On March 11, 1954, the Seattle Buddhist Temple received Betsuin status, and its many accomplishments were recognized by the mother temple in Japan. Because the Seattle Betsuin Buddhist Temple has been such a vital part of China Town and the history of Seattle, the temple was included in the China Town Historic District in 1986 when the district was listed in the National Register of Historic Places. (Courtesy of Seattle Buddhist Temple Archives Collection.)

Six

Mount Zion Baptist Church

Mount Zion Baptist Church is perhaps one of the most well-known icons of the civil rights movement. The church was founded in 1890 and has the largest African American congregation in the state of Washington. From its beginnings, it was steeped not only in spirituality but also civil rights for racial minorities, the working poor, and any oppressed group.

In 1890, a group of African Americans began meeting in homes to worship. Some attended other Seattle churches, such as the First Baptist Church; however, many members wanted their own church to reflect their own method of worship. Rev. George T. Burchett, who was pastor of the First Baptist Church, encouraged the establishment of the startup church and even donated temporary space in a store at Fourteenth Avenue and East Madison Street that would be used as the church's first house of worship and Sunday school.

The new church was organized on February 18, 1894, and incorporated in 1903. The original members included Austin Anderson, Mrs. Braxton, Robert A. Clark, Mrs. E.W. Butler, Mr. and Mrs. Robert A. Clark, Elize Washington, Mr. and Mrs. Shephard, and B.F. Ward.

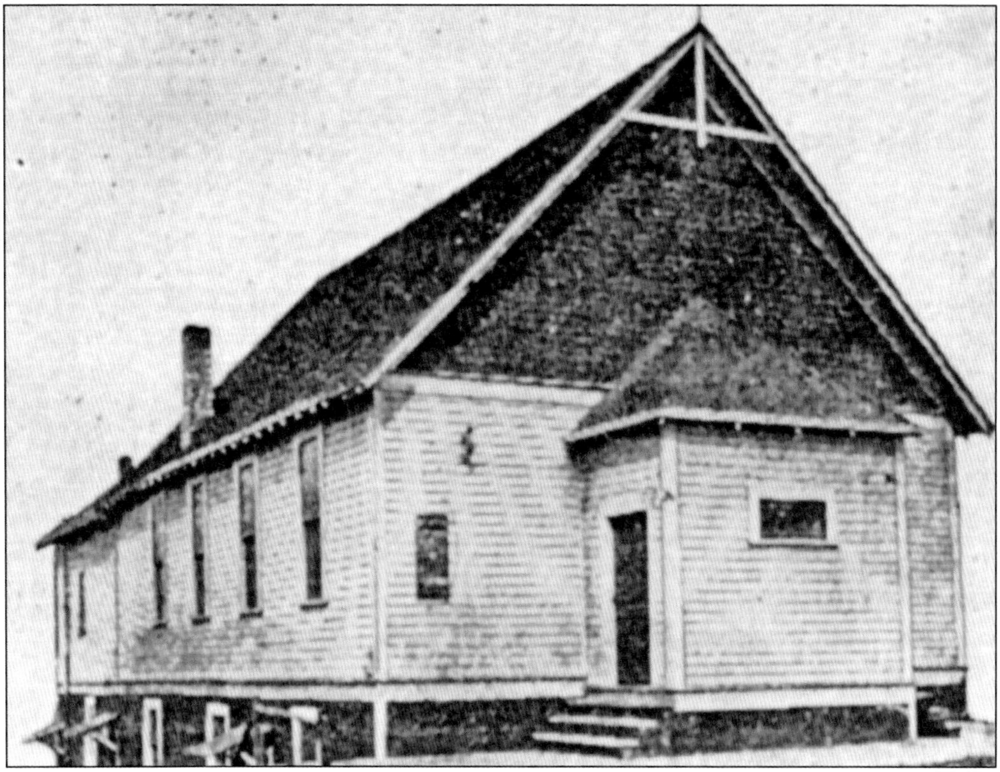

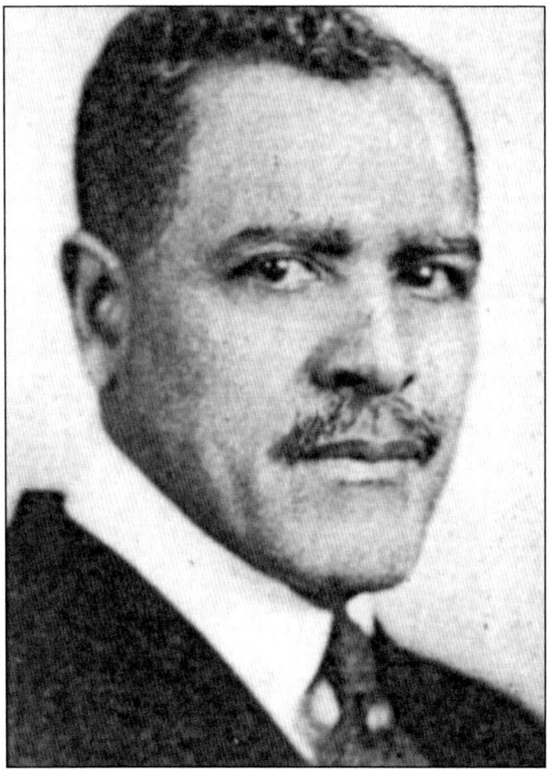

In 1907, after a series of locations, Mount Zion Baptist Church purchased land at Eleventh Avenue and Union Street, where the first church was built. (Courtesy of Mount Zion Archives Collection.)

During its early years, Mount Zion's pastors' tenures were very short. The ministers usually stayed from eight months to two years before moving on. However, in 1912, the pastorship of Mount Zion began to stabilize with the arrival of Rev. W.D. Carter on November 12. Reverend Carter served from 1912 to 1925, and under his leadership, the church's congregation grew exponentially. (Courtesy of Mount Zion Archives Collection.)

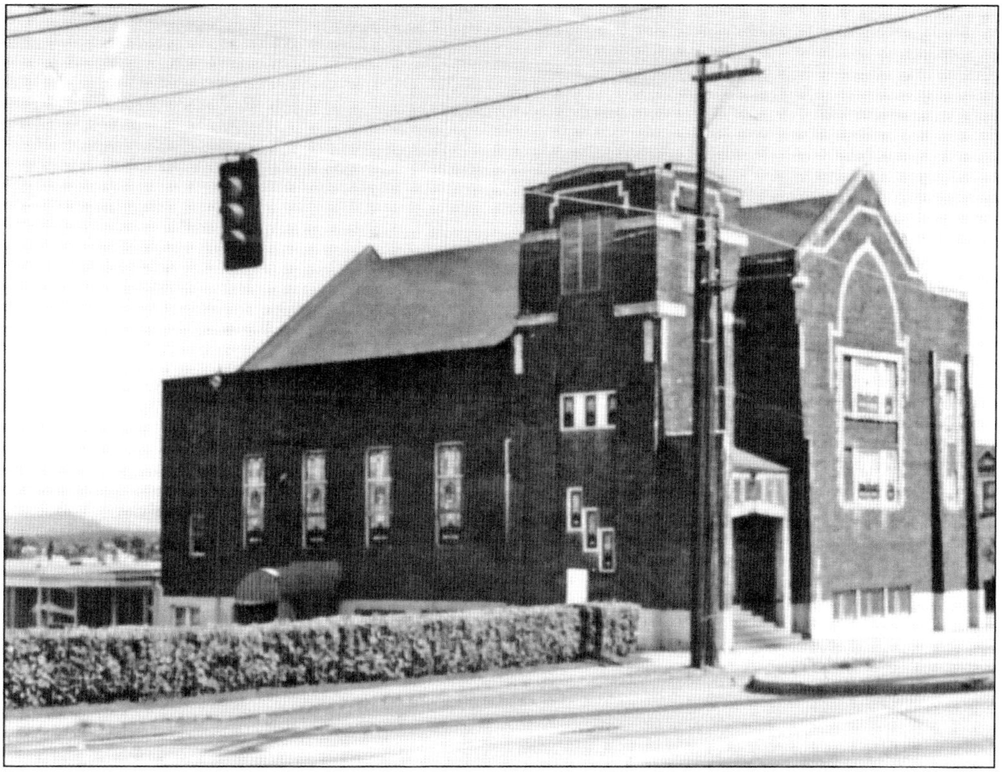

The congregation soon outgrew the small church, and in 1918, Reverend Carter approved the purchase of an eight-room house at Nineteenth Avenue and East Madison Street. In 1920, the house was repurposed and remodeled as a bigger sanctuary with a 700-seat capacity. Reverend Carter also started work in political, social, and educational advocacy. (Courtesy of Mount Zion Archives Collection.)

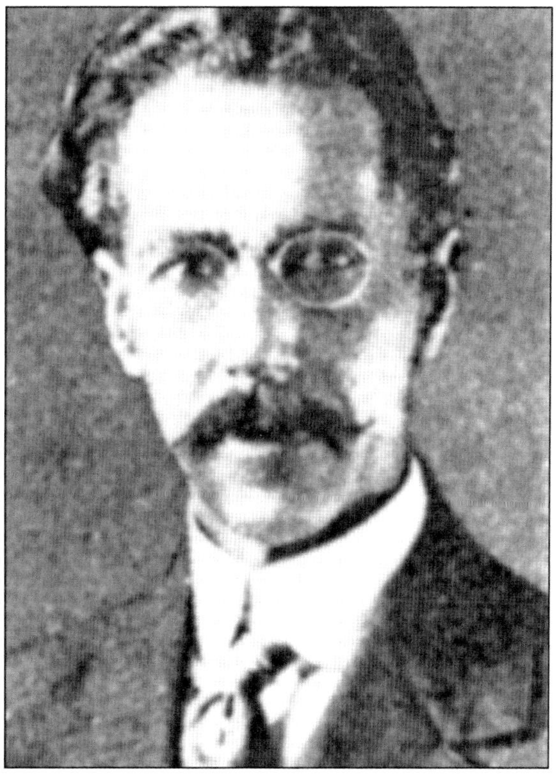

Rev. Sterling Moore was pastor from 1925 to 1932 and was instrumental in eliminating much of the church's debt. He also continued the church's advocacy work. (Courtesy of Mount Zion Archives Collection.)

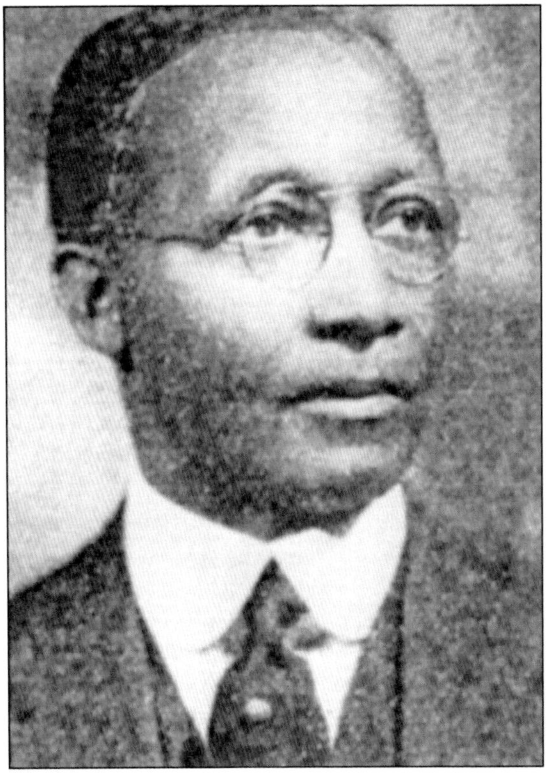

Rev. Taylor M. Davis pastored the church from 1932 to 1940. He had the unenviable task of guiding the congregation through the Great Depression, which for most people did not end until 1939. More than 13 million Americans were unemployed, and almost half the country's banks failed. (Courtesy of Mount Zion Archives Collection.)

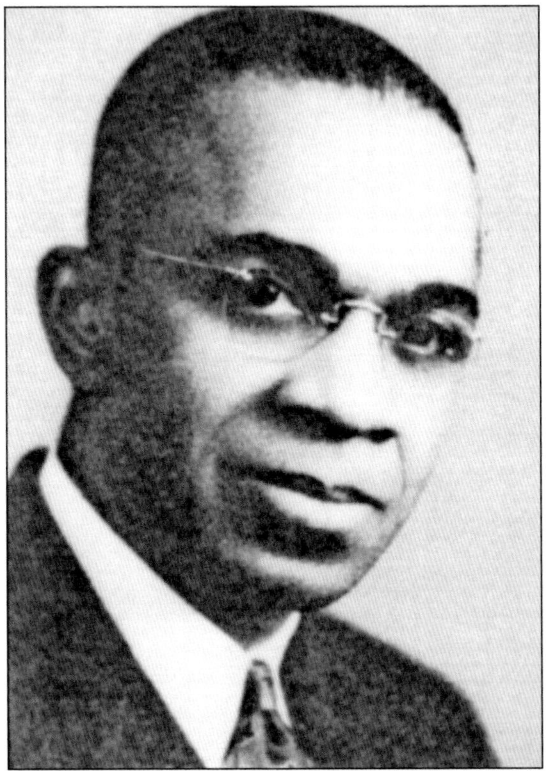

From 1940 to 1942, Rev. Fountain E. Penick was pastor. Under his leadership, the church purchased two additional lots to expand. At the time, Mount Zion was Seattle's only African American Baptist church. Under his leadership, the Brotherhood was formed. Reverend Penick left Mount Zion to organize another church in Seattle. (Courtesy of Mount Zion Archives Collection.)

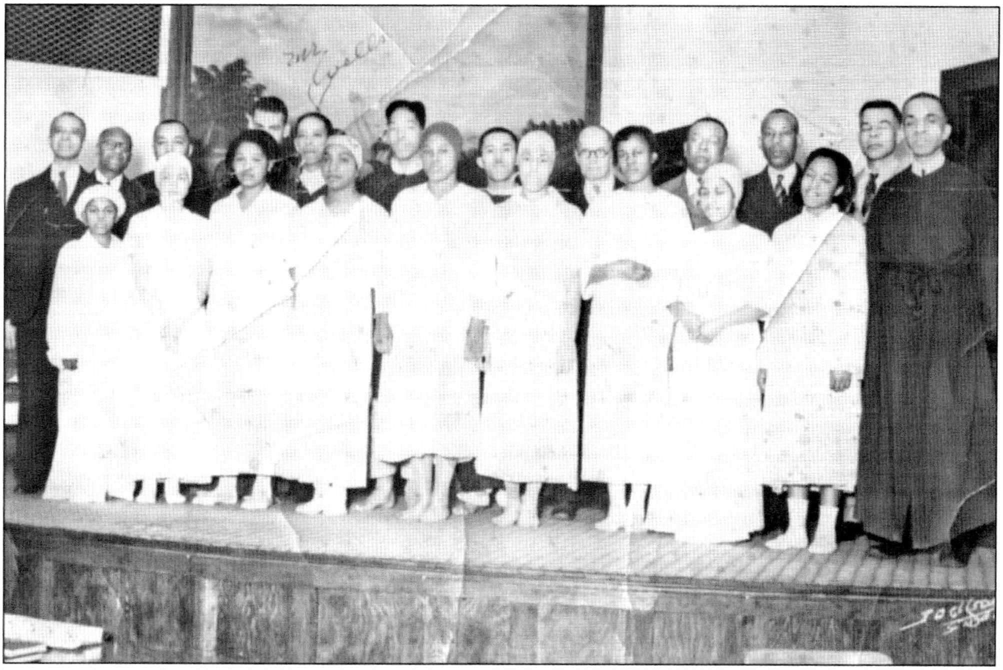

Reverend Penick is about to perform a baptism. At most Baptist churches, the person being baptized is submerged in a pool of water. (Courtesy of Mount Zion Archives Collection.)

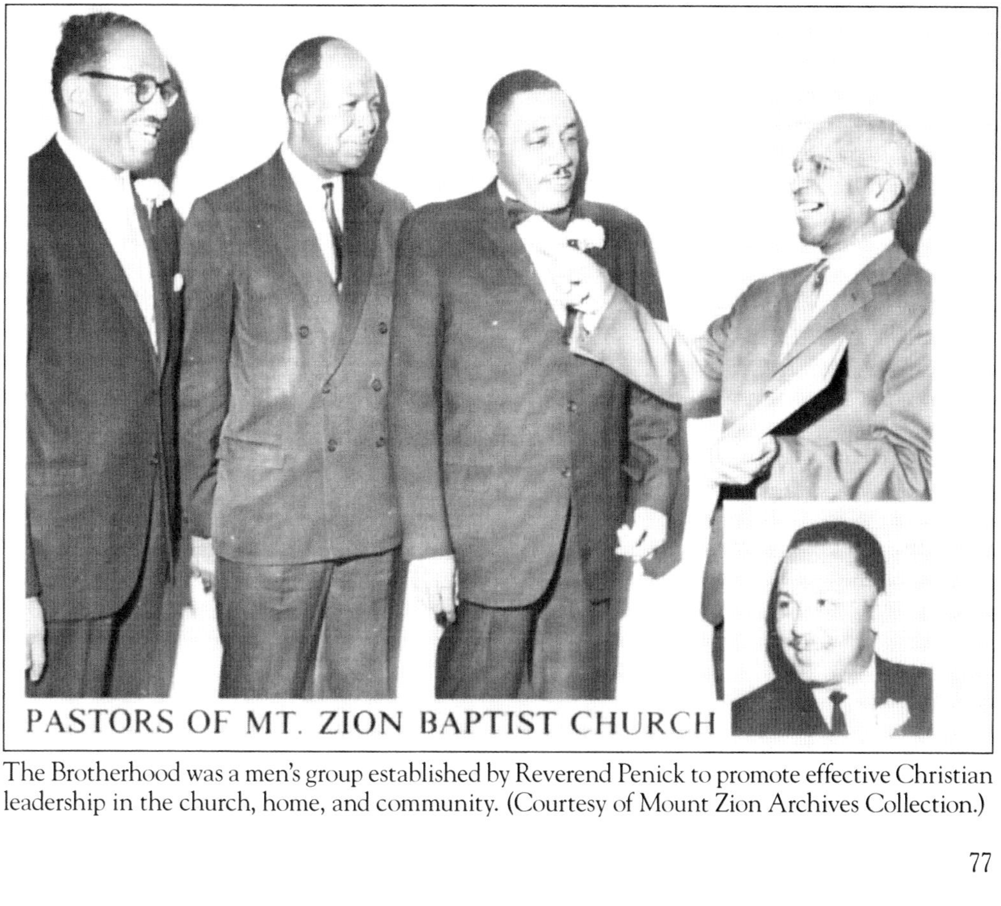

The Brotherhood was a men's group established by Reverend Penick to promote effective Christian leadership in the church, home, and community. (Courtesy of Mount Zion Archives Collection.)

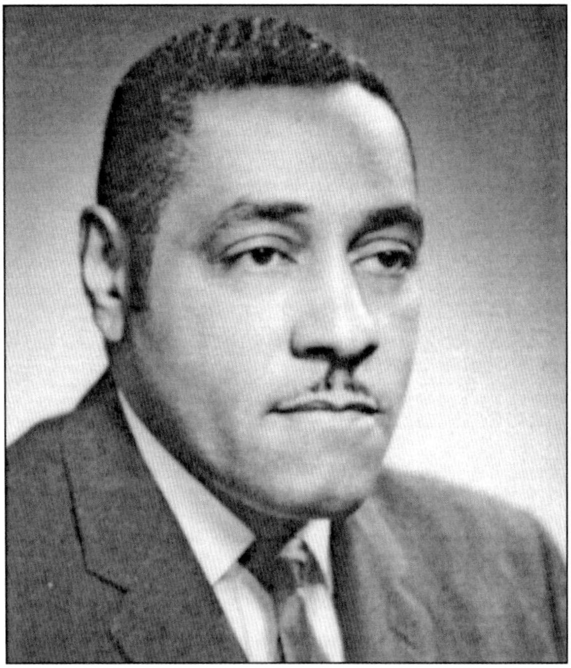

Rev. F. Benjamin Davis pastored Mount Zion from 1942 to 1955. The start of World War II brought many African Americans to Seattle, including military personnel and people coming to work for companies such as Boeing that were dedicated to the war effort. During this period, Mount Zion's membership more than doubled. Revered Davis was a tireless worker. He began the church's nursery school and purchased a Sunday school bus to more actively involve families in worship. (Courtesy of Mount Zion Archives Collection.)

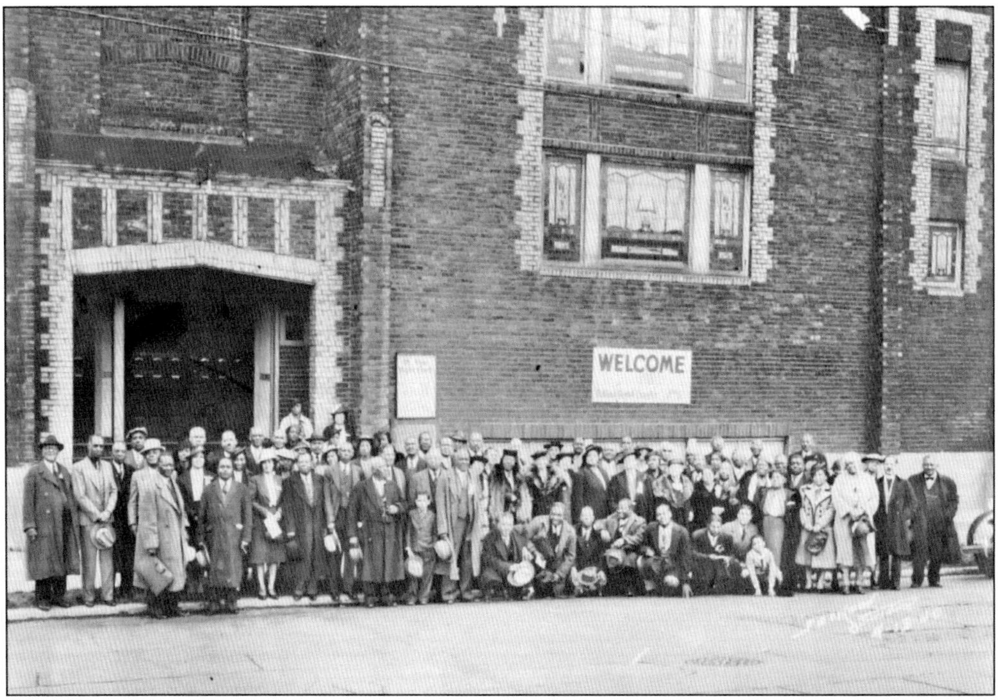

Reverend Davis also solidified the church's affiliation with the National Baptist Convention. Reverend Davis continued the church's civil rights commitment as he and the church itself were becoming more influential in political and social issues in the city. He ran for the city council in 1946, and although he lost, he received more than 25,000 votes in a city of only 4,000 black voters. Delegates of the Washington State Baptist Convention are pictured around 1942. (Courtesy of Mount Zion Archives Collection.)

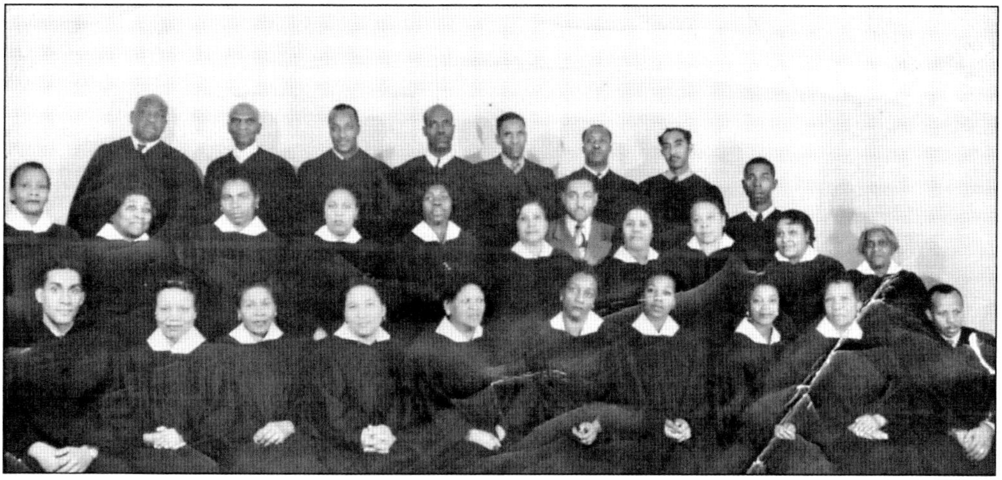

Reverend Davis named a music director, Kenneth Stovall, who instituted a senior and youth choir. The music became one of the welcoming features of Mount Zion's services. The church choir became renowned. (Courtesy of Mount Zion Archives Collection.)

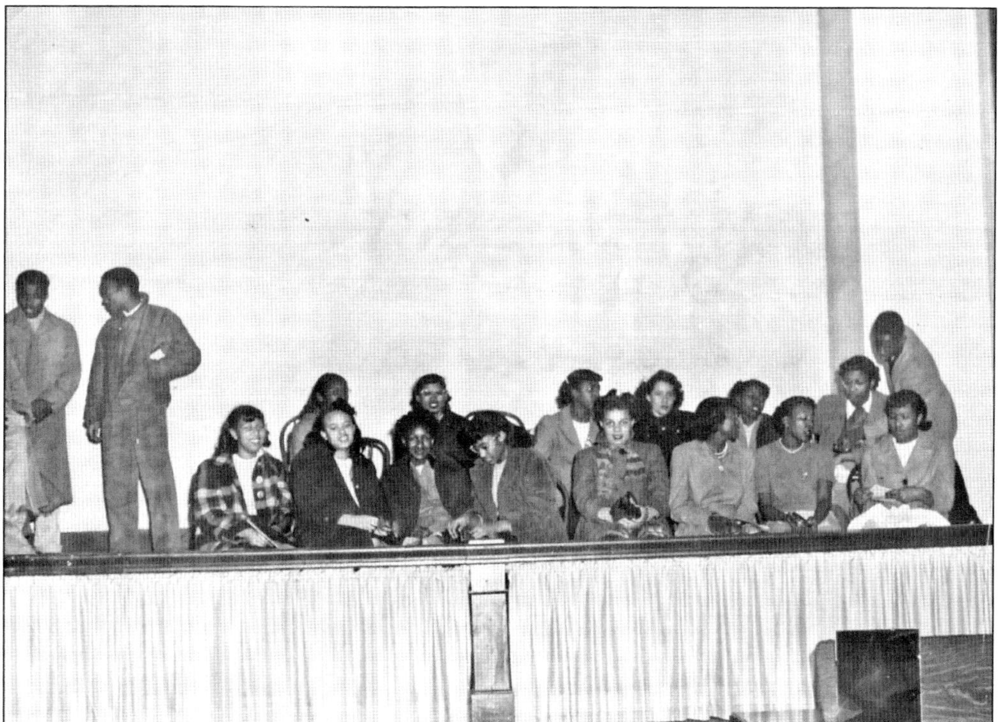

Choir rehearsal takes place at Mount Zion around 1948. Choir members included a young future music legend, Quincy Jones, standing at right. (Courtesy of Mount Zion Archives Collection.)

MOUNT ZION PASTORS

(Not Pictured)

Rev. Anderson - 1890

Rev. Calvin Williams - 1894

Rev. R.W. Jennison - 1896

Rev. Simons - 1896

Rev. J. C. Pegram - 1897

Rev. Eugene Harris - 1898

Rev. Prince - 1899

Rev. George Maney - 1900

Rev. Gordon McPherson - 1907

Rev. Walker - 1908

Rev. Wiggins - 1908

Rev. R. H. Thomas - 1910

Rev. Lyman Smith - 1911

Rev. William Hammon - 1911

Rev. William Barry - 1912

Rev. Gil B. Lloyd was pastor from 1955 to 1958. Under his leadership, the building fund grew, and he also helped develop the Women's Society. (Courtesy of Mount Zion Archives Collection.)

Women's Day is pictured at Mount Zion around 1956. The Women's Society participated on councils and oversaw congregational activities. (Courtesy of Mount Zion Archives Collection.)

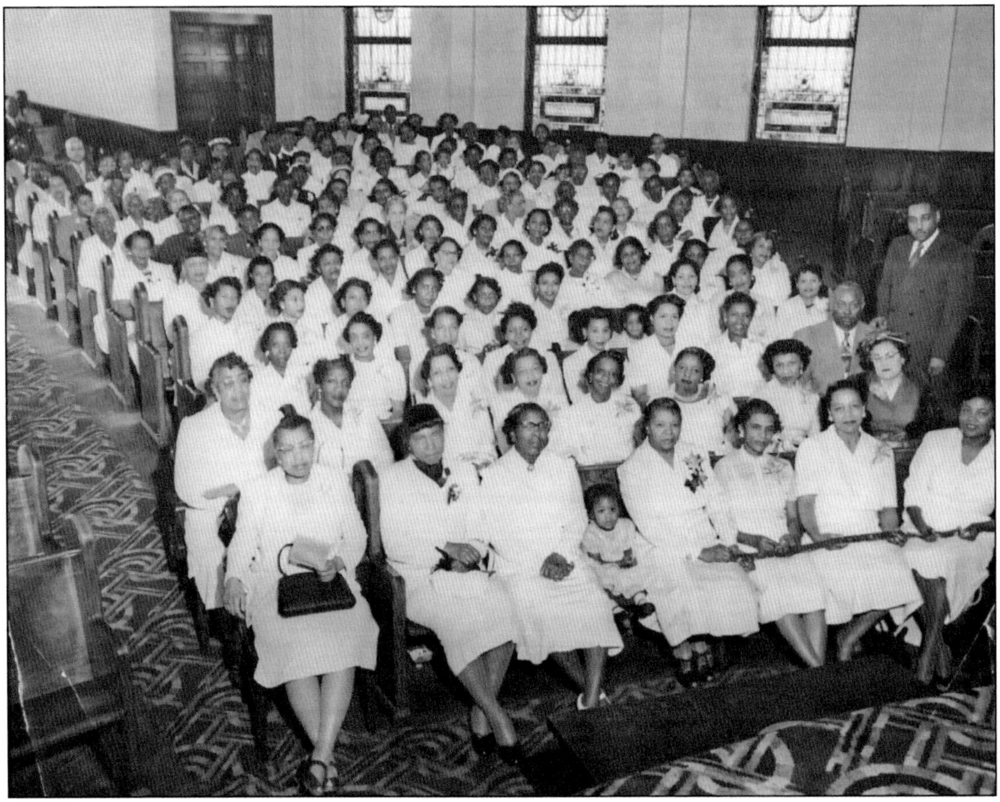

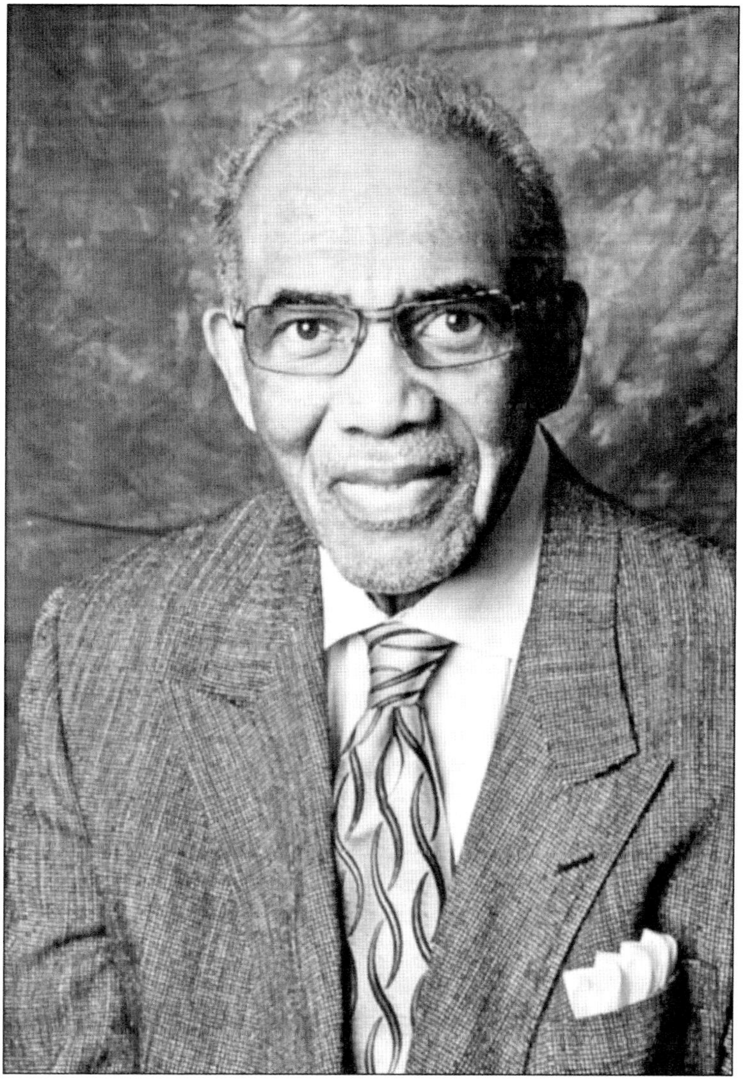

In 1958, the Reverend Dr. Samuel Berry McKinney arrived as pastor of Mount Zion. His continuous 40-year pastorship was the longest in the church's history. He retired in 1998 but came out of retirement and served again from 2005 to 2008. He became one of the more iconic civil rights leaders in the state of Washington and the nation. Reverend McKinney was born on December 28, 1926, in Flint, Michigan. His father was a Baptist minister and a civil rights advocate. The family moved to Ohio, and while he was growing up, his father would often invite civil rights leader Thurgood Marshall to his church to speak. Reverend McKinney attended Morehouse College, an all-male historically black college in Atlanta that has produced Rhodes scholars and is the alma mater of many African American leaders. While there, he and Dr. Martin Luther King Jr. were roommates and would often discuss how they would effect change in the world. Reverend McKinney initially wanted to become a civil rights attorney, but after much discussion and soul searching, they both decided to become ministers. Reverend McKinney said he saw no difference between being a minister and being a civil rights leader because both aimed to end the suffering of people. He graduated from Morehouse in 1949 and from New York's Colgate Rochester Divinity School in 1952; he received his doctorate degree in 1975 from Colgate Rochester Crozier Divinity School. (Courtesy of Mount Zion Archives Collection.)

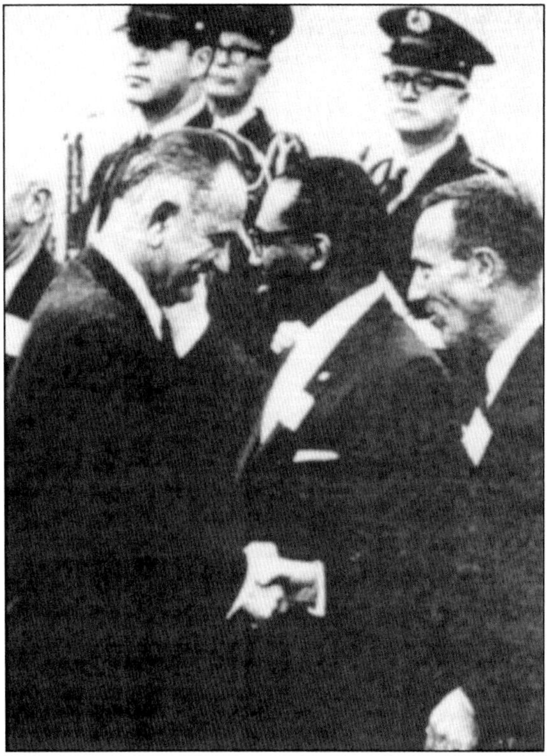

Dr. McKinney soon became one of the leading voices on civil rights, and Mount Zion became a focal point for spiritual enrichment and civil rights activities as well. During the 1960s, he marched in the streets of Seattle alongside other civil rights organizations such as the NAACP and CORE for equal rights, equal job opportunities, equal housing, and equal education for minorities, the poor, and all other disenfranchised people. His voice was so strong that local and national political leaders made Mount Zion a mandatory stop on their path to an election. Here, Pres. Lyndon Johnson meets with Reverend McKinney during his reelection bid. (Courtesy of Mount Zion Archives Collection.)

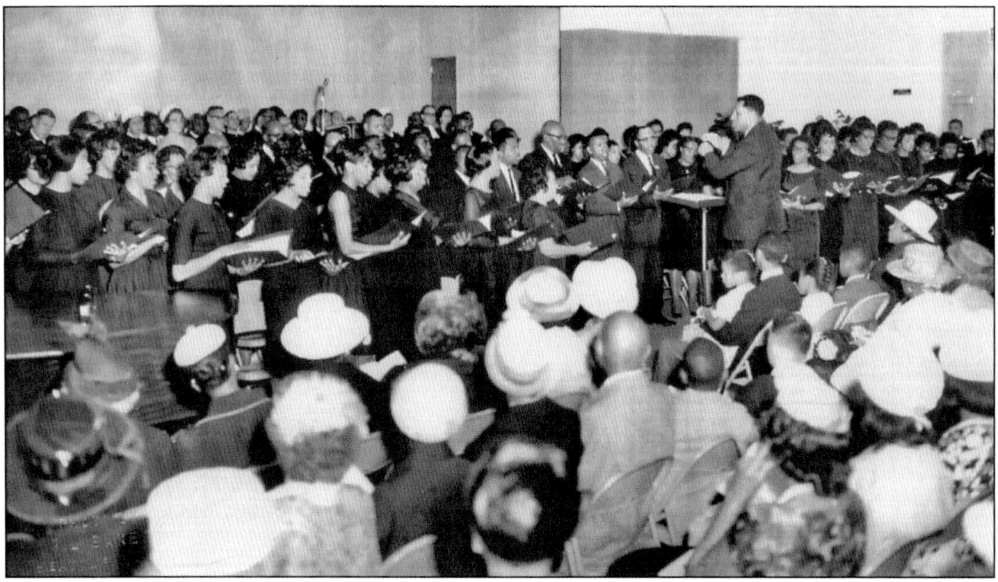

In 1961, Reverend McKinney invited his old friend Dr. Martin Luther King Jr. to speak in Seattle. Mount Zion didn't have enough space to accommodate the expected crowd, so Reverend McKinney arranged with another church to hold the event. Word got out that Dr. King, who was considered very controversial at the time, was speaking, and the church cancelled the event. However, Temple de Hirsch stepped in and offered its synagogue, and the event went on as planned. Plymouth Congregational Church held a reception for Dr. King after his speech. (Courtesy of Mount Zion Archives Collection.)

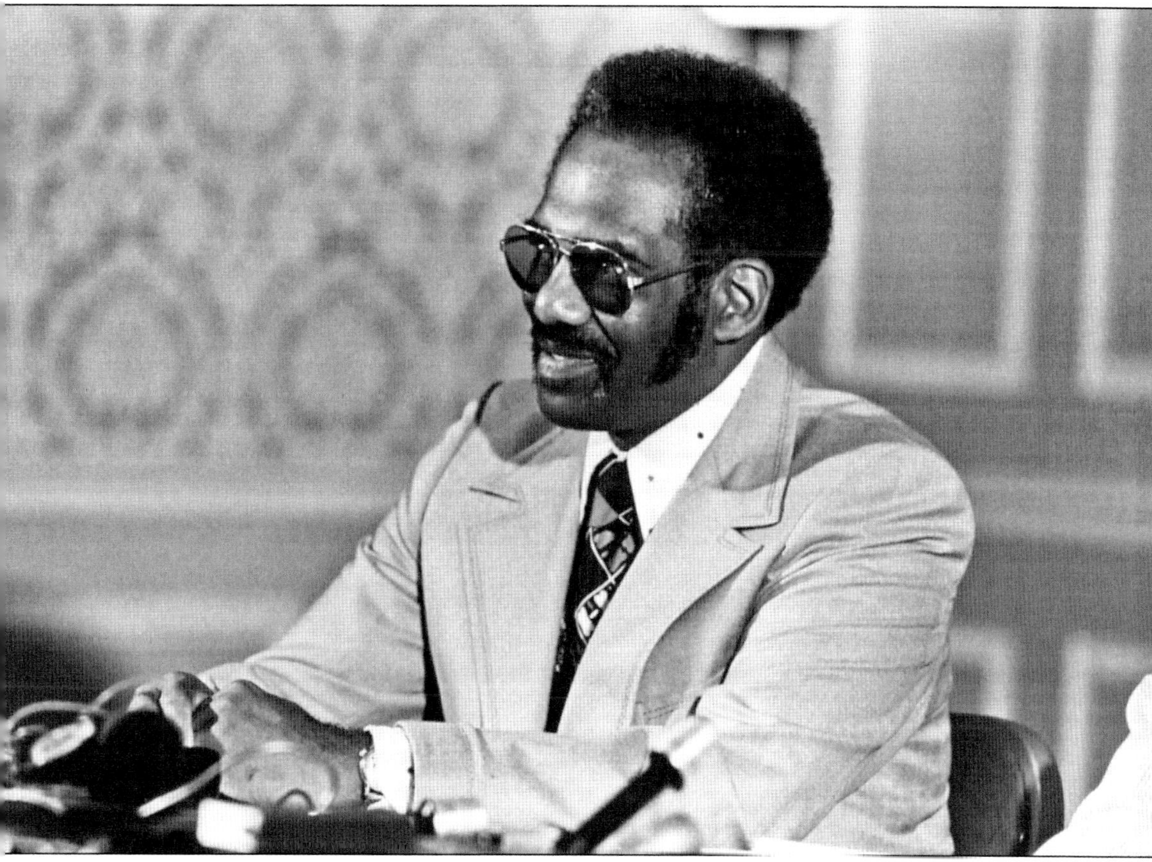

In 1963, Rev. McKinney joined Dr. King for the March on Washington for Jobs and Freedom, which was attended by more than 250,000 people. In 1965, he marched with Dr. King again during the historic Selma-to-Montgomery march in support of the passage of the Voting Rights Act. In 1966, he cofounded the Seattle Opportunity Industrialization Center, a nonprofit community vocational training center. Under his leadership, the Samuel Berry McKinney Manor, which houses the elderly and the working poor, was constructed and completed in 1998. He also helped to develop the Mount Zion preschool and kindergarten and the Ethnic School, and helped to establish an annual $20,000 scholarship fund. In 1985, he was arrested for protesting apartheid in South Africa. Reverend McKinney is pictured at a Seattle City Council meeting. (Courtesy of Mount Zion Archives Collection.)

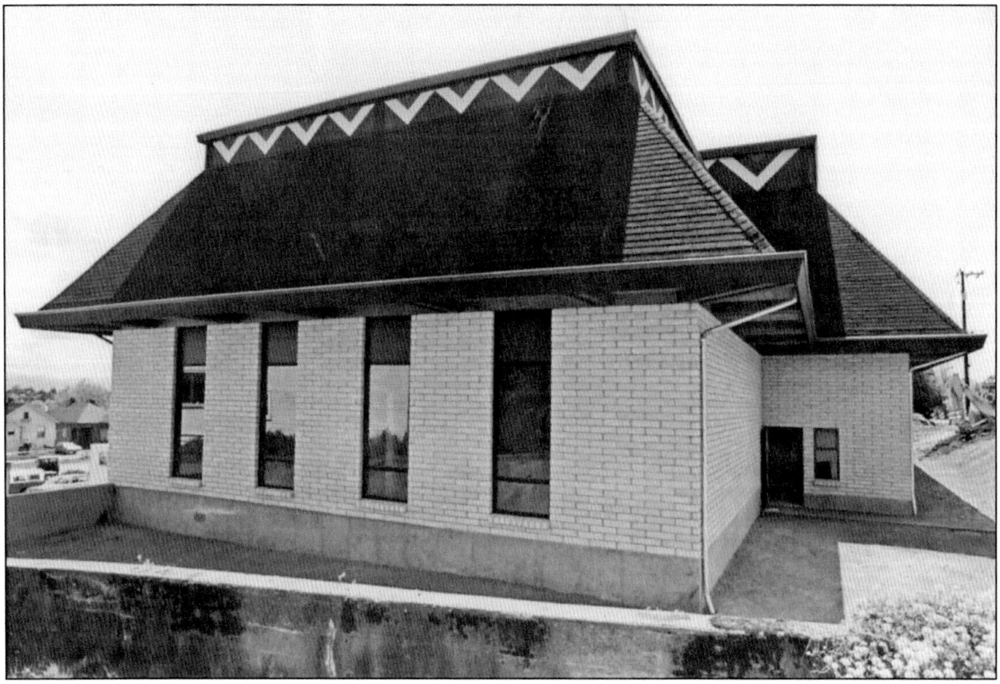

In 1975, Mount Zion's third building was designed with an African theme. (Courtesy of Mount Zion Archives Collection.)

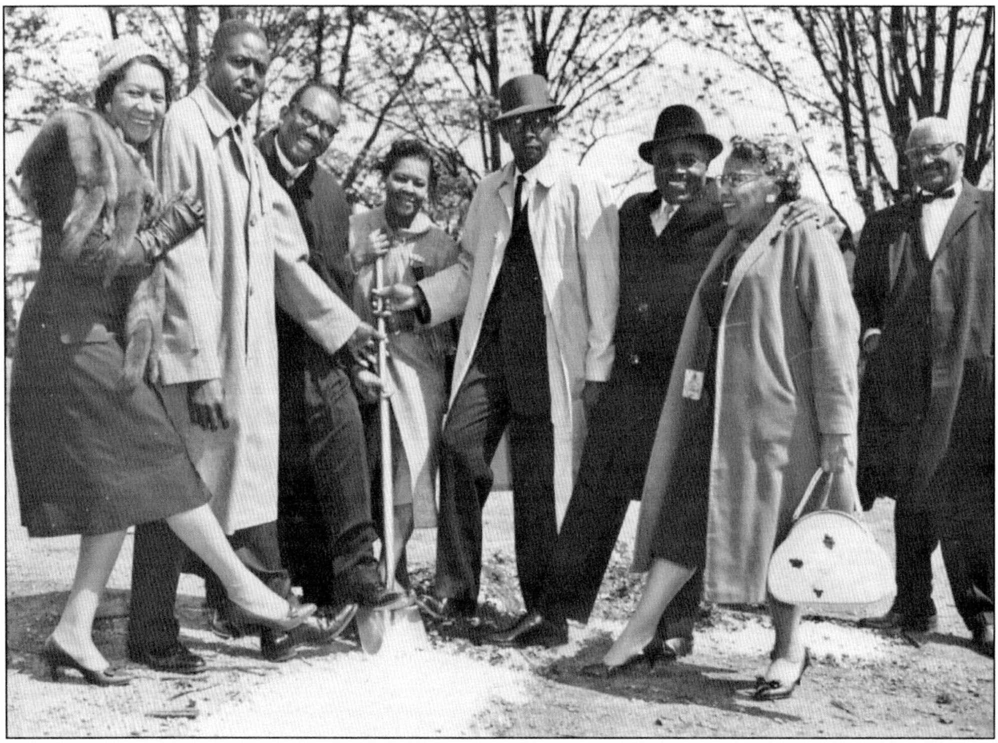

The ground-breaking ceremony for the new fellowship hall is pictured around 1960. (Courtesy of Mount Zion Archives Collection.)

The interior of the church has 18 stained-glass windows known as *The Church of the World*, honoring people who have made an impact or contribution to African American life. Those honored include Booker T. Washington, Martin Luther King Jr., and abolitionists Harriett Tubman (below) and Frederick Douglass (right). The stained-glass windows are one of a kind and were made specifically for Mount Zion. The windows were designed by Douglas Phillips of Cleveland, Ohio, the only black owner of a stained-glass studio in the United States at that time. (Both photographs by Marilyn Morgan, courtesy of Mount Zion Archives Collection.)

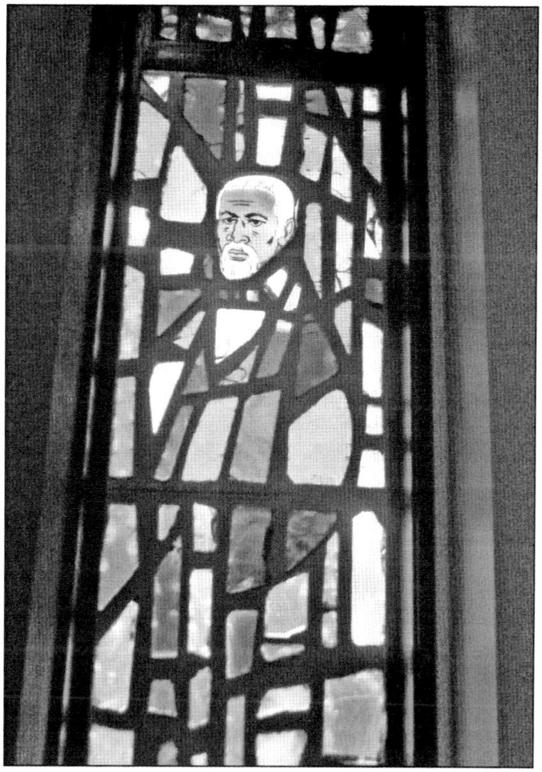

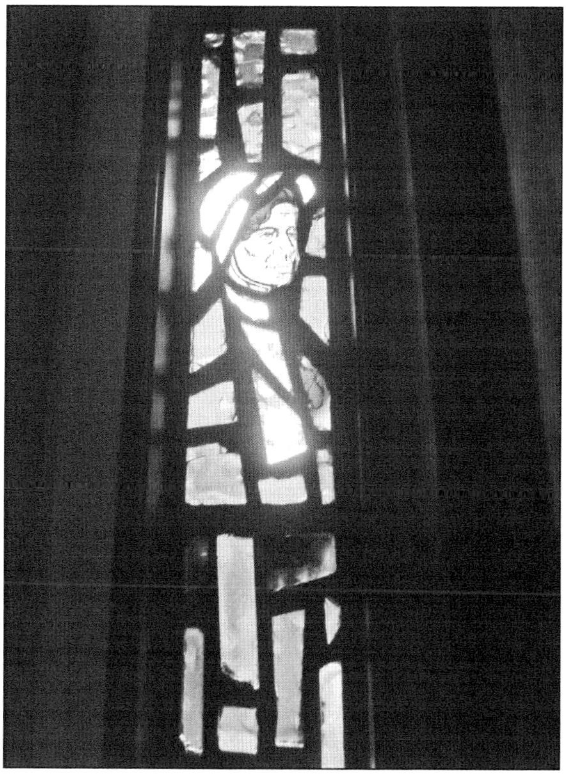

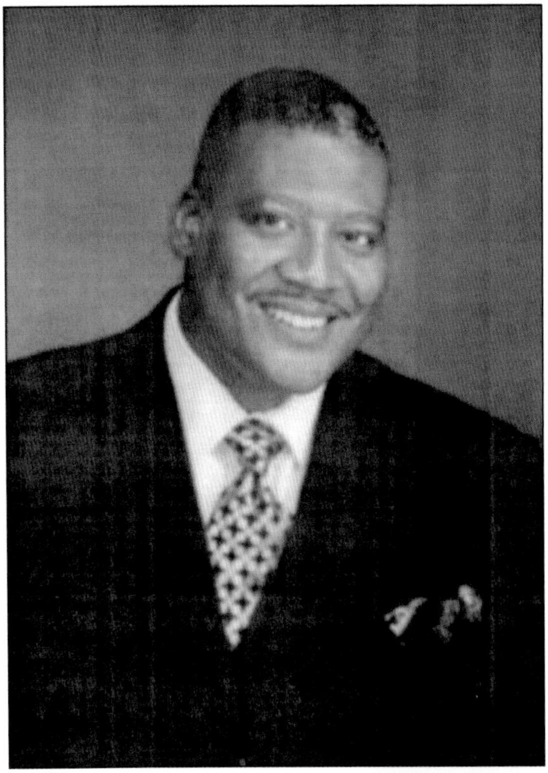

Reverend McKinney retired in 1998, leaving behind a long legacy. Rev. Leslie David Braxton took over as senior pastor but resigned in 2005 after his tenure was met with tension and derision. Reverend McKinney was asked to return in 2005 and stayed until his second retirement in 2008. (Courtesy of Mount Zion Archives Collection.)

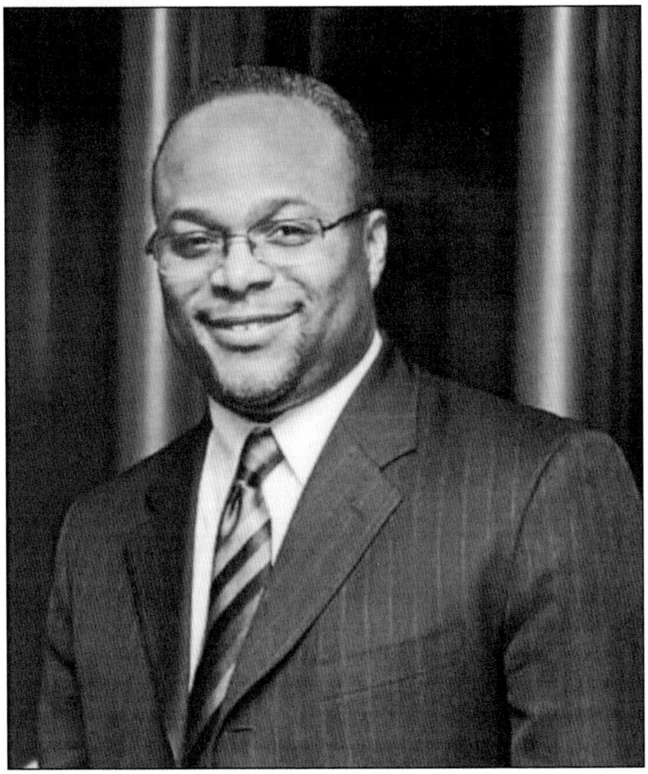

In 2008, Rev. Aaron Williams became the church's senior pastor. (Courtesy of Mount Zion Archives Collection.)

Seven

SEATTLE FIRST BAPTIST CHURCH

In 1869, Seattle was a rapidly growing town with a population of more than 1,100 people. It was also a town of 13 saloons that were apparently well patronized.

That December, 11 people met at the home of Edward and Abbie Hanford to establish a church. They were Edward Hanford, Abbie Hanford, Thaddeus Hanford, Frank Hanford, L.S. Rogers, Delia Rogers, W.L. Rogers, Lucy Rogers, L.J. Holgate, A.O. McAllister, and S.P. Andrews. The committee members were pioneers in Seattle. For example, John C. Holgate was one of the first people to make the Puget Sound his home. The committee signed an article of faith to establish Seattle First Baptist. The first service was on New Year's Day 1870 at the home of the Hanfords. Since a building had not been erected, the church members met at various homes.

The new church needed a building and a minister to carry out its work and to attract more members. Toward that end, Elizabeth Holgate bought and donated land at Fourth Avenue between Cherry and James Streets for a church. It was a small wooden structure. On August 25, 1872, a dedication ceremony was held, and in April 1873 a new pastor, Rev. James Freeman, arrived to lead the congregation. Reverend Freeman was from Boston, Massachusetts, and his intention was to stay with the church for at least a year. However, he was an older man, and the rough-and-tumble pioneer life proved to be too much, so he returned to Boston within a few months. During its early years, the church saw a series of pastors come and go. On April 6, 1875, the church welcomed a new pastor, Rev. J.A. Wirth, who served until 1883. The next pastor was Dr. D.J. Pierce, who served from 1883 to 1888. A graduate of New Hampton Institute and of Newton Theological Seminary, he believed strongly in missions; from 1883 to 1892, Seattle First Baptist became the mother church of several churches, including Scandinavian Baptist (1883), Japanese Baptist (1891), and Chinese Baptist (1892).

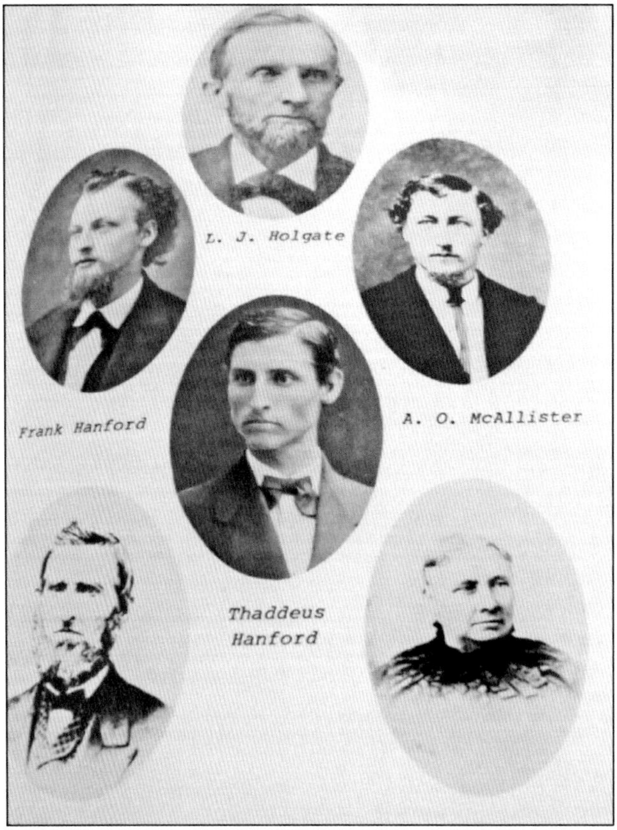

Some of the founders of Seattle First Baptist Church are pictured here. They met in 1869 at the home of L.S. Rogers to form the church. Clockwise from top are L.J. Holgate, A.O. McAllister, Abbie Hanford, Edward Hanford, Frank Hanford, and Thaddeus Hanford at center. (Courtesy of Seattle First Baptist Church.)

Seattle First Baptist Church's first building is pictured in 1885. (Courtesy of Seattle First Baptist Church.)

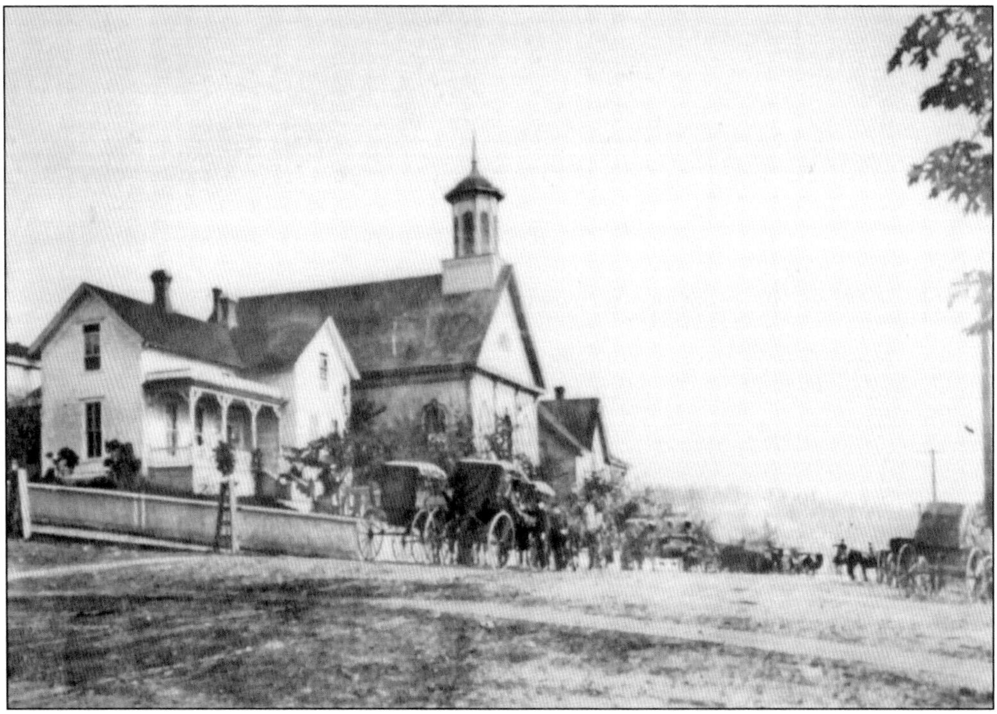

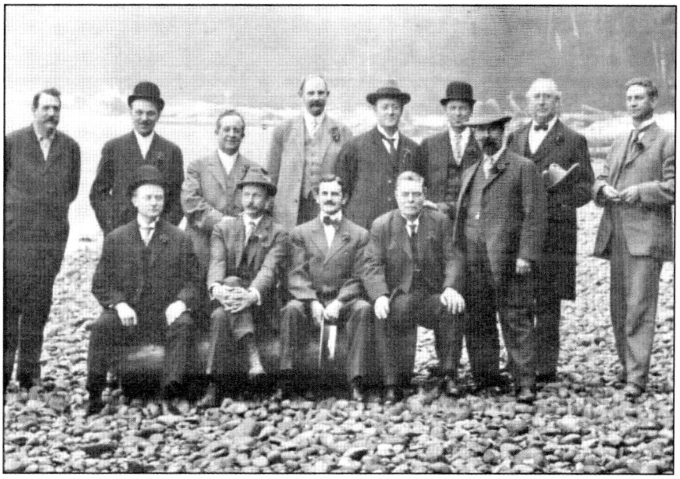

Dr. Pierce was succeeded by Rev. Robert Whitaker, who served from October 1888 to October 1889. The Great Seattle Fire of June 6, 1889, occurred during his tenure. The fire destroyed almost the entire downtown business and residential area. However, Seattle First Baptist was spared, as the fire stopped just short of the church. The Building Committee is pictured. (Courtesy of Seattle First Baptist Church.)

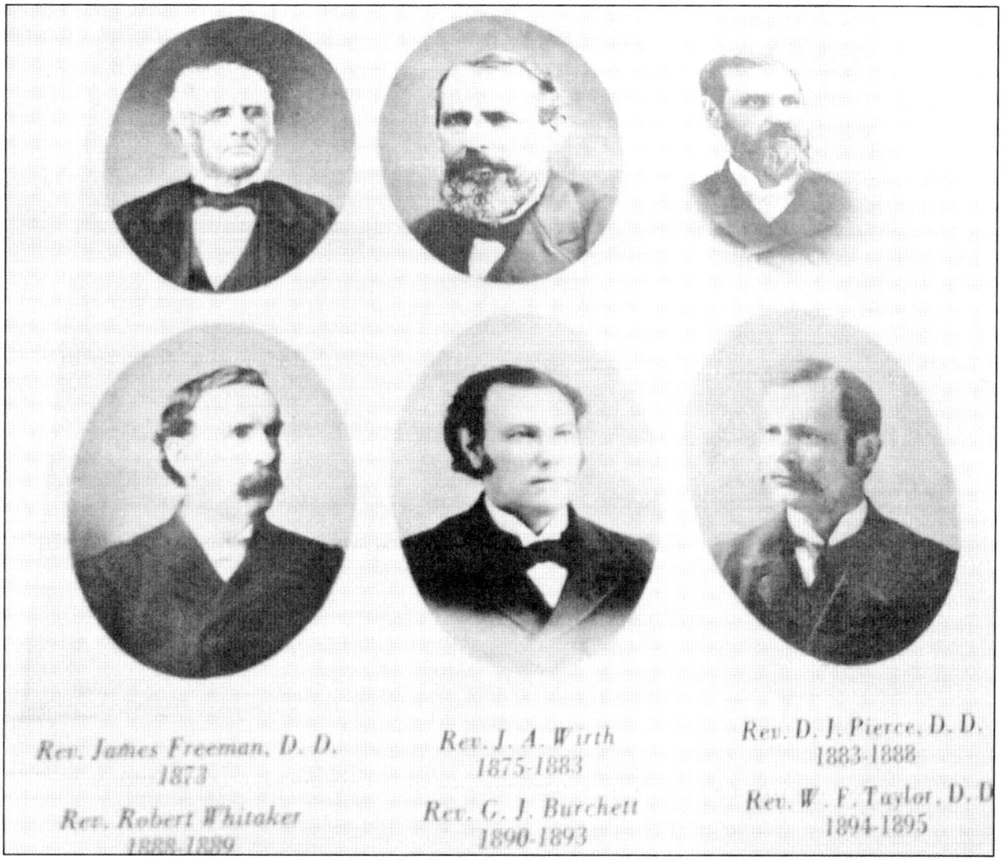

Rev. G.J. Burchett was the fifth pastor and served from January 11, 1890, to 1893. The church's congregation had increased significantly during this period and was continuing to grow. The congregation had outgrown the quaint, original church, and Reverend Burchett wanted to start a committee to raise funds to build a new church. However, these efforts were thwarted by a short depression for the city. In 1893, a drop in the US gold reserves resulted in a national depression. Seattle, still trying to recover from the Great Seattle Fire, was hit hard by the downturn. The city didn't fully recover until 1898. (Courtesy of Seattle First Baptist Church.)

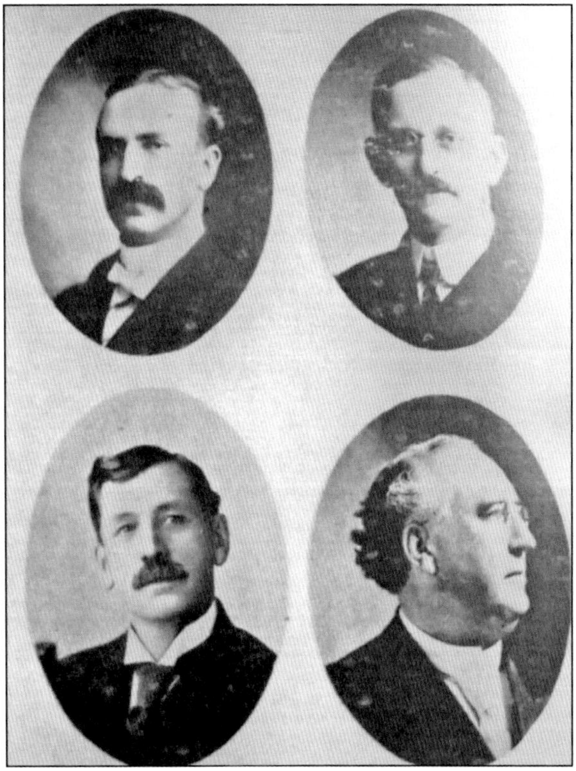

When Dr. W.F. Taylor became the sixth pastor on June 17, 1894, the congregation had outgrown the church, and services were held at the Seattle Theater at the corner of Third Avenue and Cherry Street. Rev. Louis S. Bowerman (top left) of Randolph, Massachusetts, became the church's seventh pastor on October 27, 1896, and stayed until 1902. The eighth pastor, Dr. J.O. Rust (top right), served from November 25, 1903, to May 1904. His tenure was cut short by his unexpected death. Rev. Myron Haynes (bottom left) became the ninth pastor and served from September 1905 to September 1907. Dr. Benaiah L. Whitman (bottom right) became the 10th pastor in January 1908. (Courtesy of Seattle First Baptist Church.)

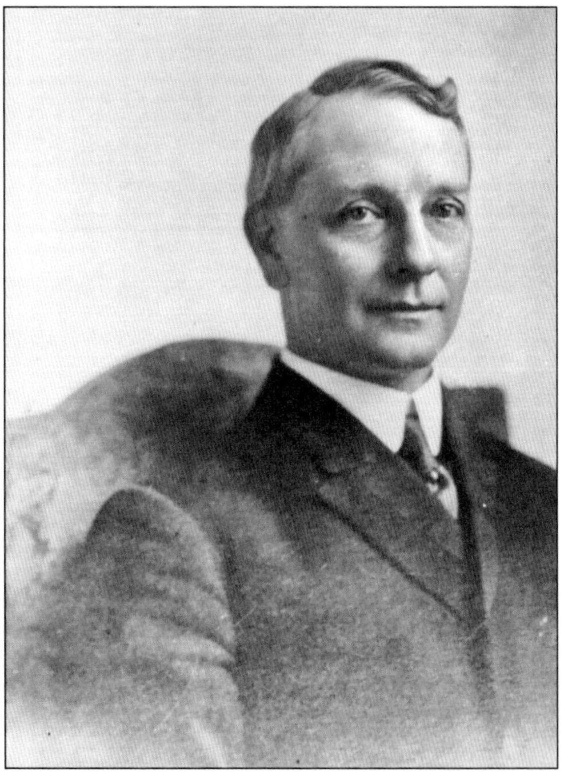

The congregation needed a place to worship, and Temple de Hirsch opened its doors to Seattle First Baptist on February 2, 1908. Under Dr. Whitman's leadership, property for a new church was purchased at Harvard Avenue and Seneca Street (the church's present location). Dr. Whitman was instrumental in crafting what the church would be, and the cornerstone was laid on October 12, 1910. Dr. Carter Helm Jones (pictured) preached the first service at the new church on September 15, 1912. Dr. Jones remained with the church until February 1, 1918. (Courtesy of Seattle First Baptist Church.)

Seattle First Baptist had seen great turnover in its pastors over the years, but that situation began to stabilize starting in the 1920s. Only three pastors served over the next 35 years. Dr. Ambrose M. Bailey (pictured) served from April 3, 1920, to September 1, 1928. He became known as "Seattle's Fighting Parson" for bringing to light what he charged as "the mayor and police running a lawless town." Pastor Bailey had a reputation as a man of the people—he would walk among the homeless on Seattle's Skid Row, giving them money, food, and comfort. (Courtesy of Seattle First Baptist Church.)

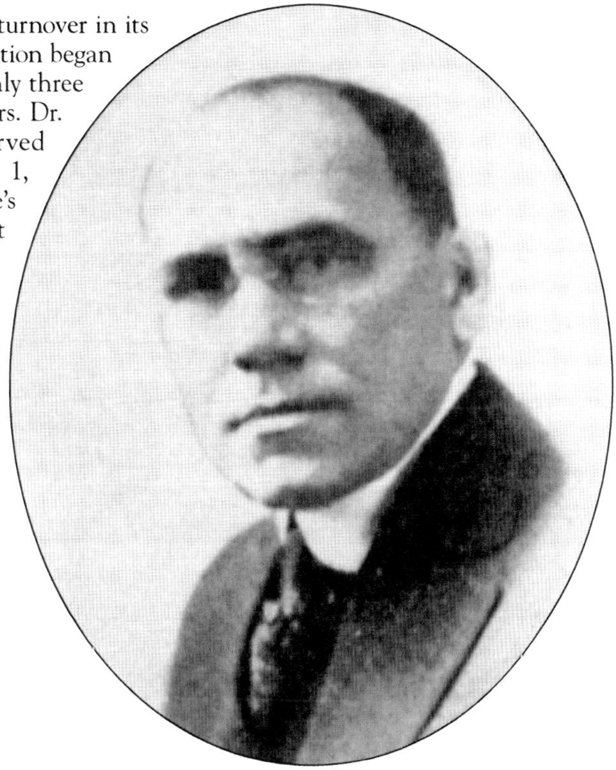

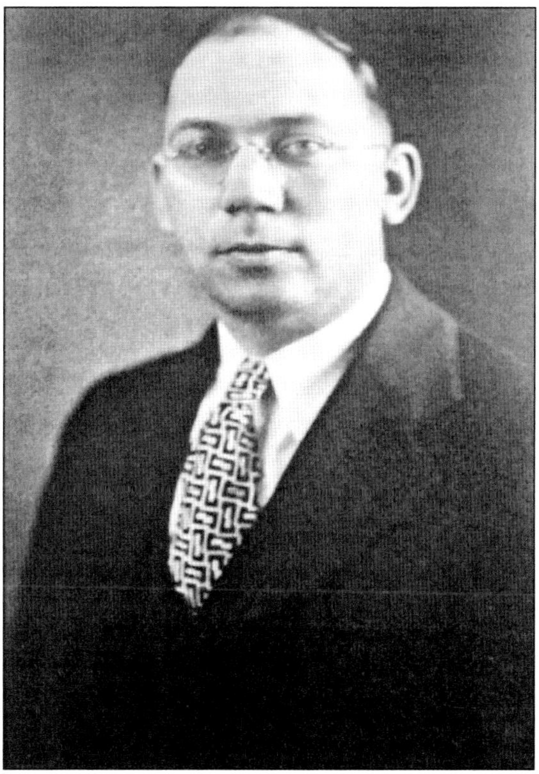

Dr. Elmer A. Fridell served from 1929 to 1937 and was described as scholarly and soft-spoken. He was a man of peace, and his sermons often reflected his beliefs, with titles such as "What Would Happen if the US Disarmed." During World War I, he went into the Army as a private and became a noncommissioned officer. Perhaps the horrors of war shaped his perspective. After his military experience, he became a pacifist and worked for peaceful solutions to conflicts. He received his degree from what is now the American Baptist Seminary of the West in 1922. Dr. Fridell also did graduate work at the University of California and the Pacific School of Religion. (Courtesy of Seattle First Baptist Church.)

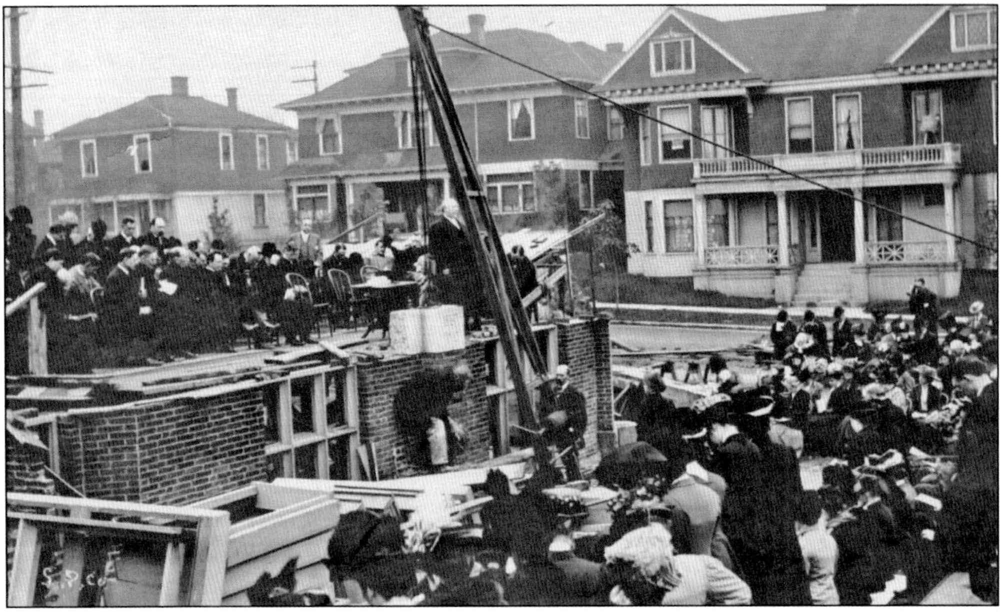

During Dr. Fridell's tenure, the church began to focus on Christian education. The church expanded its Sunday school facilities. The old Minor hospital was purchased and repurposed for an education hall. Dr. Fridell was well traveled and continued to travel to Europe and other continents. He wrote about his experiences in the church's newsletter, the *Herald*, which later became the *Spire*. Dr. Fridell was often called a communist because of his views on nonviolence and civil rights for all. Under Dr. Fridell's tenure, the church's congregation grew significantly, and the church was on stable ground financially. He resigned in 1937 to teach at Berkeley Baptist Divinity School. He died in 1978 at the age of 85. (Courtesy of Seattle First Baptist Church.)

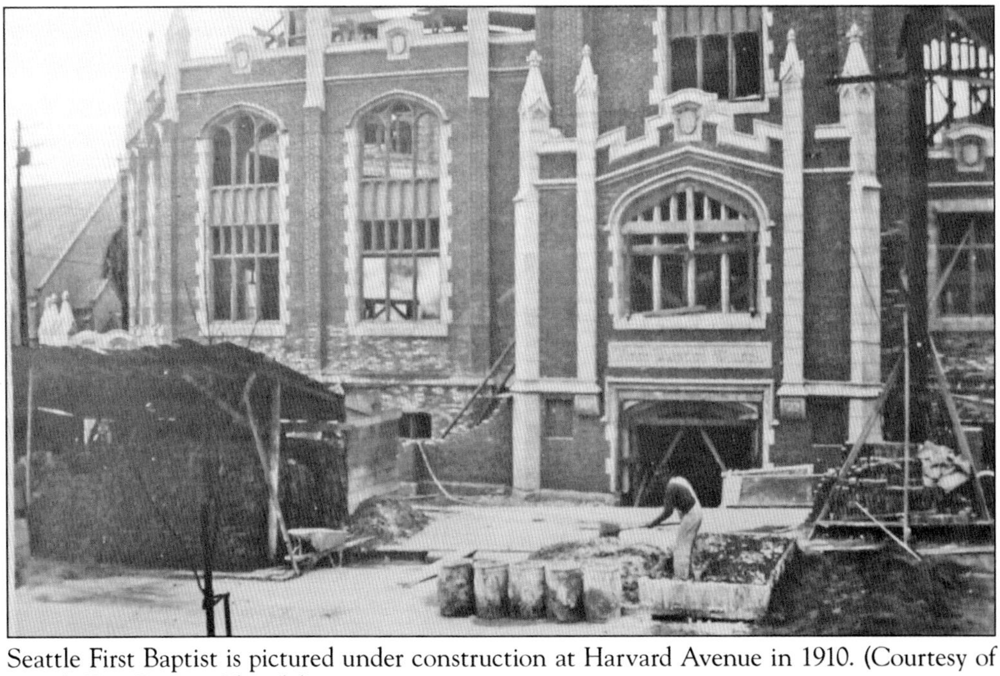

Seattle First Baptist is pictured under construction at Harvard Avenue in 1910. (Courtesy of Seattle First Baptist Church.)

This postcard shows Seattle First Baptist Church in 1913. (Courtesy of Seattle First Baptist Church.)

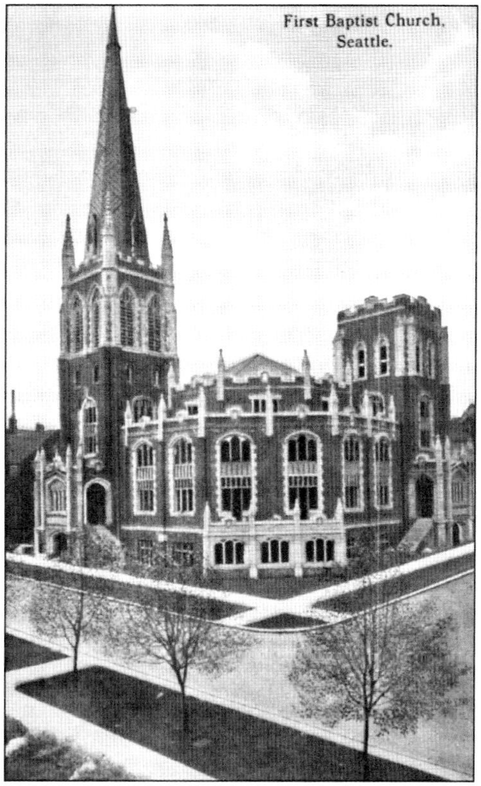

Girls of the Sunday school class at Seattle First Baptist are pictured around 1910. (Courtesy of Seattle First Baptist Church.)

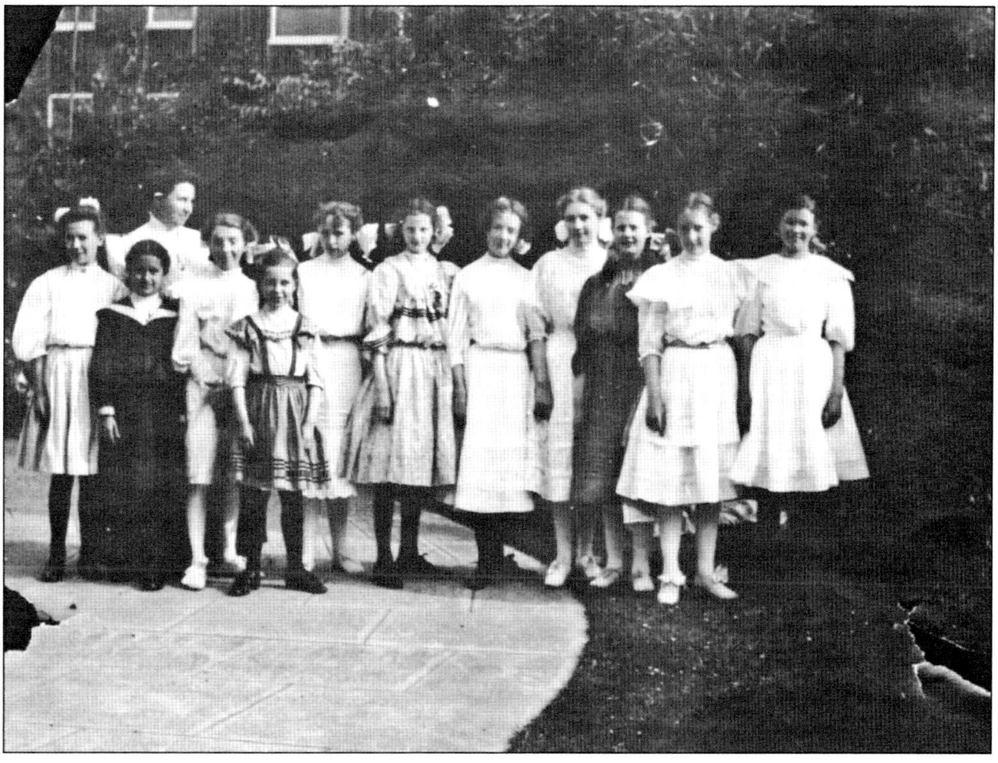

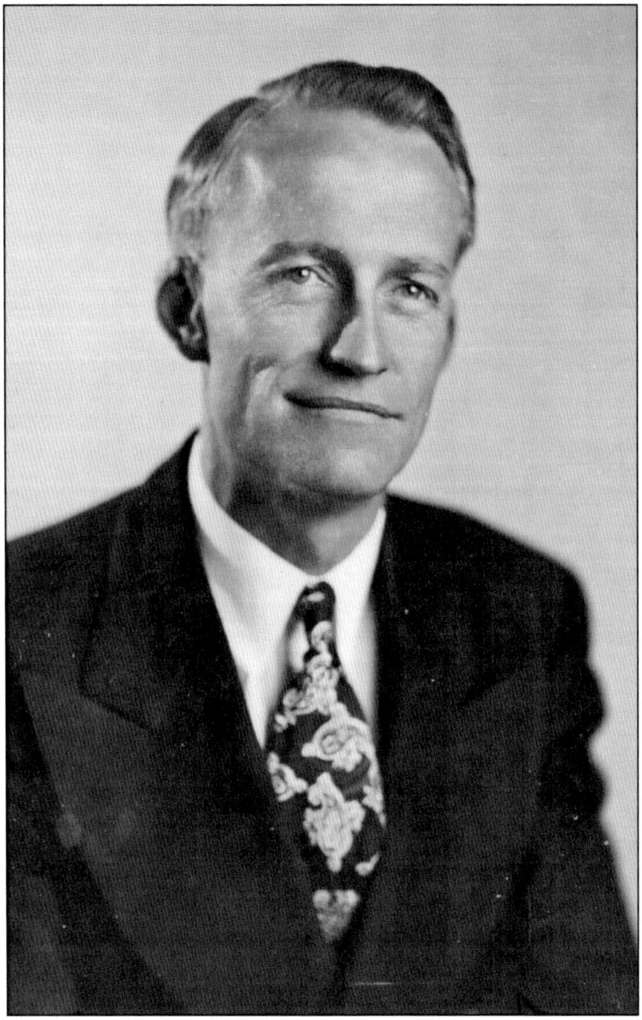

Dr. Harold V. Jensen (1938–1954) served as minister of Seattle First Baptist for 16 years, the longest-serving pastor in the church's history. He was born in Wisconsin in 1901 and was the son of a minister. He graduated magna cum laude from Andover Newton Theological Seminary. Dr. Jensen guided the church through some tough times, including World War II. A few days after the bombing of Pearl Harbor, Dr. Jensen wrote to the congregation through the newsletter: "our relationship with Japanese-Americans gives us a great opportunity. In the name of Christ, let us not be less but more friendly to them. A cherry greeting would be a wholesome antidote to the inevitable rebuffs they will receive." When many Japanese citizens were placed in internment camps, members of Seattle First Baptist stored household goods for them. Dr. Jensen fought hard against internment—he protested and went to court fighting for Japanese Americans whose property was seized. He received threats for his efforts. He visited the internment center at Camp Harmony in Puyallup, where he led internees in communion. He was assisted by Kaoru Ichihara, a member of Seattle First Baptist. Even after the war ended in 1945, anti-Japanese sentiment was still high. An editorial in the *Seattle Star* called for the formation of posses to turn the Japanese back at the city line. Dr. Jensen called for peace and understanding, saying, "they have been examined by the FBI, by Army Intelligence, and by Naval Intelligence. Many of their sons have given their lives in combat—let's welcome them home." The Seattle community stood behind Dr. Jensen. (Courtesy of Seattle First Baptist Church.)

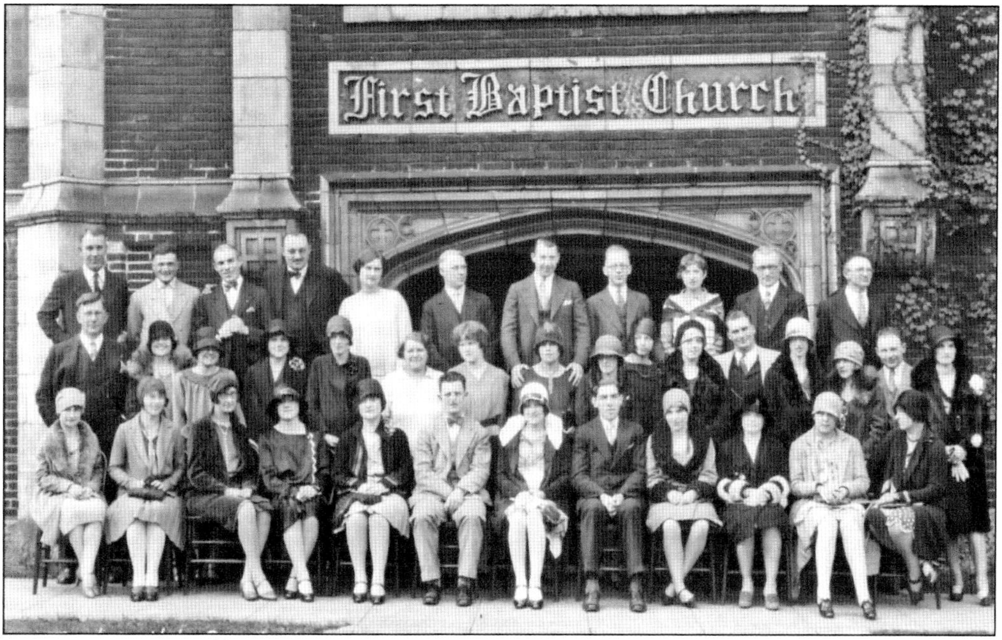

Dr. Jensen continued his work aiding war victims around the world, including those who suffered in Nazi war camps. He resigned in 1954. During his tenure as pastor, the congregation grew from 1,840 to 2,223 and missionary giving was at an all-time high. He and his wife, Marie, were killed in a traffic accident in 1968. Attendees at the church's 10th birthday breakfast are pictured in 1920. (Courtesy of Seattle First Baptist Church.)

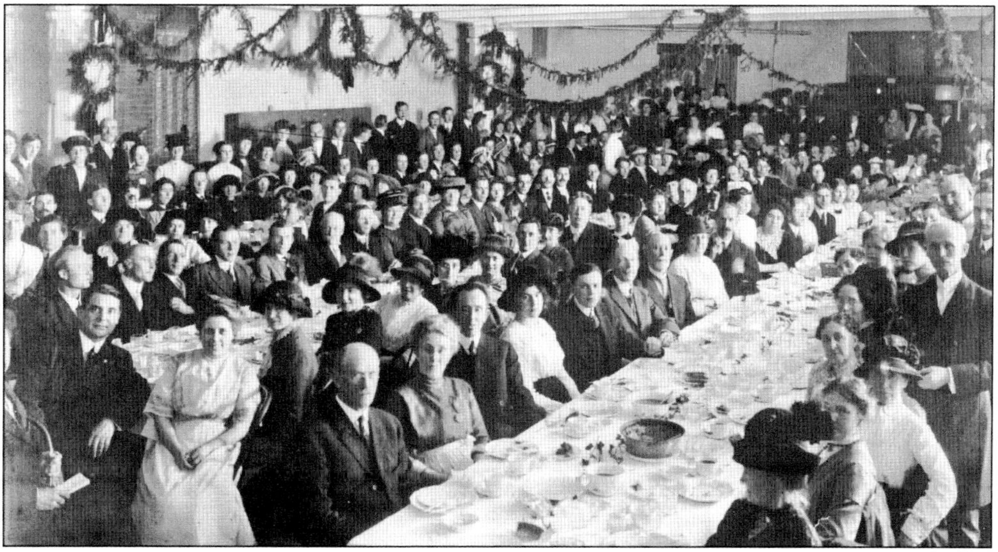
Dr. John Skoglund served from 1954 to 1958. Under his tenure, the sanctuary was remodeled in time for the American Baptist Convention, which drew missionaries from all over the world. Dr. Max Webster Morgan served from 1959 to 1962. He valued music and choirs and initiated two during his tenure: the youth choir (directed by Marion Merriwether) and the children's choir (directed by Mildred Vogue). Reverend Morgan was president of the Church Council of Greater Seattle. Pictured is a banquet in the fellowship hall around 1913. (Courtesy of Seattle First Baptist Church.)

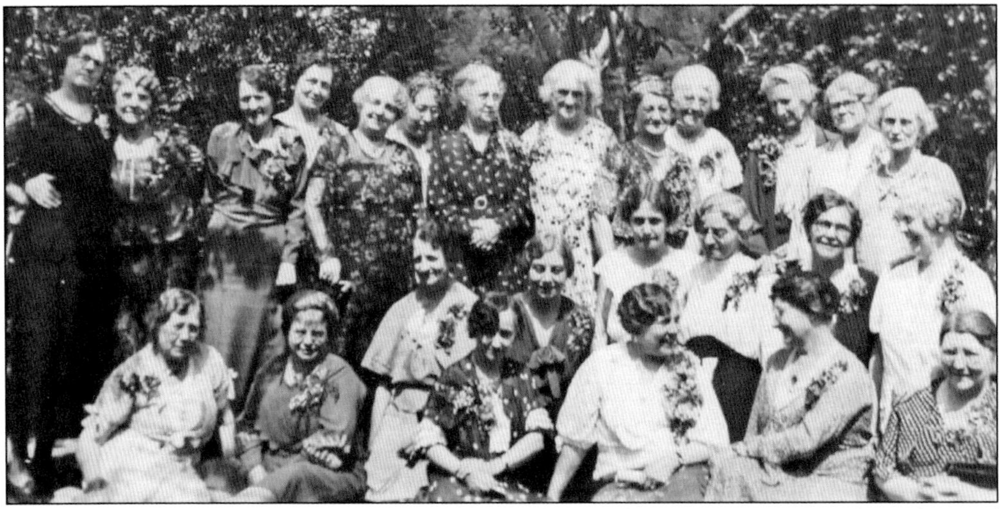

Dr. August M. Hintz (1963–1976) was a very vocal advocate for open housing, racial equality, and help for the poor and called for churches to have a role in resolving community problems. He was one of 45 American Baptist ministers who called for the de-escalation of the war in Vietnam, and he preached against the death penalty. Under his leadership, the church set aside $15,000 to assist in low-income housing, $2,000 for a scholarship fund for central-area young people, and $1,000 for a halfway house for alcoholics. Seattle First Baptist Church deaconesses are pictured in 1921. (Courtesy of Seattle First Baptist Church.)

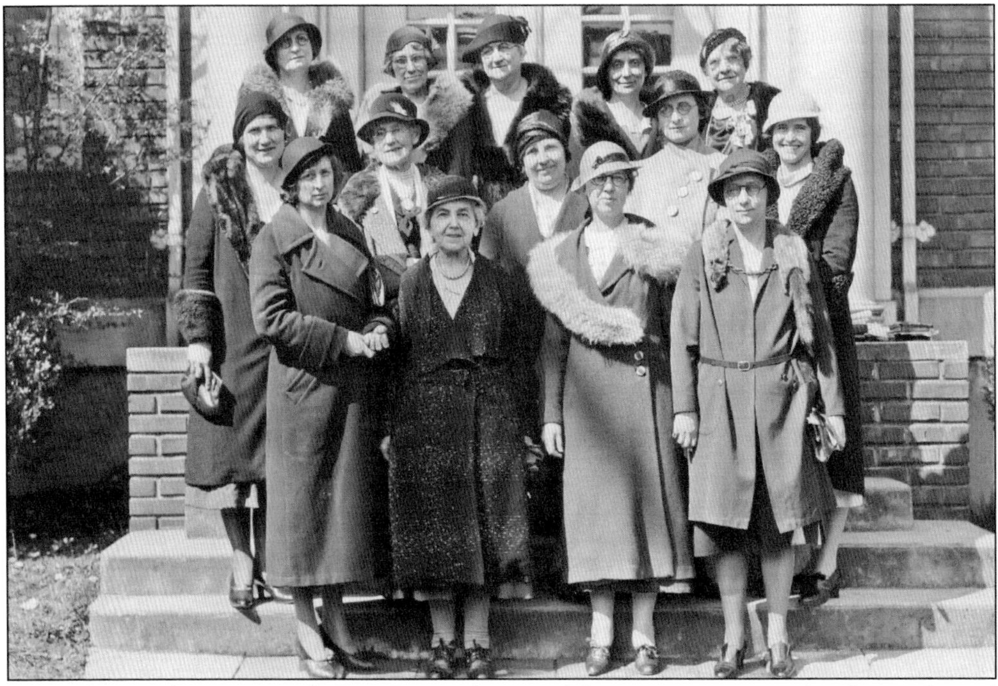

Throughout its history, Seattle First Baptist has stood for peace, justice, civil rights, and equal treatment for all. The church has supported and fought for Native Americans, Chinese immigrants, Japanese Americans, African Americans fighting for civil rights, and the lesbian, gay, bisexual, and transgendered community in their fight for human rights. That legacy continues today. The Women's Society Circle is pictured around 1930. (Courtesy of Seattle First Baptist Church.)

Eight

Plymouth Congregational Church

During the mid-1800s, Seattle was a town of a little more than 1,100 people, most of whom were men looking for Western adventure. Jobs mostly consisted of working for sawmills and other lumber-related work.

On October 16, 1869, an organizing committee consisting of John Sanderson, Stephen Andrews, William Baxter, A.N. Merrick, J.T. Jordan, Dr. George V. Calhoun, D.R. Lord, C.P. Stone, and Rev. John F. Damon (who would become the church's first pastor) met at Yesler Hall, a room above Kellogg's Drug Store, to establish the Plymouth Congregational Church. John and Caroline Sanderson were from Massachusetts. Other churches had been established in the tiny town (Catholic and Methodist among them), but the couple were descendants of people who had arrived in America on the *Mayflower* and wanted to bring that Plymouth spirit and Congregationalism to their newly adopted town.

The first service was held on January 16, 1870. The services attracted a large audience, estimated at around 100 people.

In 1871, members of the newly formed church embarked on constructing a building to house their place of worship. Arthur Denny (one of the founders of Seattle) donated the land at Second Avenue between Spring and Seneca Streets, and the lumber was donated by William Renton from his mill. The dedication ceremony was held in August 1873. Reverend Damon's health had become an issue, so he resigned in 1871. Rev. Norman McLeod became the new pastor, but he resigned in 1874. Rev. J.F. Ellis of Oregon became the new pastor in July 1876. The church began to grow under his leadership: membership grew to 135, and the Sunday school and young people's program also grew. The church was also able to relieve most of its debt.

As more people arrived in Seattle, Plymouth became a mother church by helping to establish other congregations in outlying areas. Plymouth quickly established and became known for its outreach programs. During the depression of 1893, Plymouth Congregational was a strong supporter of Seattle's missions by helping to feed and house the hungry and homeless.

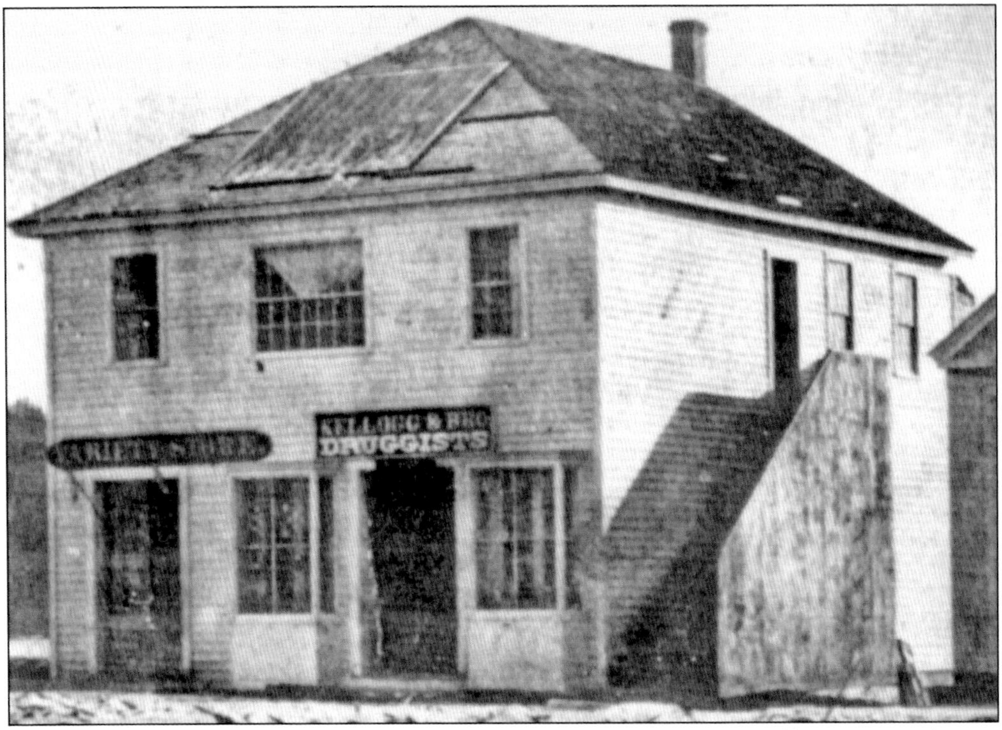

Plymouth Congregational's first meeting was held in 1869 in Yesler's Hall in a room above a Pioneer Square drugstore. (Courtesy of Plymouth Congregational Church.)

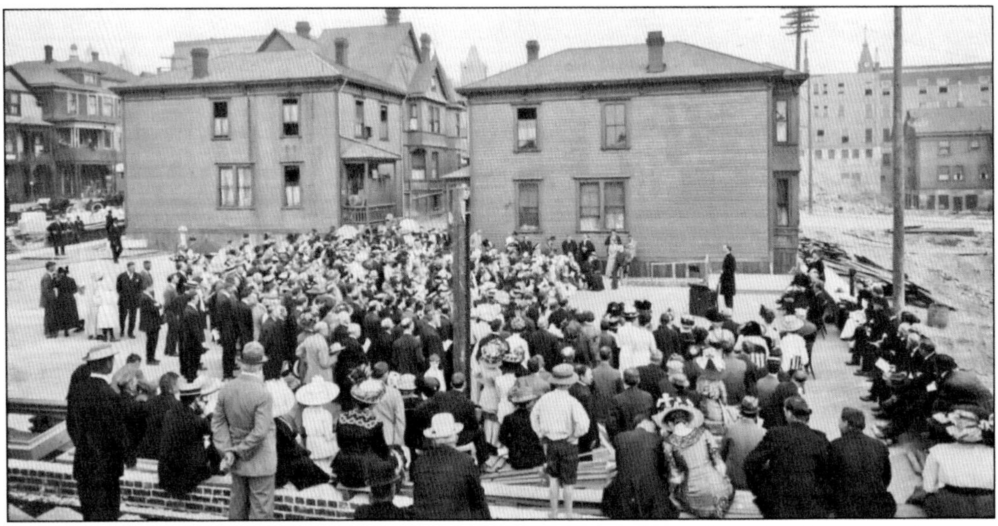

On June 6, 1889, the Great Seattle Fire quickly spread through 58 blocks in the downtown business district. Some churches were destroyed, but Plymouth Congregational was spared. The Seattle area rebounded, and most wood-frame buildings were replaced by stone and brick buildings. Plymouth had outgrown its church and wanted to update its structure to a more modern one. The congregation voted to sell the lot and building at Second Avenue for $32,000 and bought two lots at Third Avenue and University Street. Seattle was growing: between 1890 and 1900, the city's population grew to more than 80,000, and by 1910, the population reached more than 240,000. (Courtesy of Plymouth Congregational Church.)

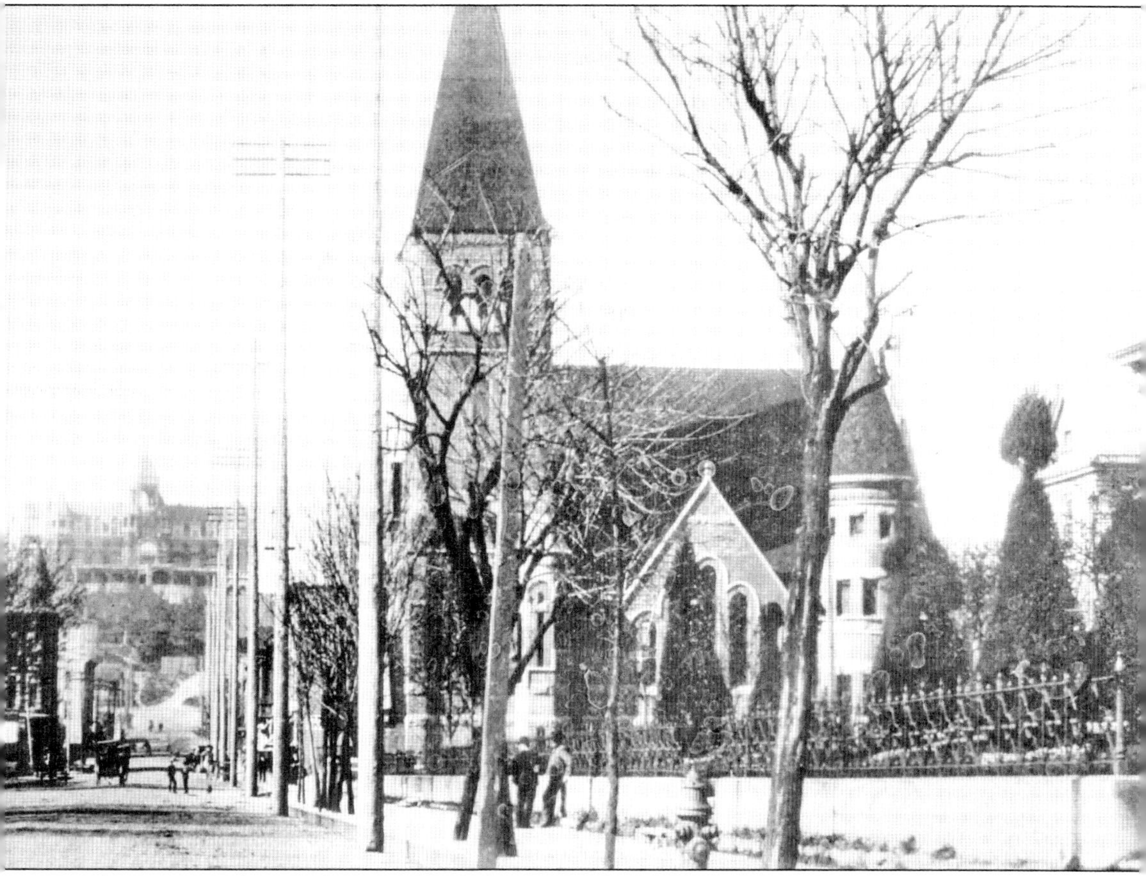

In the summer of 1891, the new church began to take shape, and it was completed in a short time. The new church could seat 800 people. A new focus was placed on music, and a 12-member choir consisted of very talented singers. By 1893, the church could easily fill its 800-seat capacity. (Courtesy of Plymouth Congregational Church.)

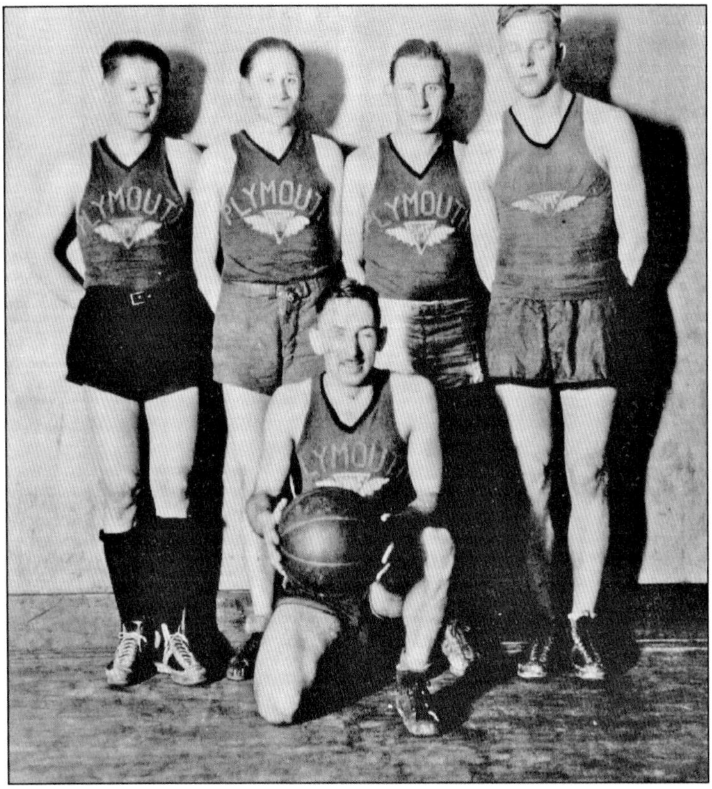

Plymouth became a center of social life, with activities at the church almost daily; it developed boys' programs (they played basketball in the church's gym, went fishing, and did a host of other activities) and even hosted the National American Woman Suffrage Association. The church hosted the event partly because the pastor at the time, Rev. Dr. Frances Van Horn, and the board of trustees were strong supporters of the women's suffrage movement. (Courtesy of Plymouth Congregational Church.)

The congregation had outgrown its original church, and a new church was built at Third Avenue and University Street. Plymouth had an open house after the dedication. The church was state-of-the-art for its time. There was a gymnasium, large Sunday school quarters, a men's club, and a women's association parlor. There was also a new organ, because music was one of the interesting features of the church; in fact, the choir had a reputation throughout the Northwest. (Courtesy of Plymouth Congregational Church.)

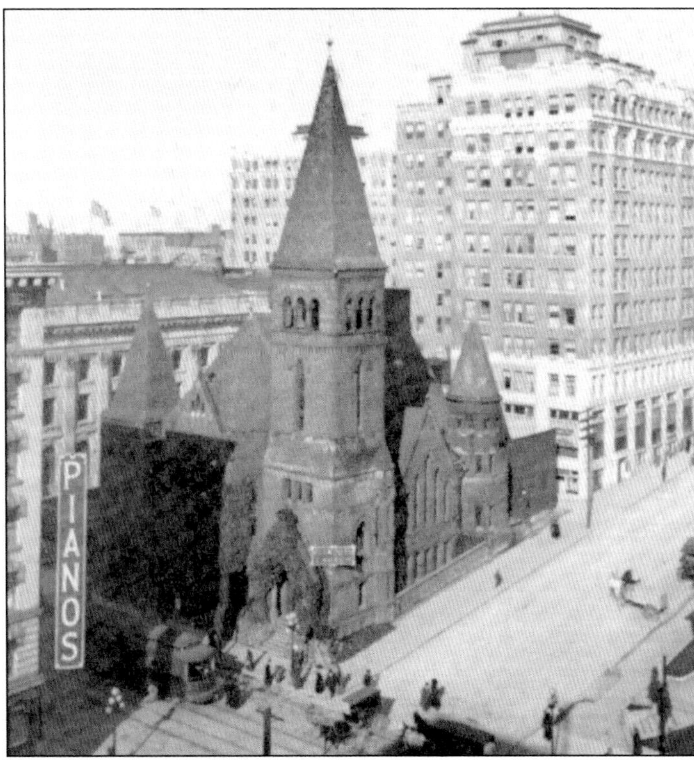

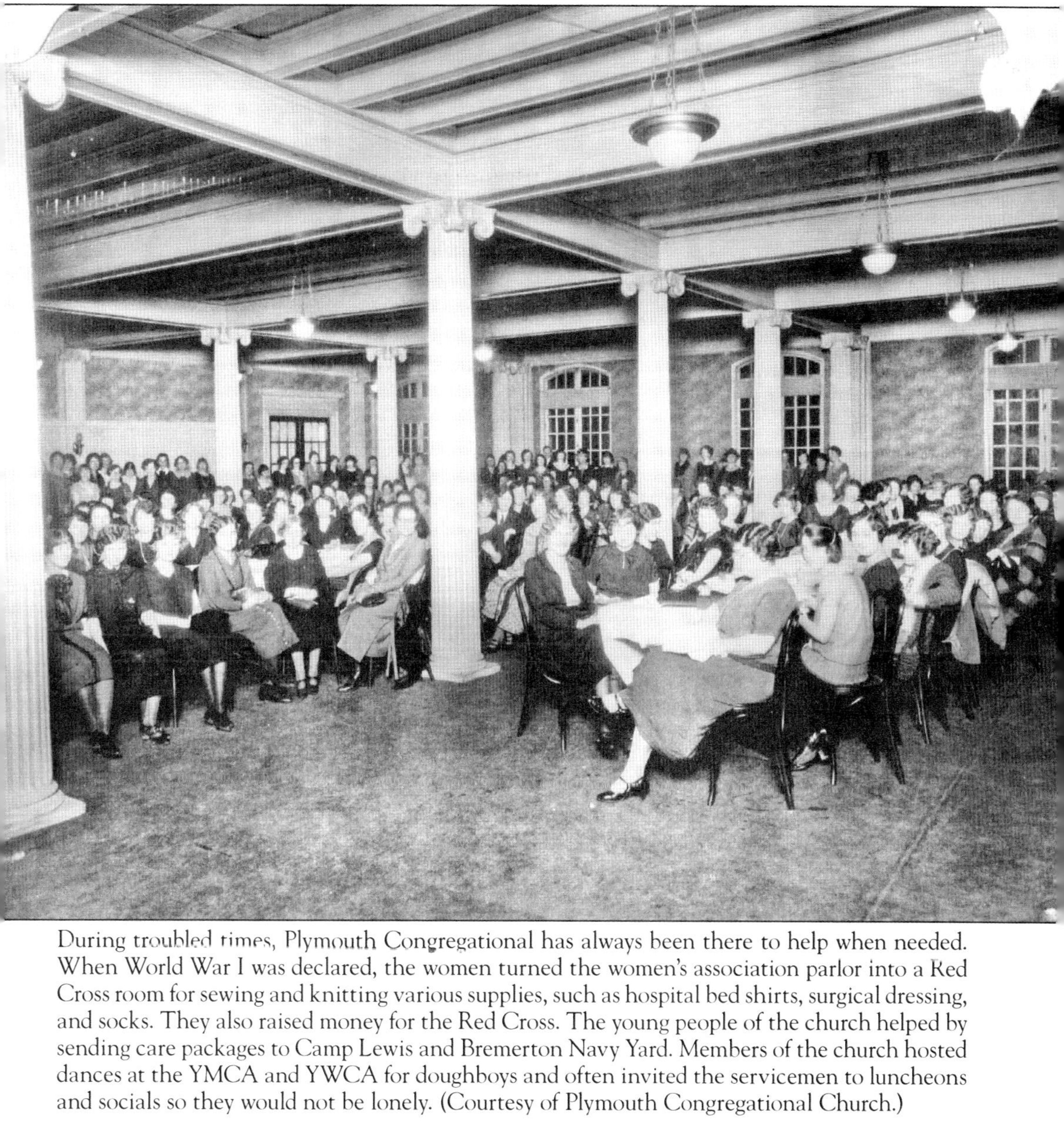

During troubled times, Plymouth Congregational has always been there to help when needed. When World War I was declared, the women turned the women's association parlor into a Red Cross room for sewing and knitting various supplies, such as hospital bed shirts, surgical dressing, and socks. They also raised money for the Red Cross. The young people of the church helped by sending care packages to Camp Lewis and Bremerton Navy Yard. Members of the church hosted dances at the YMCA and YWCA for doughboys and often invited the servicemen to luncheons and socials so they would not be lonely. (Courtesy of Plymouth Congregational Church.)

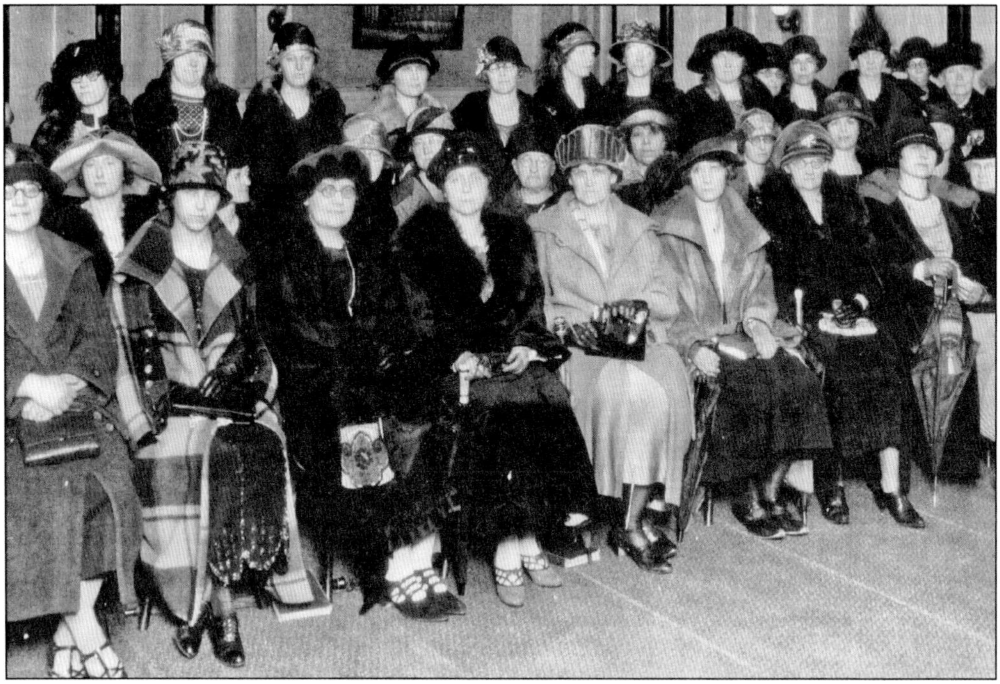

In the 1920s, Plymouth Church (under the leadership of Dr. Chauncey Hawkins) developed many community service programs, including a free health clinic. It also organized the Plymouth Girls' Club, a nondenominational social organization for single working women from 18 to 40. (Courtesy of Plymouth Congregational Church.)

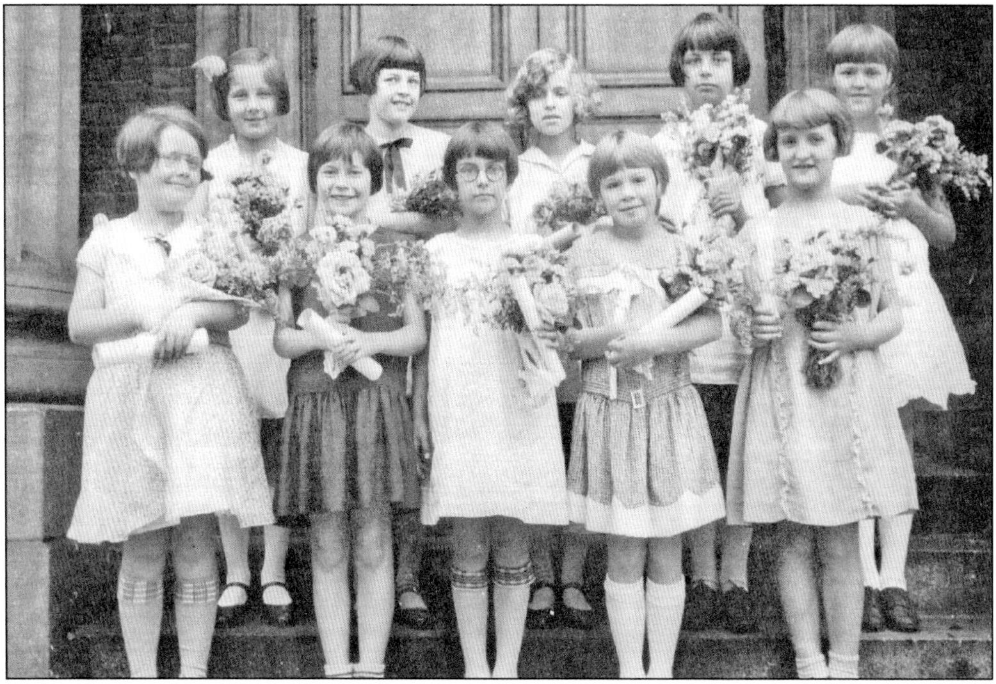

Girls are pictured at their first communion on the steps of Plymouth Congregational around 1920. (Courtesy of Plymouth Congregational Church.)

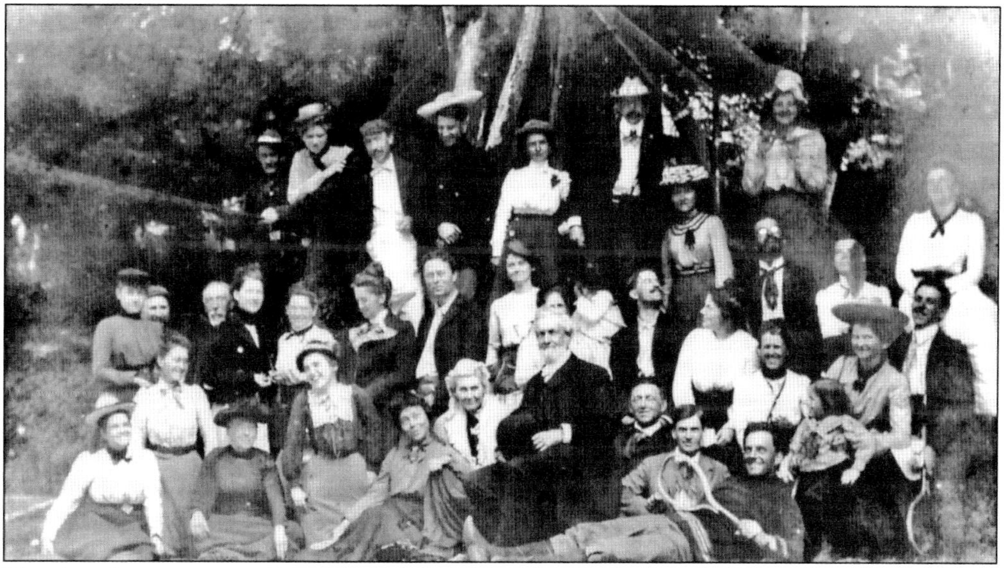

The church was an integral part of the lives of its parishioners. Here, people enjoy a church picnic around 1900. (Courtesy of Plymouth Congregational Church.)

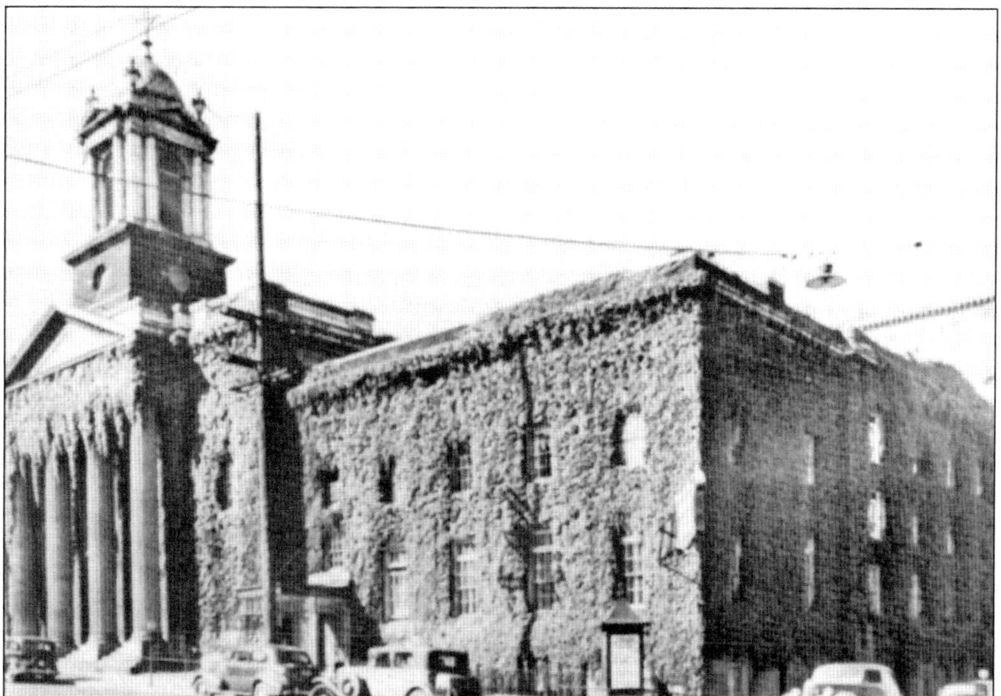

Once again, the influx of new members had outgrown Plymouth Congregational, and a third church was built at Sixth Avenue and University Street. The church was dedicated in 1912. (Courtesy of Plymouth Congregational Church.)

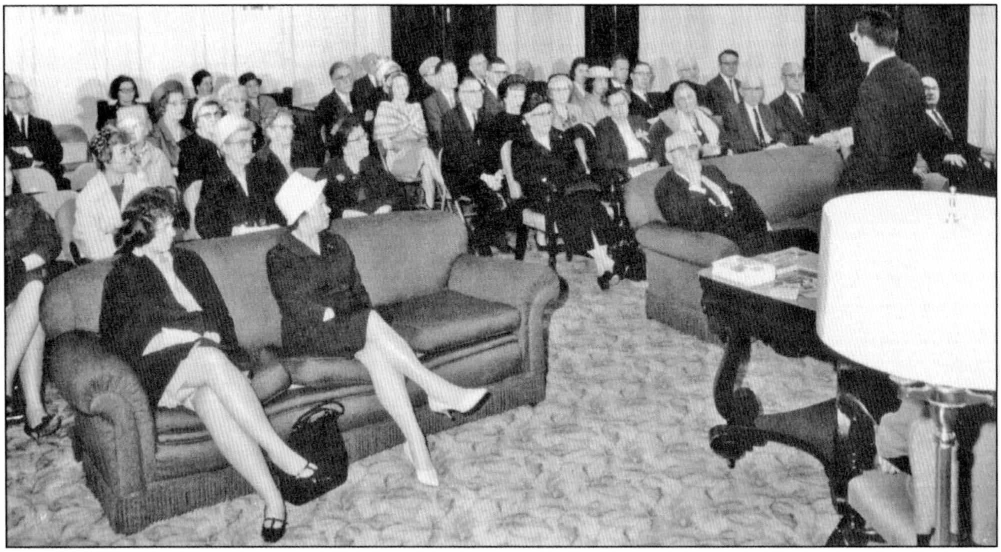

During the Great Depression, Plymouth's financial outlook was better than most churches. The church organized a relief department where members contributed blankets, clothing, food, and even jobs to those hardest hit by the Depression. The Depression soon took its toll on the church's finances, however; several programs, such as the Girl's Club and the Pilgrim Home, were discontinued. (Courtesy of Plymouth Congregational Church.)

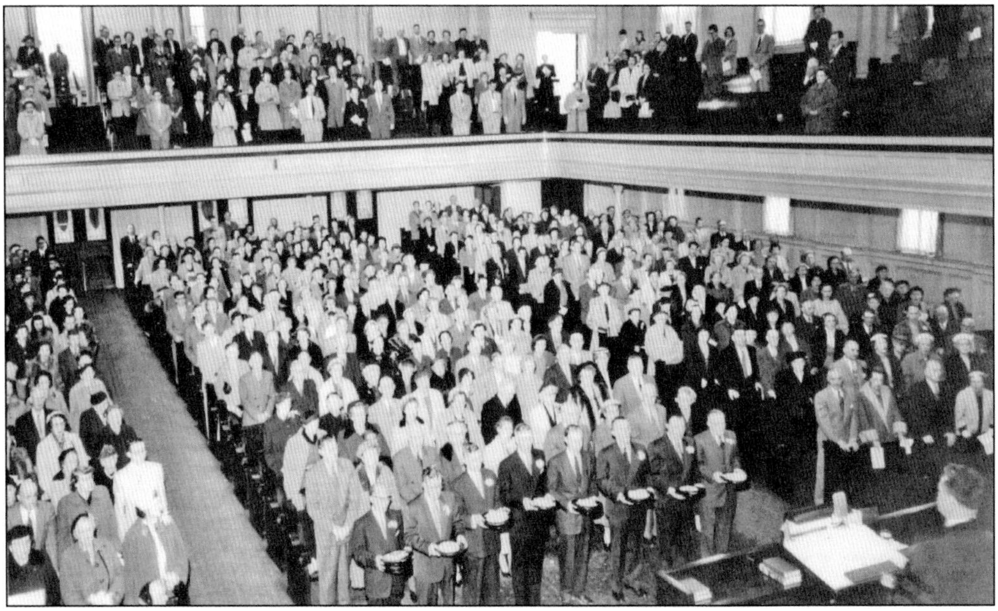

When war became a very real threat for the country, a national preparedness program was initiated. In Seattle, the Boeing workforce grew to more than 50,000 by 1944. The church hoped that war could be avoided. However, on December 7, 1941, Japan attacked Pearl Harbor. After President Roosevelt signed an executive order, many Seattle Japanese residents were sent to internment camps, most taking only what they could carry; church members assisted as much as they could. The church was also a haven for those called to war. The women's association hosted Sunday luncheons and socials for GIs and set up work rooms for the Red Cross. Pictured is a church service around 1945. (Courtesy of Plymouth Congregational Church.)

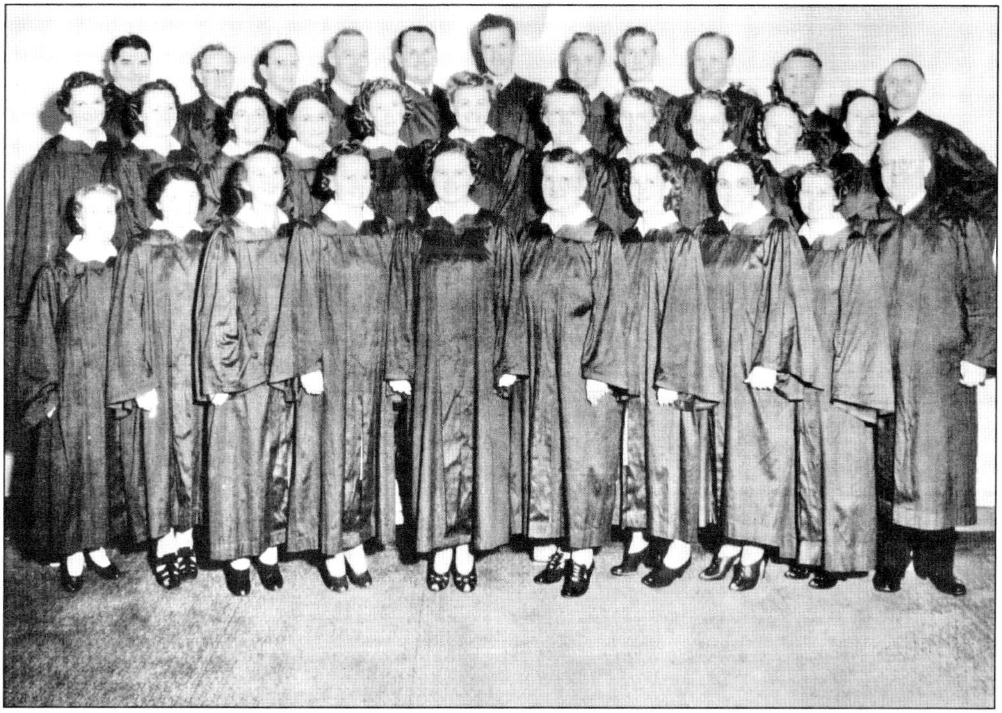

Music has always been a part of the church's services. The choirs have been renowned throughout the years. Here is the choir during the 1940s. (Courtesy of Plymouth Congregational Church.)

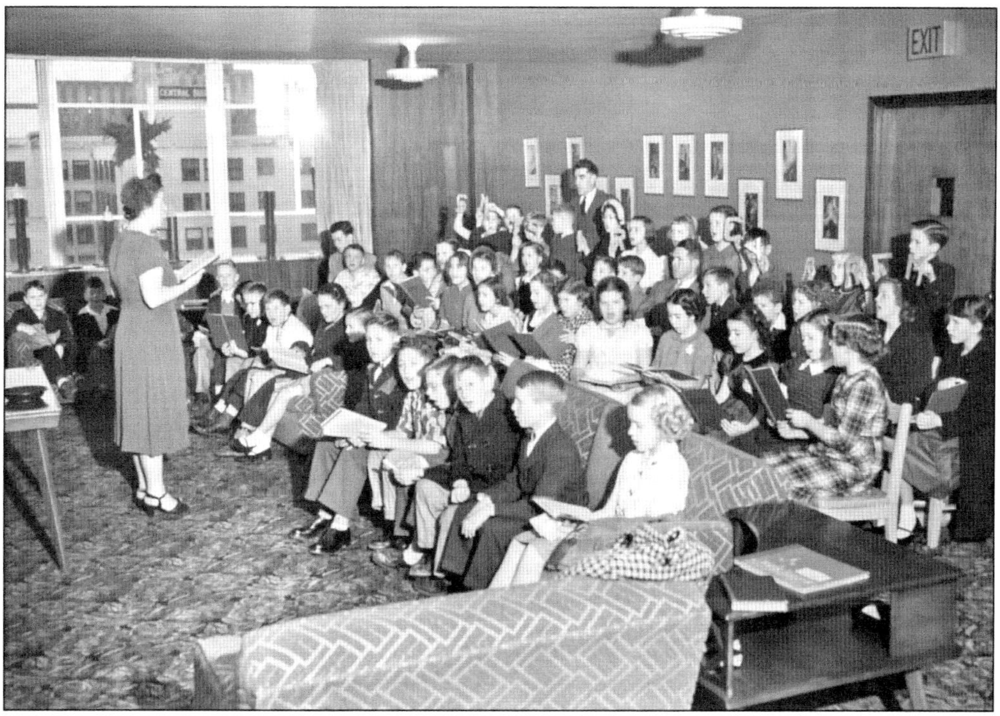

A fellowship hour with children is seen around 1955. (Courtesy of Plymouth Congregational Church.)

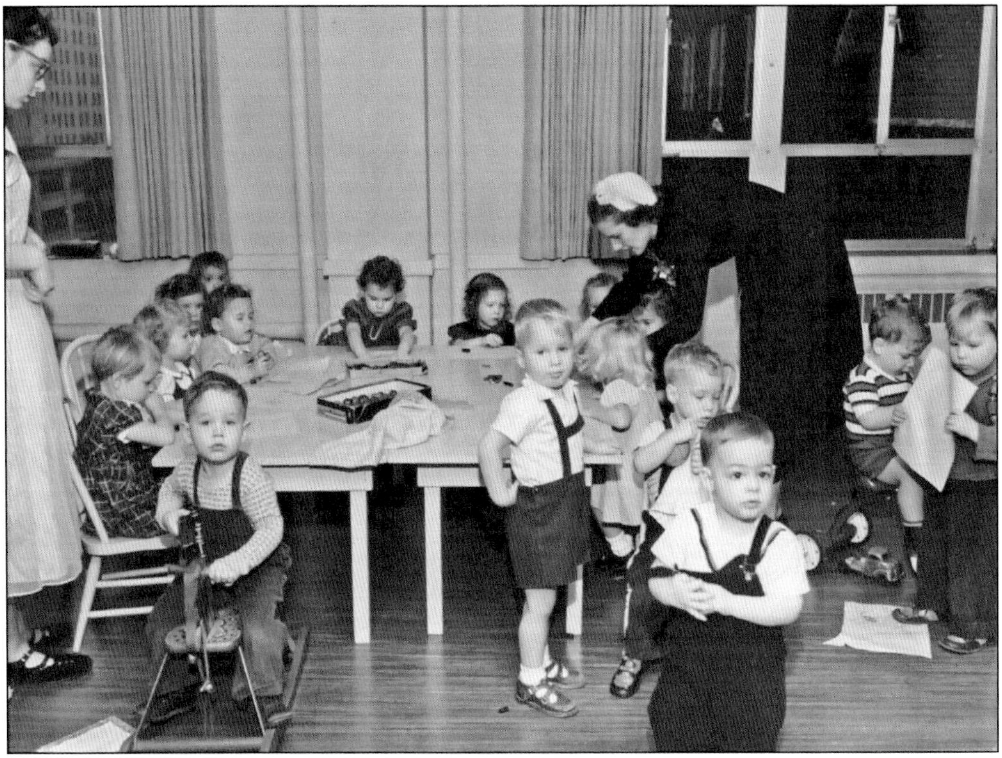

The church's nursery is pictured around 1958. (Courtesy of Plymouth Congregational Church.)

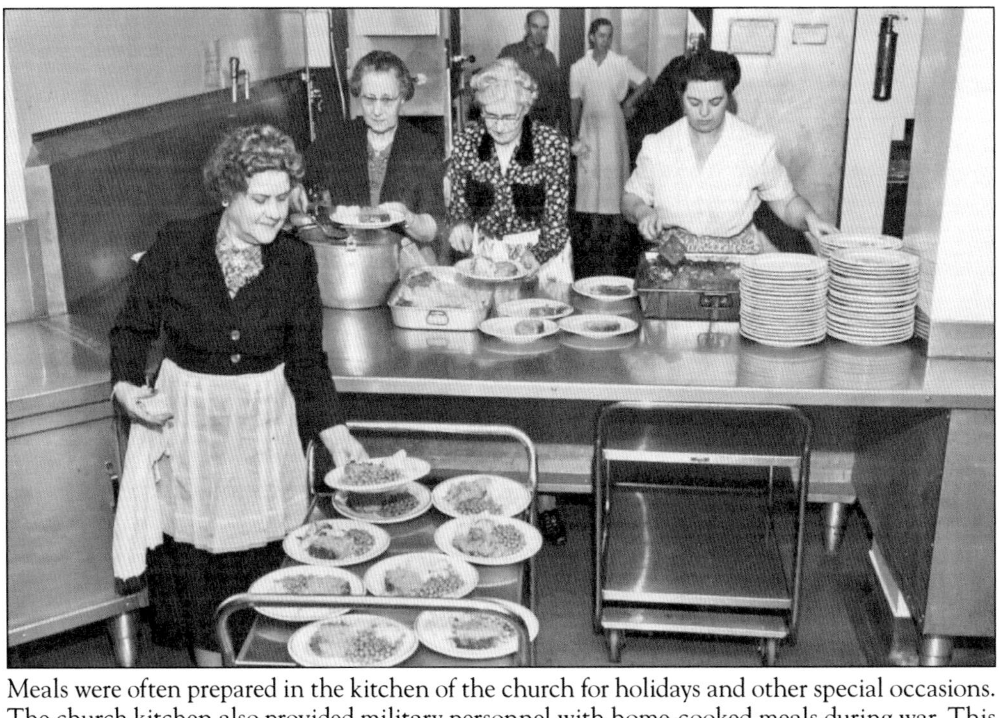

Meals were often prepared in the kitchen of the church for holidays and other special occasions. The church kitchen also provided military personnel with home-cooked meals during war. This photograph is from around 1960. (Courtesy of Plymouth Congregational Church.)

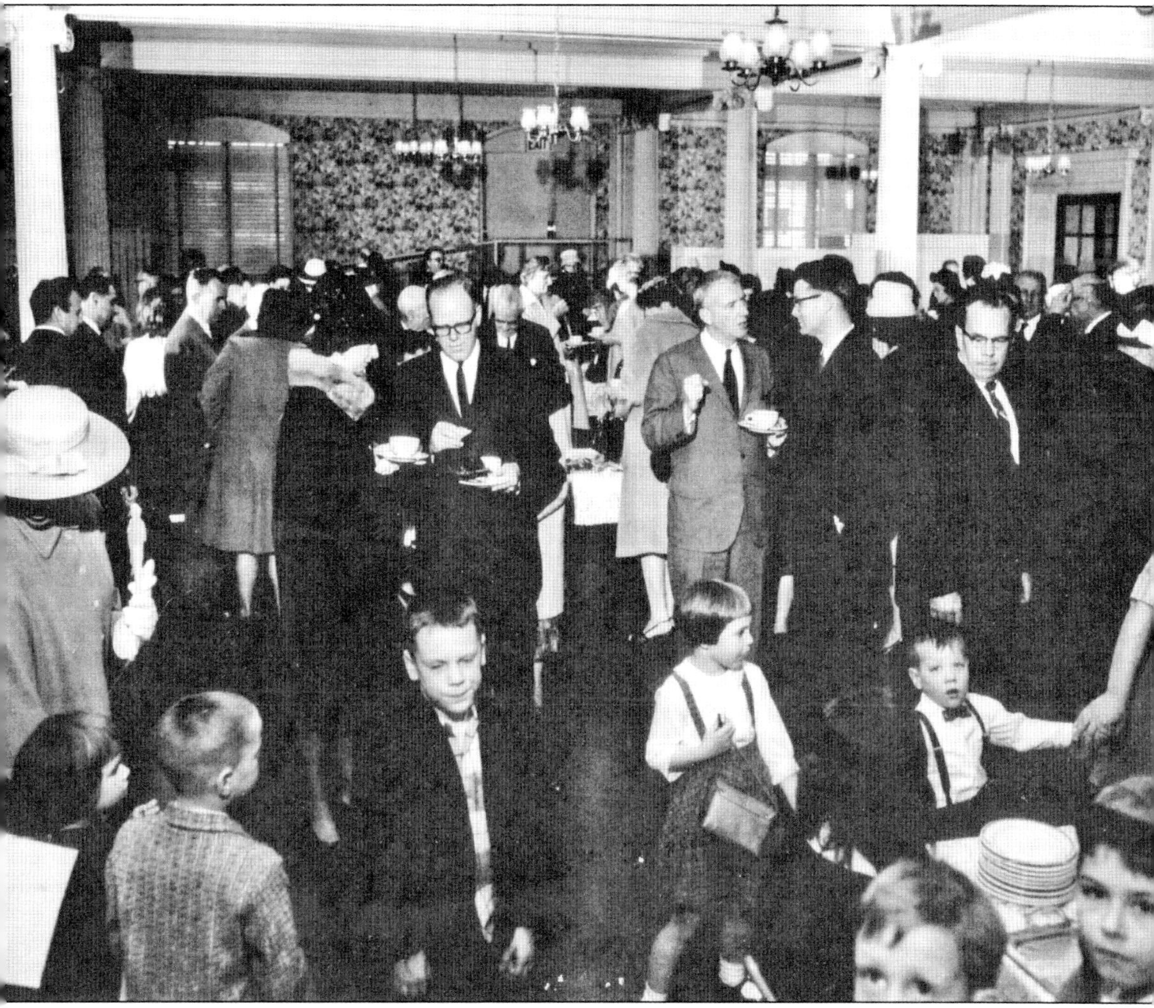

In the 1960s, Plymouth's pastor, Rev. Martin L. Goslin, hosted a show on KOMO-TV with Rabbi Raphael Levine and Fr. William Treacy. *The Challenge*, a weekly program, was considered groundbreaking at the time. It featured the Jewish rabbi, Catholic priest, and Protestant minister discussing not only religion but also world problems and social issues through different perspectives. The emphasis was on the commonality of all faiths. In 1962, Dr. Goslin announced in the church's newspaper, the *Herald*, that a national conference was using the show's format to bring together Jewish, Catholic, and Protestant groups to address racial problems. The three men of the cloth became great friends. (Courtesy of Plymouth Congregational Church.)

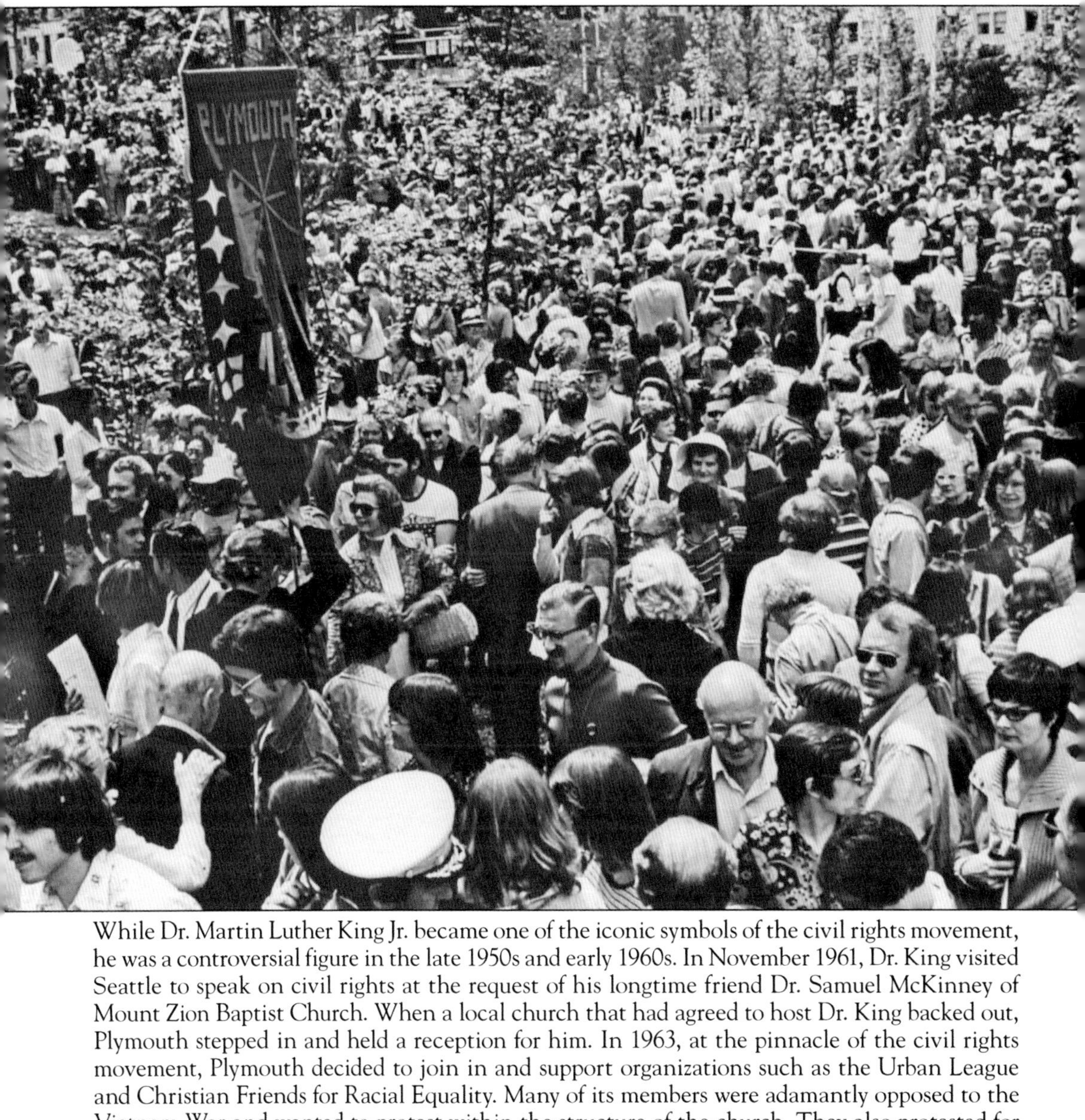

While Dr. Martin Luther King Jr. became one of the iconic symbols of the civil rights movement, he was a controversial figure in the late 1950s and early 1960s. In November 1961, Dr. King visited Seattle to speak on civil rights at the request of his longtime friend Dr. Samuel McKinney of Mount Zion Baptist Church. When a local church that had agreed to host Dr. King backed out, Plymouth stepped in and held a reception for him. In 1963, at the pinnacle of the civil rights movement, Plymouth decided to join in and support organizations such as the Urban League and Christian Friends for Racial Equality. Many of its members were adamantly opposed to the Vietnam War and wanted to protest within the structure of the church. They also protested for open housing (eliminating boundaries in neighborhoods) for all in the community. (Courtesy of Plymouth Congregational Church.)

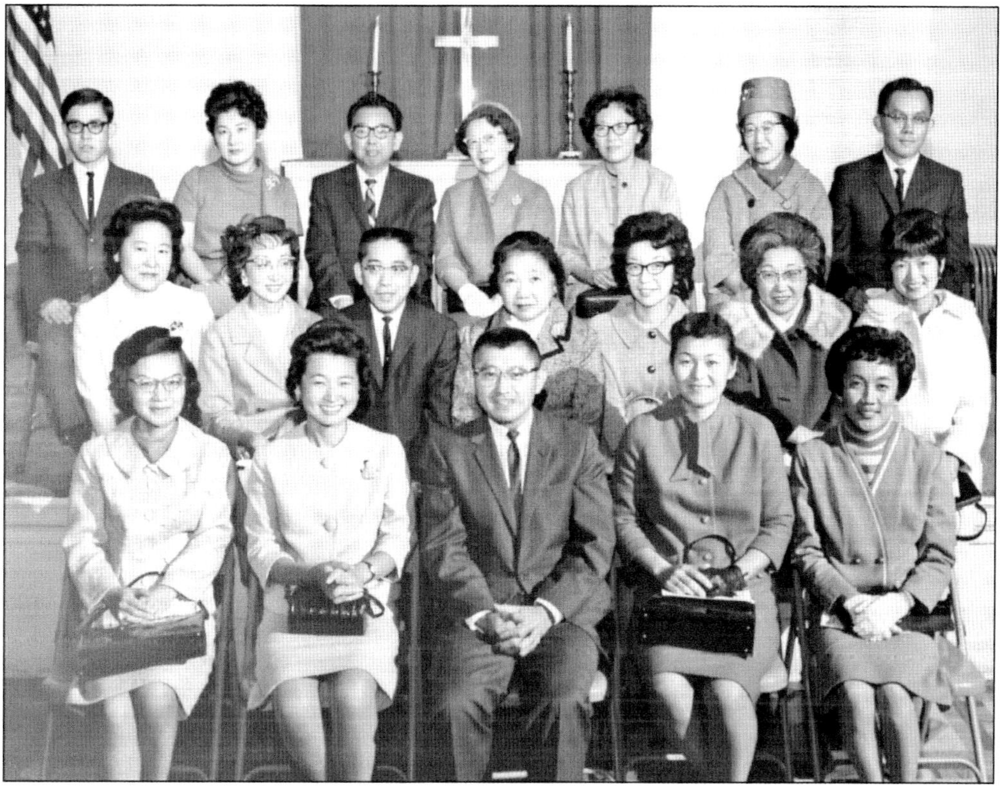

In 1965, the Seattle Japanese Congregational Church united with Plymouth. (Courtesy of Plymouth Congregational Church.)

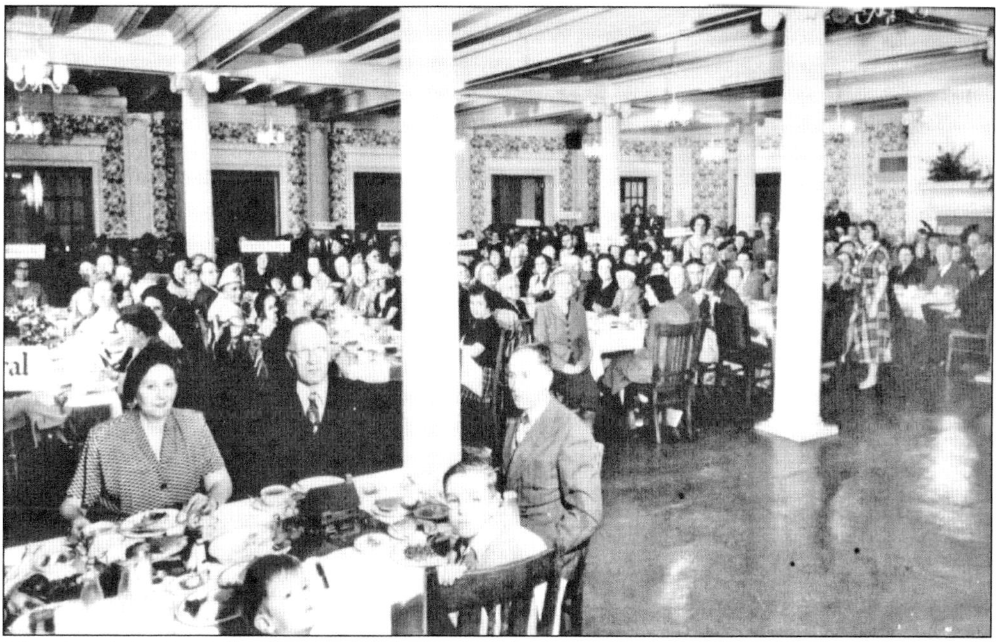

The church holds a Thanksgiving dinner around 1960. (Courtesy of Plymouth Congregational Church.)

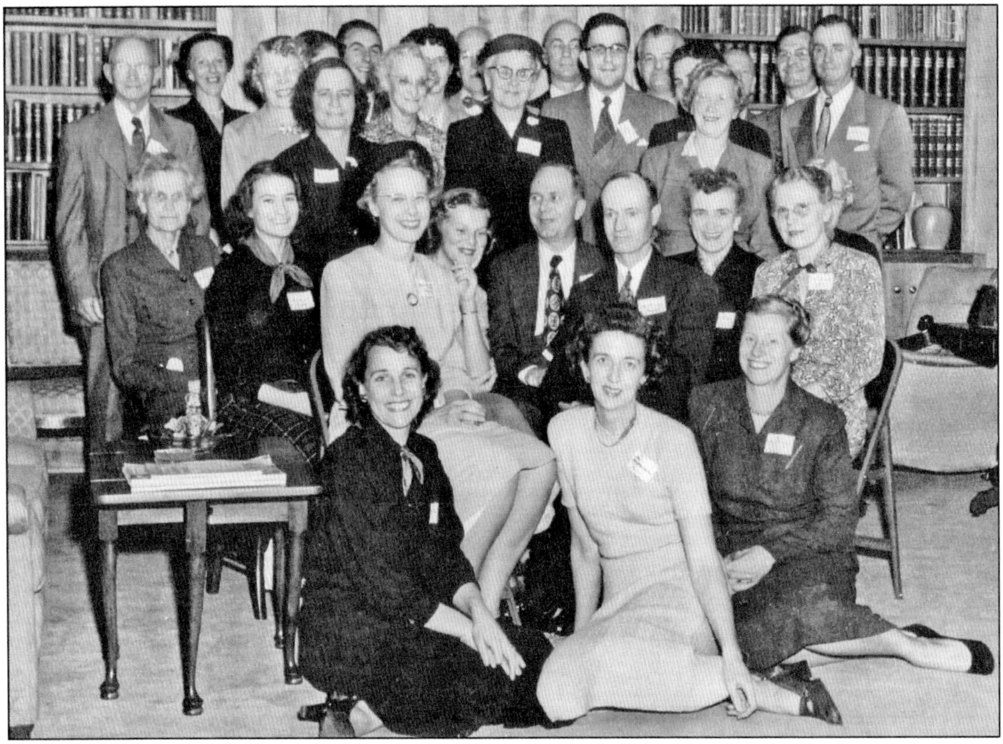

Above, the Fireside Fellowship Group is pictured around 1958. Below, the cornerstone is laid for a new church around 1967. (Both, courtesy of Plymouth Congregational Church.)

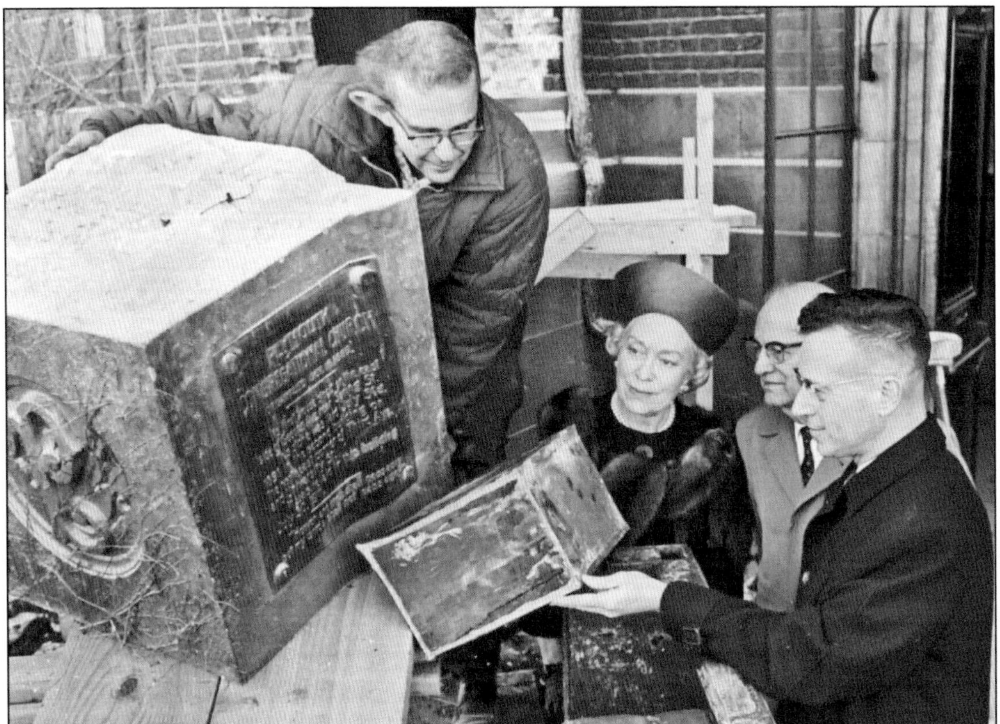

Plymouth Church had stood proud over the years, but in the 1960s, the great building's systems had become somewhat antiquated and needed repairs. Although some members wanted to restore the old church, after reviewing the architect's report, the committee concluded that restoring the building would be too expensive. While the new church was being built, church services were held at the Fifth Avenue Theater. (Courtesy of Plymouth Congregational Church.)

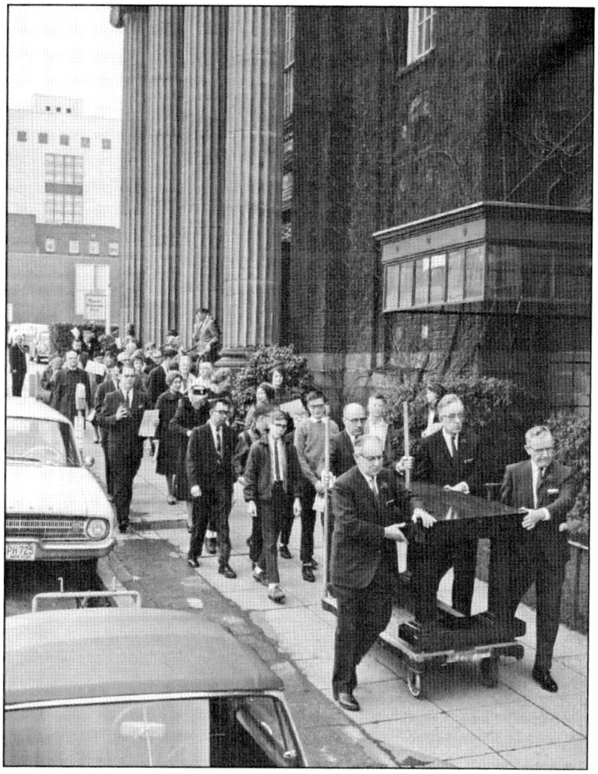

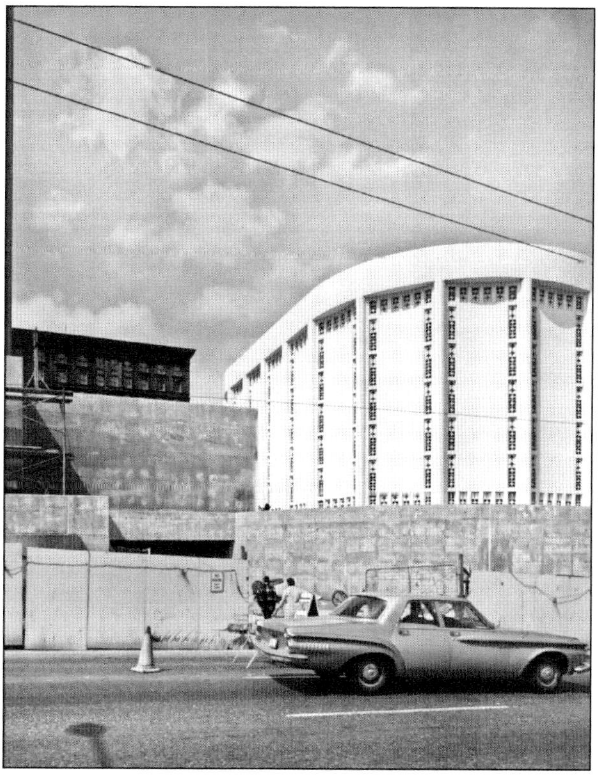

On December 4, 1963, members voted to construct a new church building. The church hired a professional fundraiser. In 1965, after the church had accepted a bid, the 16-month construction began. February 13, 1966, was the last service at the sanctuary that had been home for 54 years. (Courtesy of Plymouth Congregational Church.)

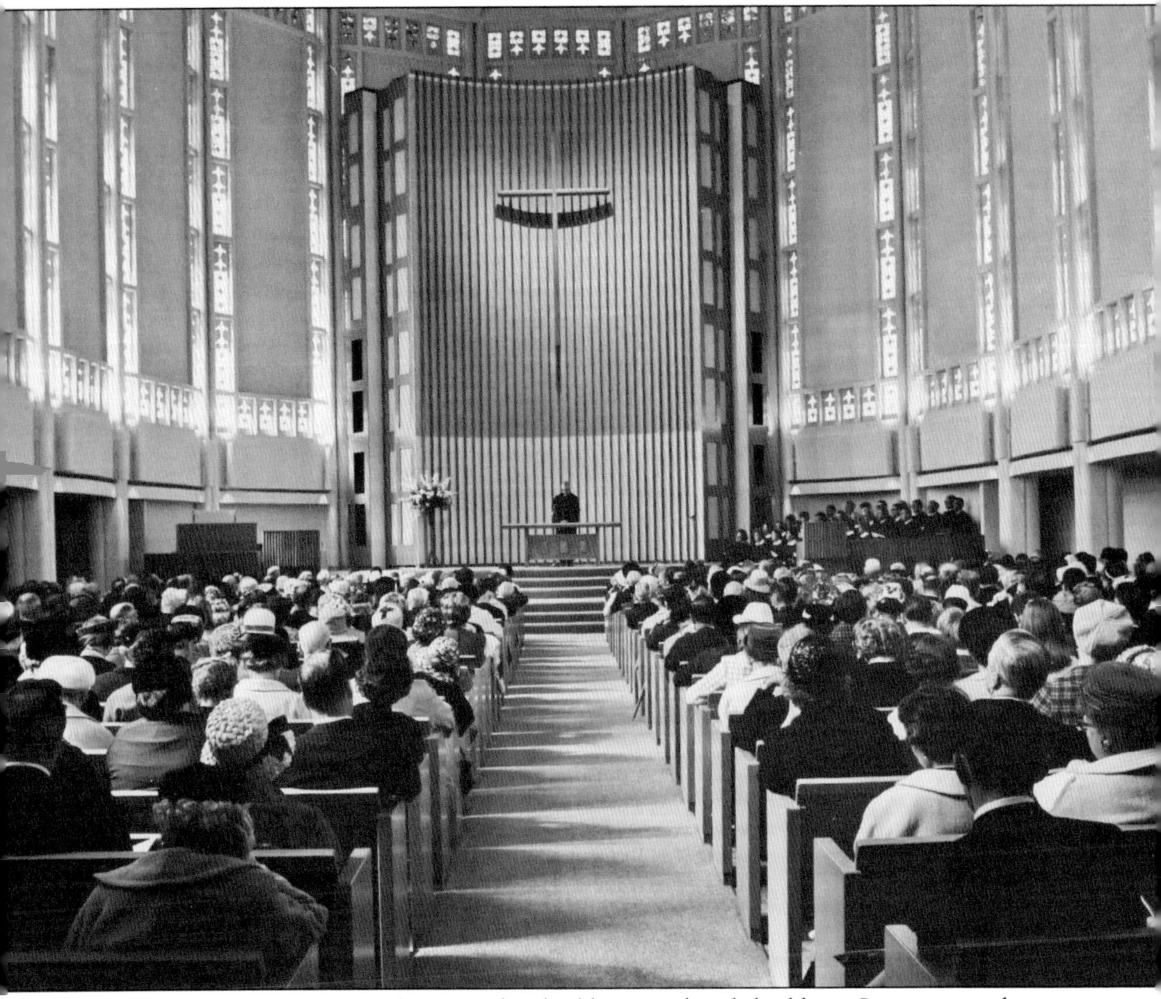

On December 4, 1963, members voted to build a new church building. Construction began in 1965 and took 16 months. The last service at the sanctuary that had been their home for 54 years was on February 13, 1966. (Courtesy of Plymouth Congregational Church.)

Nine

First Church Seattle

Founded in 1853, First Church is Seattle's first church, established two years after Seattle was homesteaded. The new residents of Seattle were truly pioneers. The founding members of the new church were Arthur and Mary Denny, John Nagle, and Catherine Blaine, the wife of Rev. David Edwards Blaine. The Blaines were newlyweds from New York State and arrived in Seattle seeking to build a new life preaching in the frontier town.

Reverend Blaine preached the very first service on December 4, 1853, at the home of Guthrie Latimer, and for the first year, First Church services were held at homes. A congregation began to form, and the need for a structure became apparent. Reverend Blaine and other settlers embarked on building a church; the land was donated by Carson Boren at Second Avenue and Columbia Street and was dedicated on May 15, 1855. It was considered a large church for the time, and it was called the "Little White Church" because it was painted white.

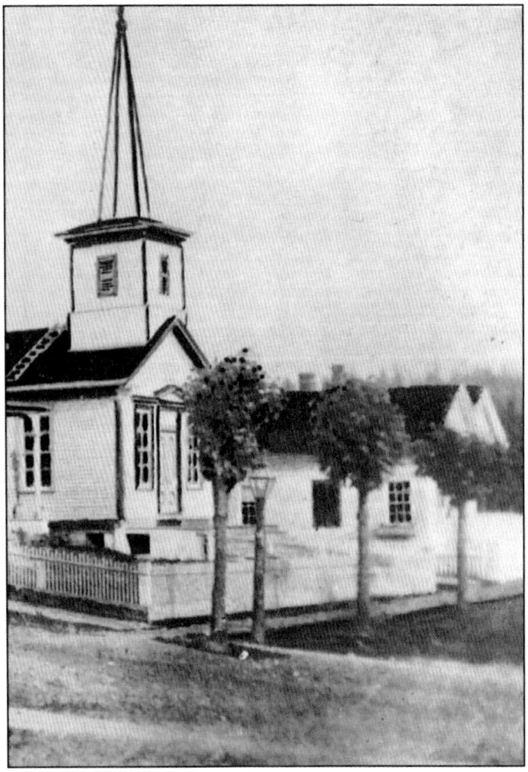

The Little White Church was dedicated in 1855. It was the first building for Seattle First Church. (Courtesy of Seattle First Church.)

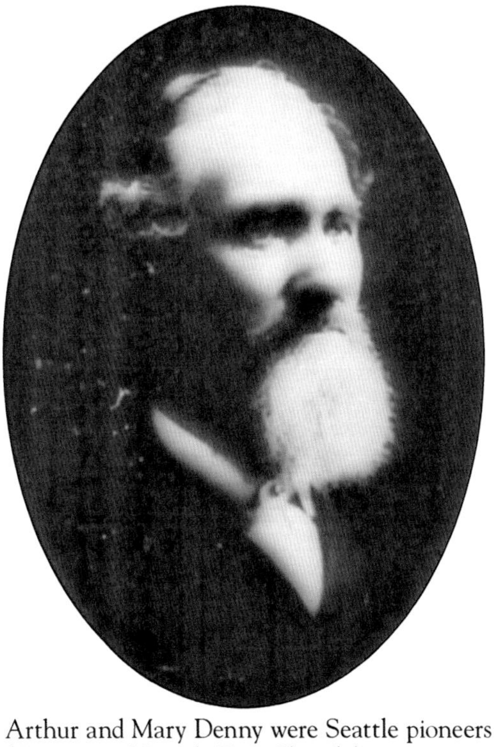

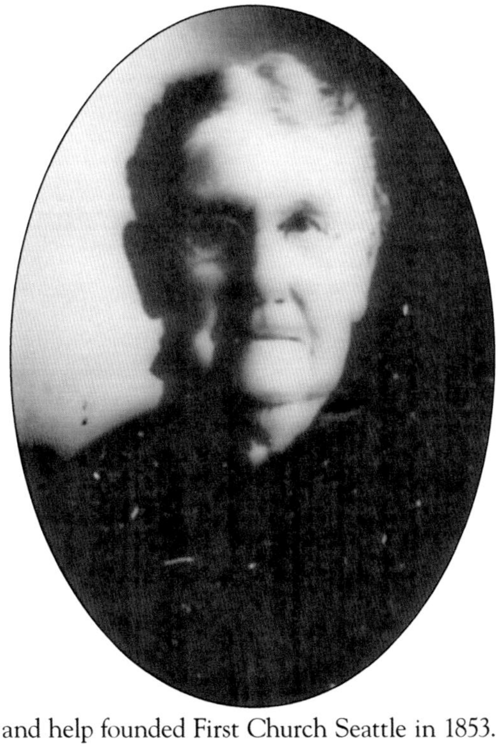

Arthur and Mary Denny were Seattle pioneers and help founded First Church Seattle in 1853. (Courtesy of Seattle First Church.)

Catherine Blaine was the wife of the first minister and was Seattle's first school teacher. She had signed the first US women's rights document in 1848, called the Declaration of Sentiments. Reverend Blaine and his wife left Seattle after about a year, leaving the new church without a minister. The church was faced with frequent turnover in minsters for the next decade. However, the new church's congregation was rapidly growing concurrently with the city. By 1876, the congregation totaled approximately 275 members. (Courtesy of First Church Seattle.)

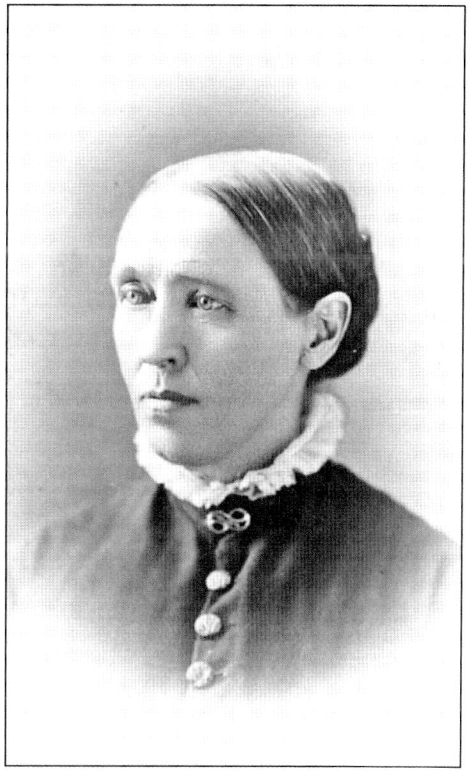

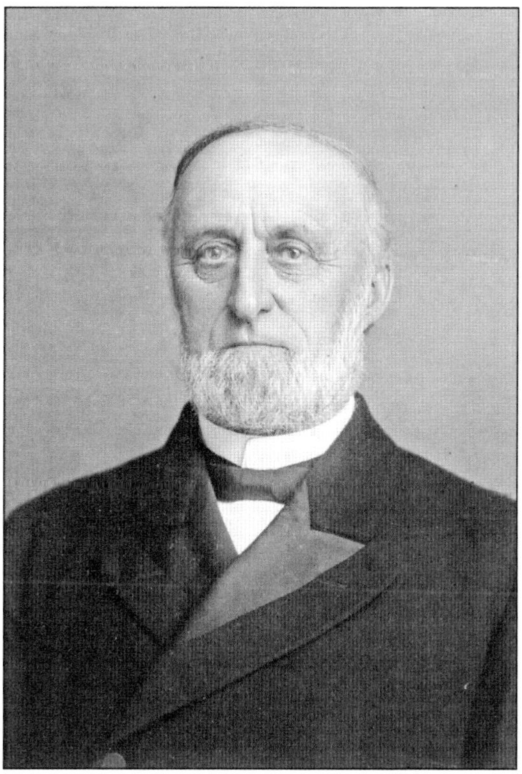

Rev. Albert Atwood was one of the church's first ministers. He was appointed in 1874. (Courtesy of First Church Seattle.)

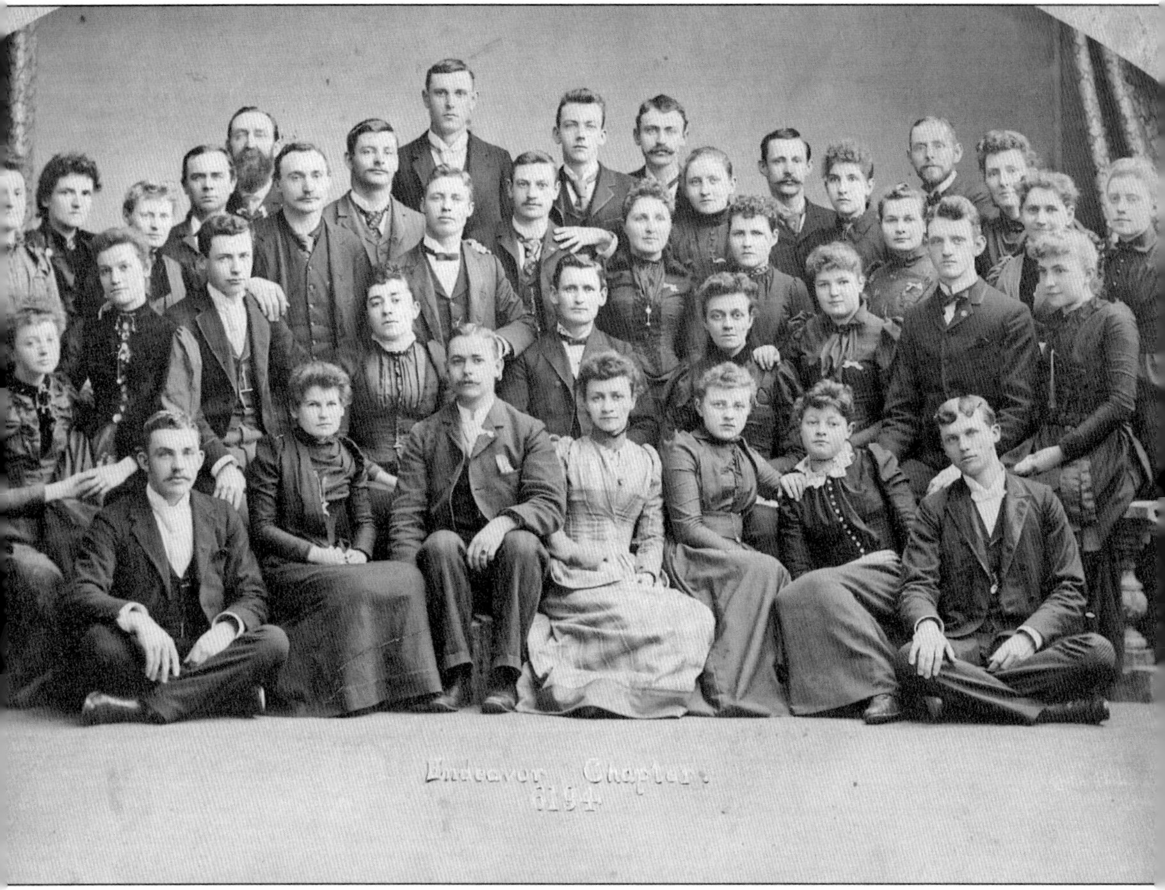

Early in its existence, First Church advocated for the rights of others. When the railroads were being built in Seattle, many Chinese immigrants came from California and Oregon to work. At first, they were welcomed because the settlers could use the help. First Church set up a school for their children in the church's basement. However, as Seattle began to grow, more Europeans begin to immigrate to the city. White workers began to complain about "cheap Chinese labor." A strong anti-Chinese sentiment began to take hold, and some Chinese workers were killed in different parts of the country. Any organization or person who helped or sympathized with Chinese workers was threatened directly or implicitly. Since First Church had helped Chinese workers by providing a school for their children, the minister and other members stood on the steps of the building for several days and nights to protect it during some of the tenser times. (Courtesy of First Church Seattle.)

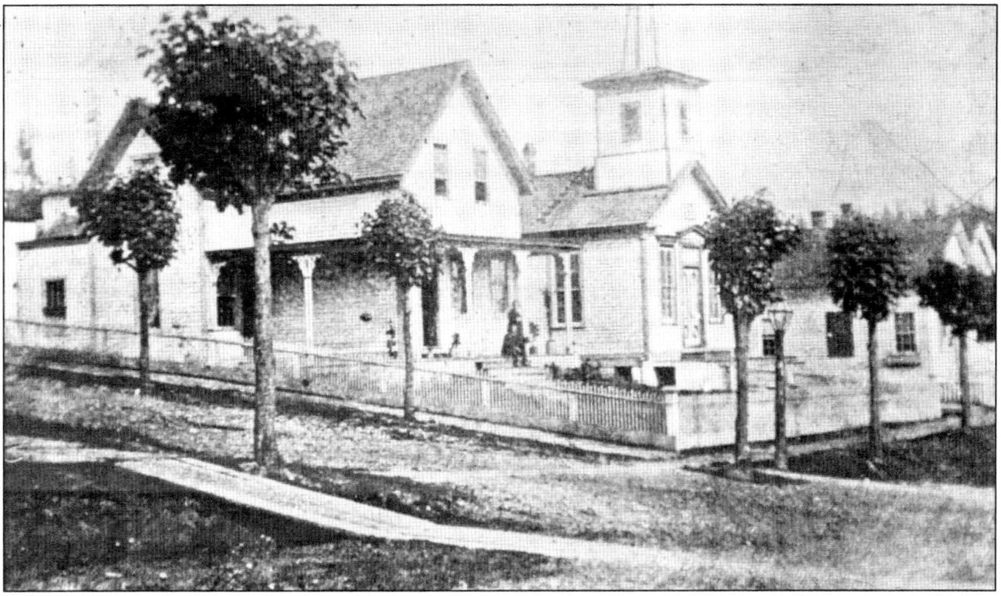

In 1889, the church's membership had outgrown the Little White Church, so a new church was built at Third Avenue and Marion Street and was dedicated in September 1889. The new church was spared by the Great Seattle Fire of June 6, 1889. (Courtesy of First Church Seattle.)

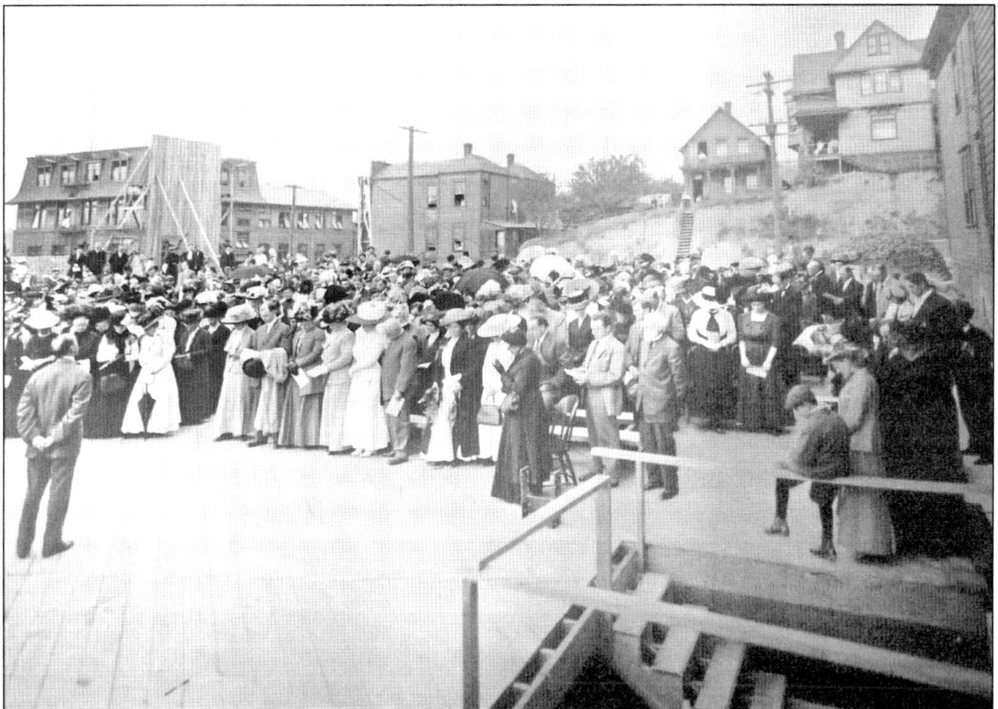

In the 1890s, Seattle was a frontier town with more than 15 saloons, and the church joined the temperance movement, organized to encourage moderation or total abstinence from alcohol. Many equated excessive alcohol consumption to destitution, crime, and marriage and health problems. (Courtesy of First Church Seattle.)

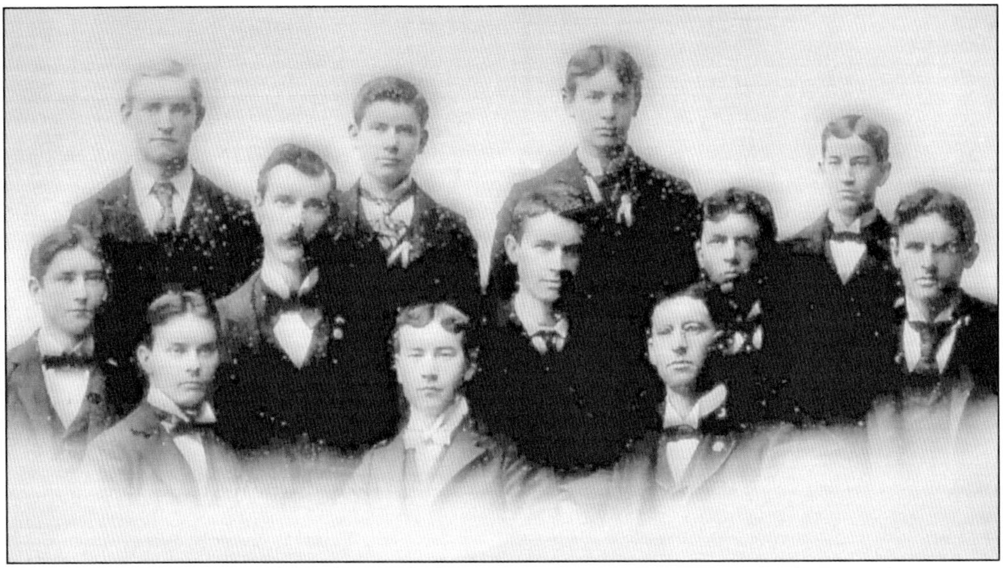

In the 1890s, during the gold rush, Seattle became a very prosperous town, and its population grew exponentially. T.S. Lippy was a First Church member who had struck gold during his prospecting days. He was very generous to First Church and the YMCA when he returned to Seattle. He was a generous benefactor of Seattle General Hospital. The hospital and school for nurses was established in 1895 and was located at 909 Fifth Avenue. It merged with Swedish Hospital in 1980. (Courtesy of First Church Seattle.)

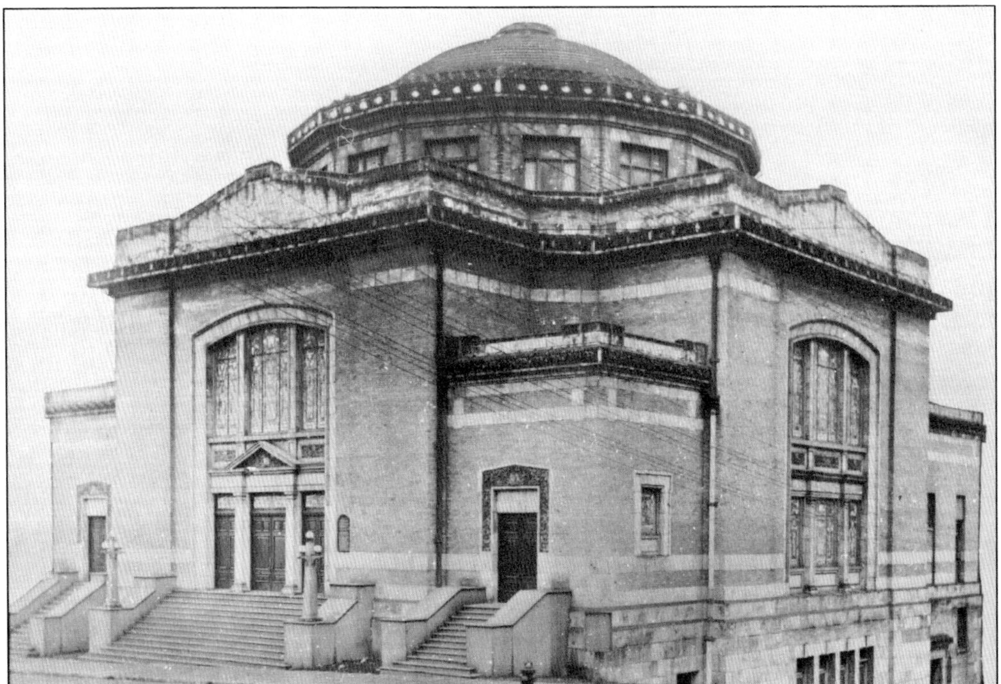

The church sold the property at Third Avenue and Marion Street and purchased property at Fifth Avenue and Marion Street to build a new church to accommodate the rapidly growing congregation; the church was dedicated in 1910. (Courtesy of First Church Seattle.)

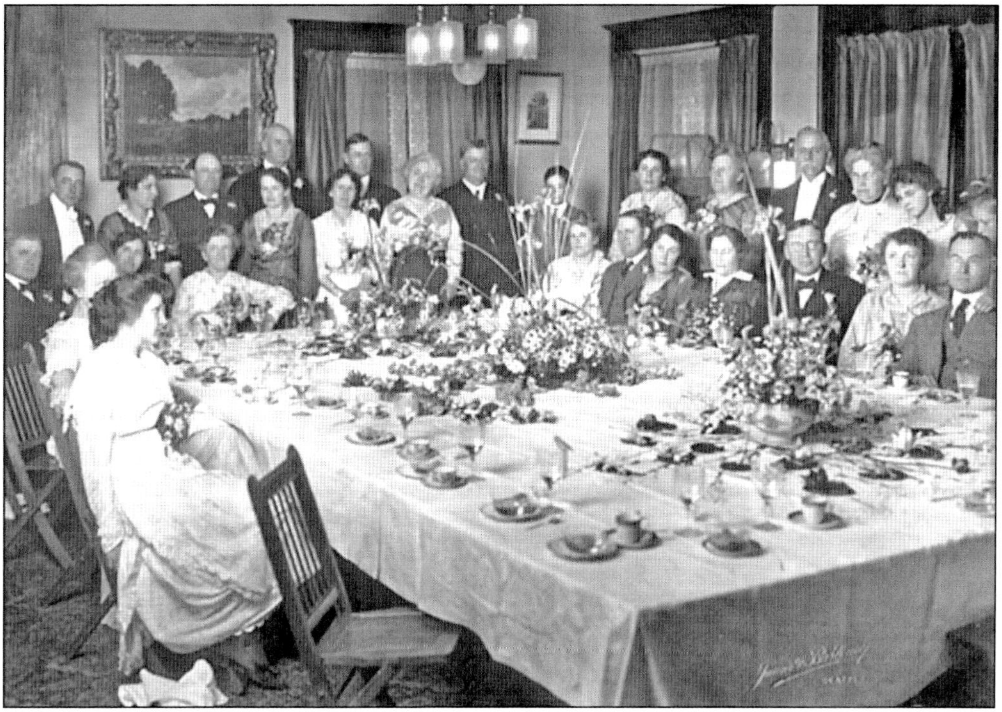

This dinner was held in honor of Adna Leonard, a First Church pastor who was elected to the Methodist episcopacy in 1916. (Courtesy of First Church Seattle.)

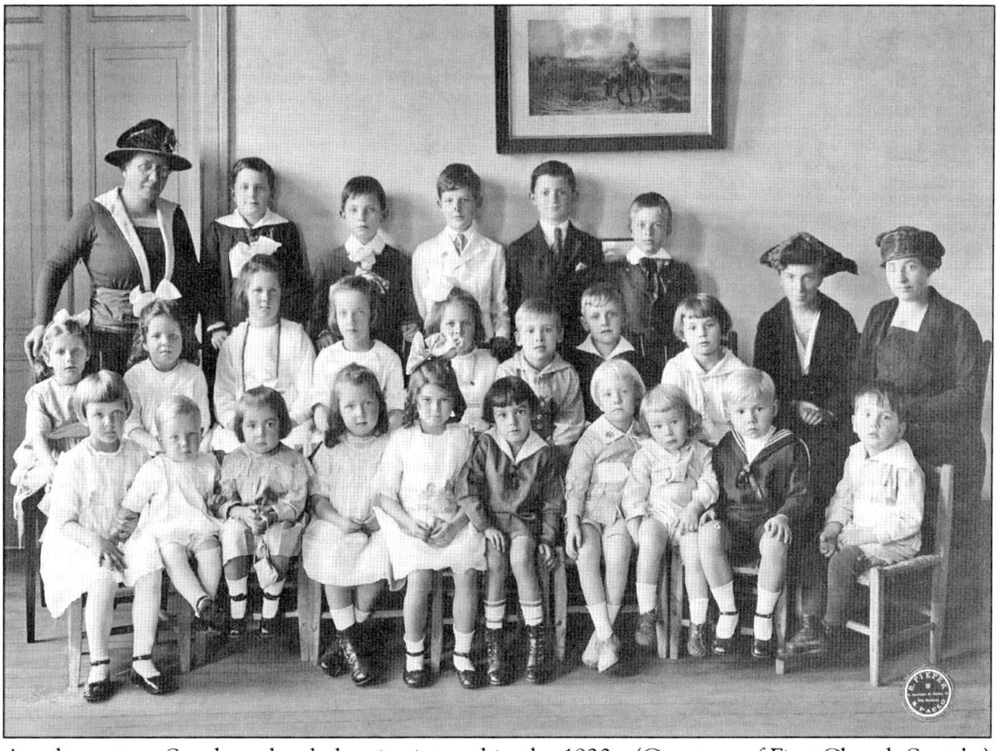

An elementary Sunday school class is pictured in the 1920s. (Courtesy of First Church Seattle.)

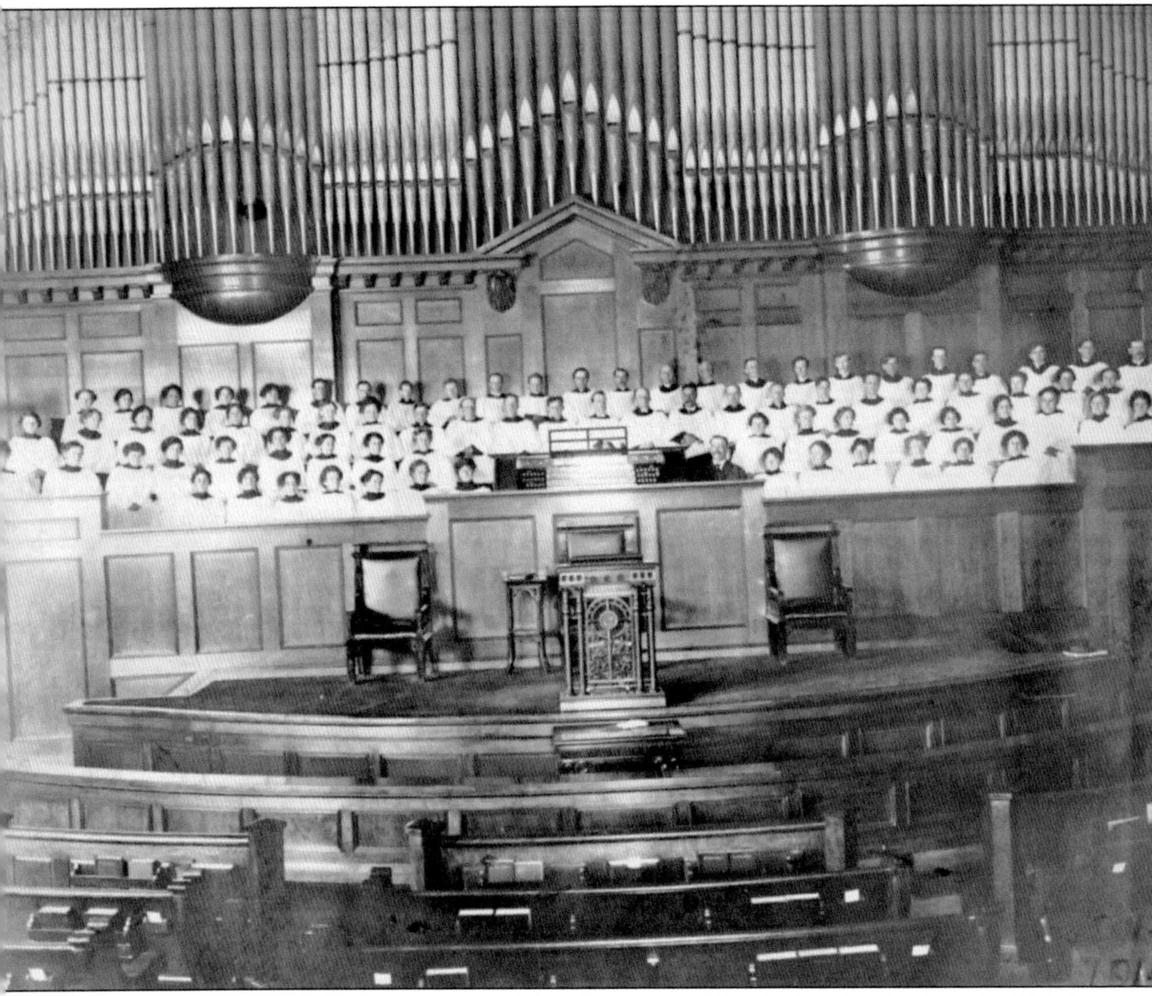

Music was an important component of church services. This is the church choir in 1914. In 1927, the church began a weekly radio broadcast on station KJR. After the Depression, the radio broadcast resumed on KEVR, which is now KING. (Courtesy of First Church Seattle.)

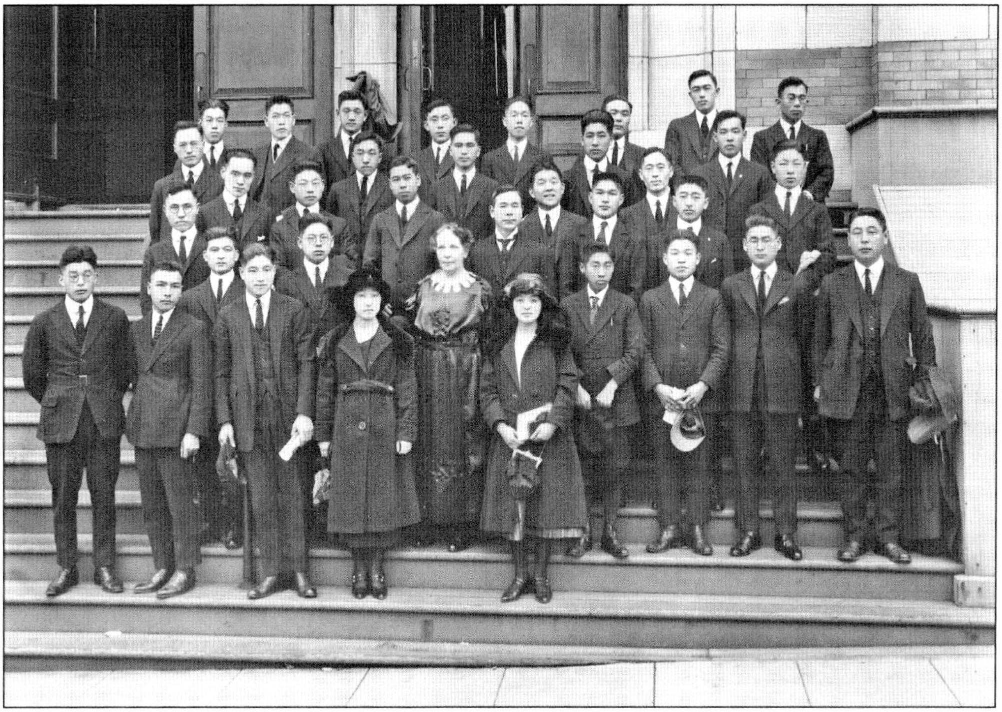

In 1919, the Seattle General Strike created money problems for the church. The church borrowed money from the national church to keep some of its ministries going, such as Bible studies for Japanese and Filipino immigrants. (Courtesy of First Church Seattle.)

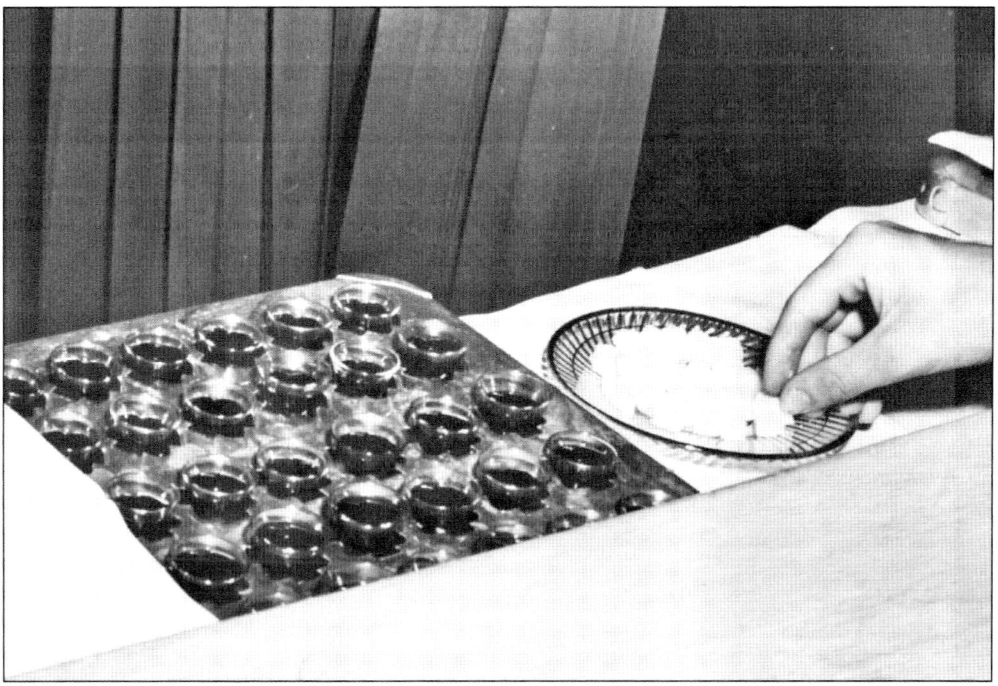

Over the years, the church has been a source of inspiration and comfort during difficult times for the country. (Courtesy of First Church Seattle.)

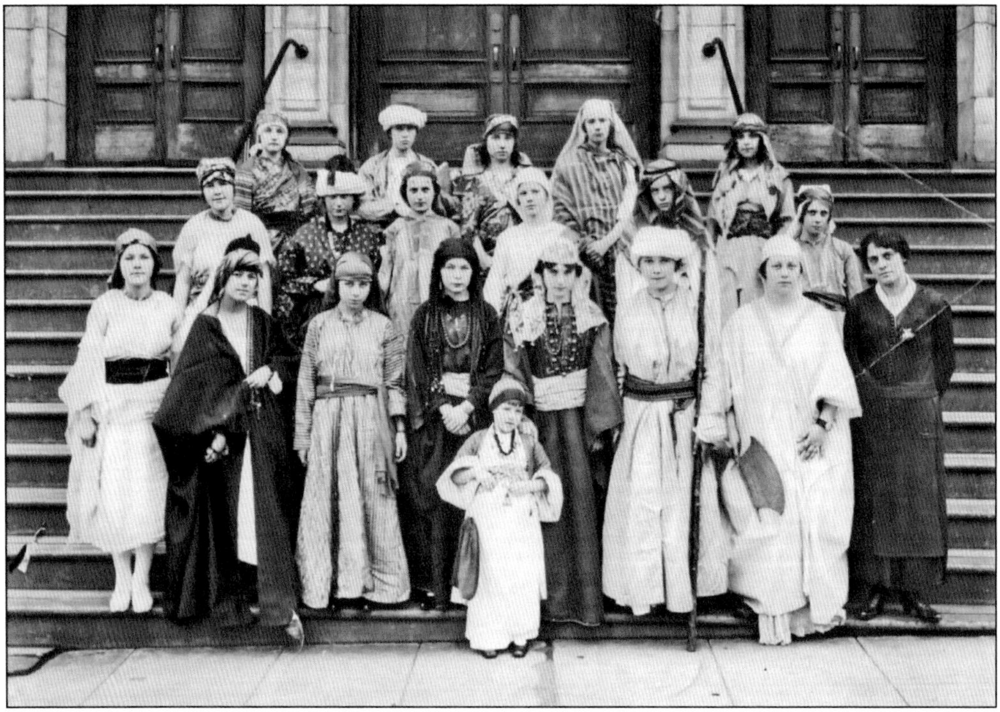

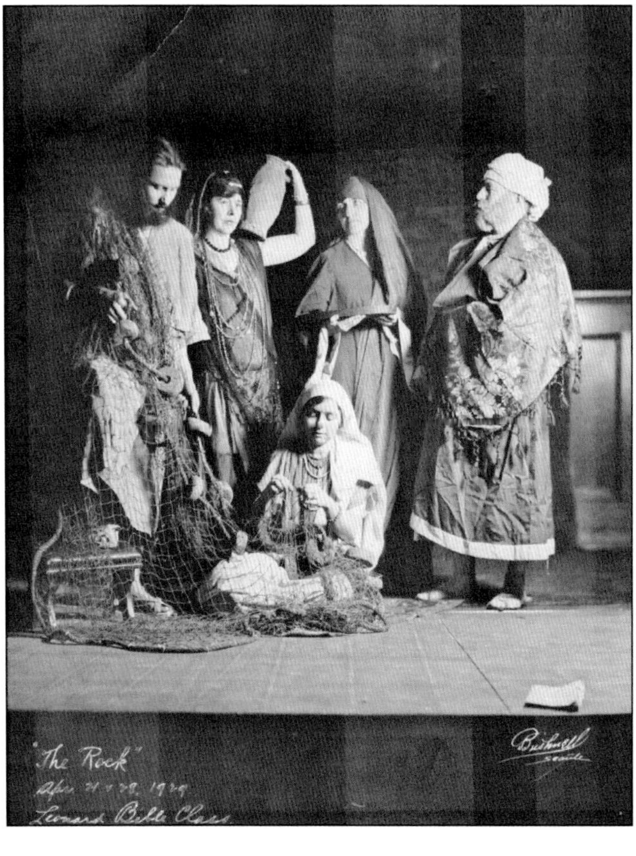

Church plays or biblical storytelling were an interesting method of reaching the congregation. Retelling the stories of the Bible through plays dates back to before the 15th century. The performers are usually very passionate about their subject, and the plays can be simplistic or very complex. (Courtesy of First Church Seattle.)

Church plays filled a vital role in demonstrating the teachings of the Bible by illustrating such themes as love, forgiveness, grace, altruism, compassion, and generosity. (Courtesy of First Church Seattle.)

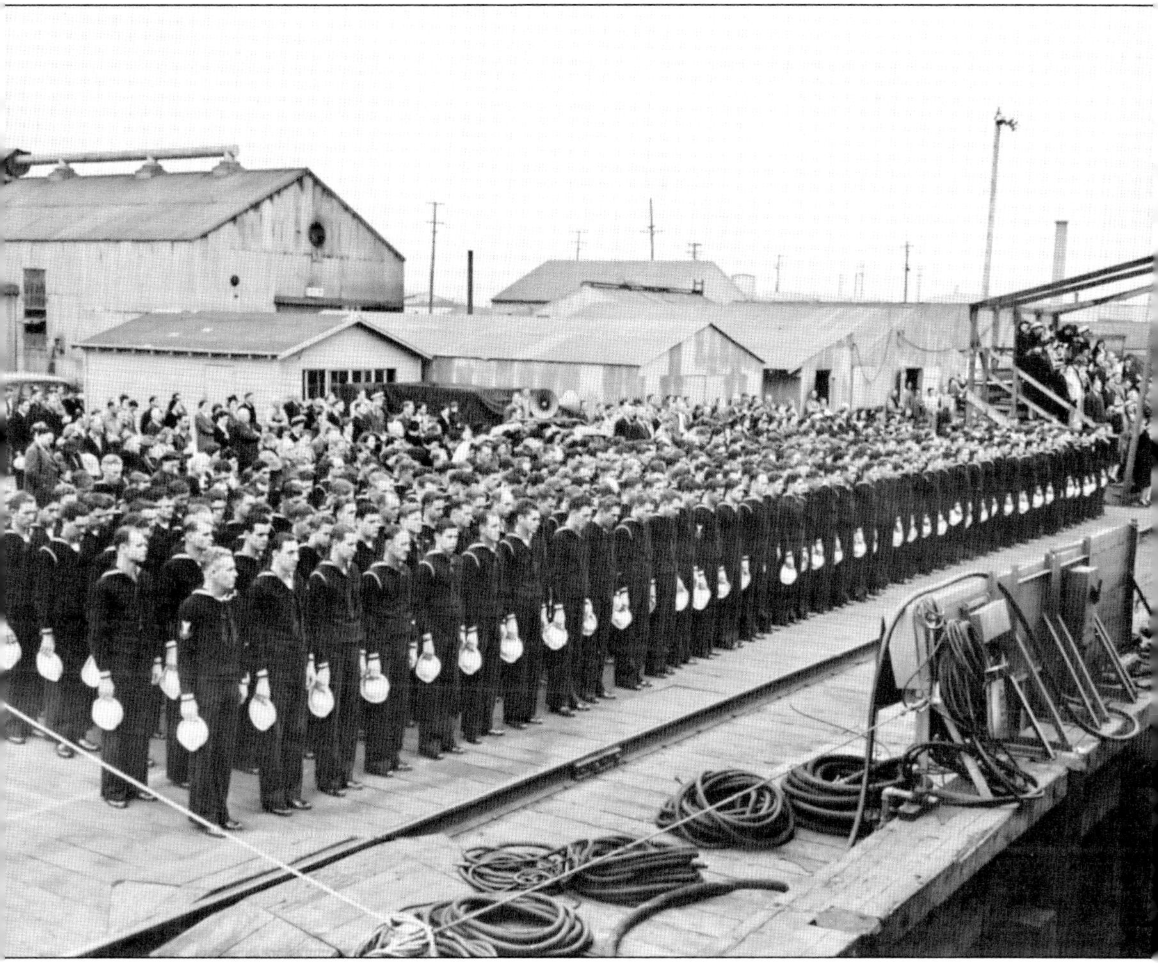

During World War I, the Ladies Aid Society established a downtown workshop for the Red Cross in support of the troops. The Ladies Aid Society was established by Catherine Blaine and was a vital part of the church and the community. Mrs. R.H. Denny donated an expensive sewing machine, and the ladies produced 856 pairs of socks, 2,895 surgical gowns and bed gowns, and 24,564 surgical dressings. In addition, the church opened its doors and sponsored luncheons and dinners for soldiers and sailors, and church members were also asked to invite the troops to their homes for meals. (Courtesy of First Church Seattle.)

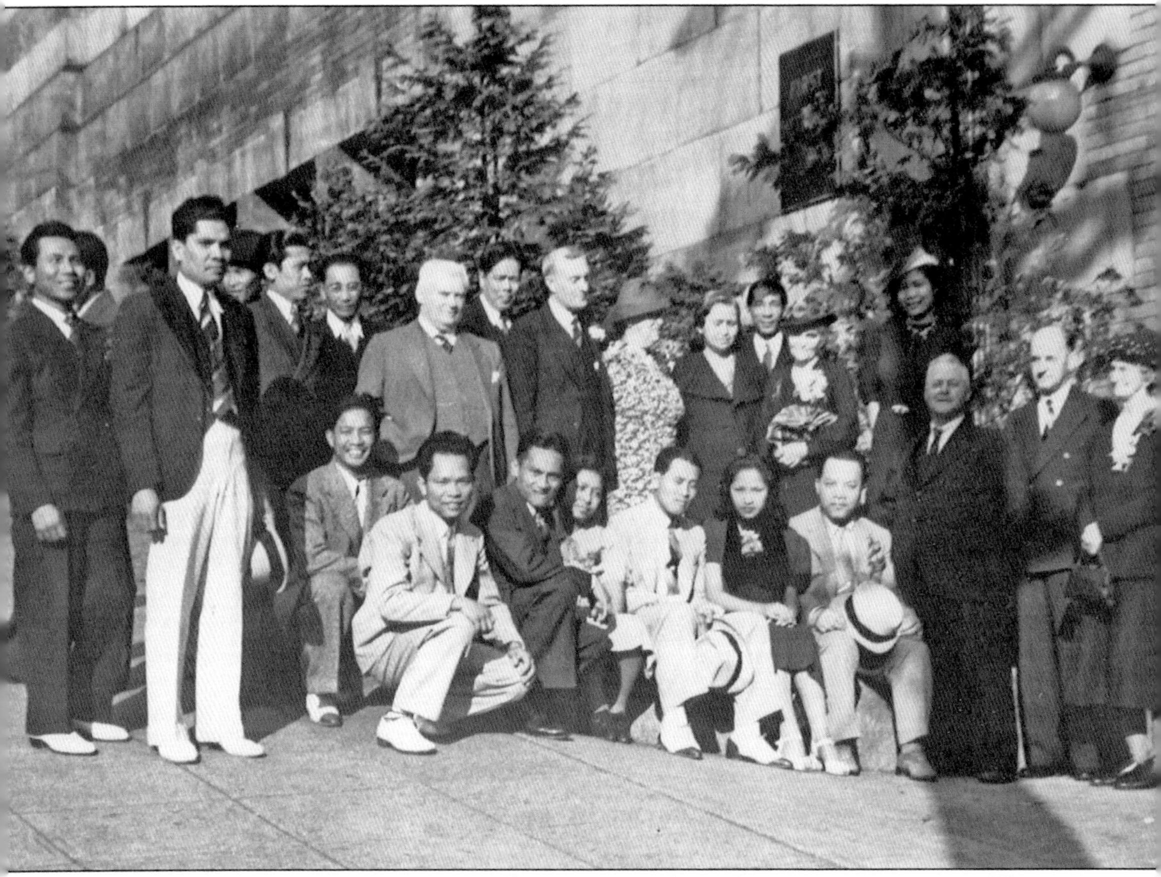

During World War II, many Japanese families were relocated to internment camps. They were put on buses and trains and often could only take the possessions they could carry, leaving most of their belongings behind. Many First Church members went to the bus and train stations to protest the internment of the Japanese, most of whom were American citizens. (Courtesy of First Church Seattle.)

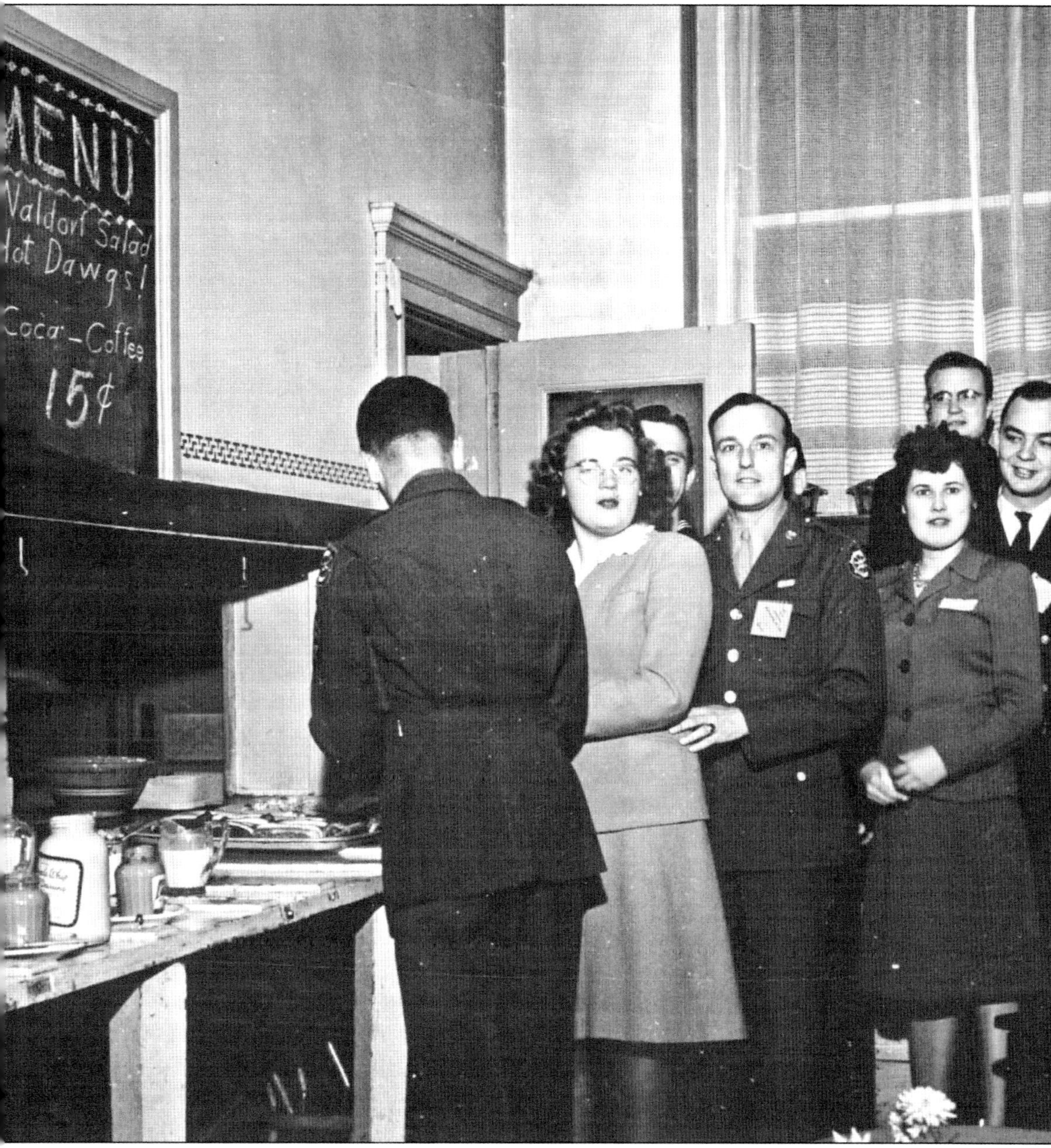

The church also supported the troops during World War II, with the Ladies Aid Society once again setting up a downtown work station to help the Red Cross. Soldiers and sailors were often invited to the church for meals and social activities. Members were again encouraged to ask the military to their homes for home-cooked meals. (Courtesy of First Church Seattle.)

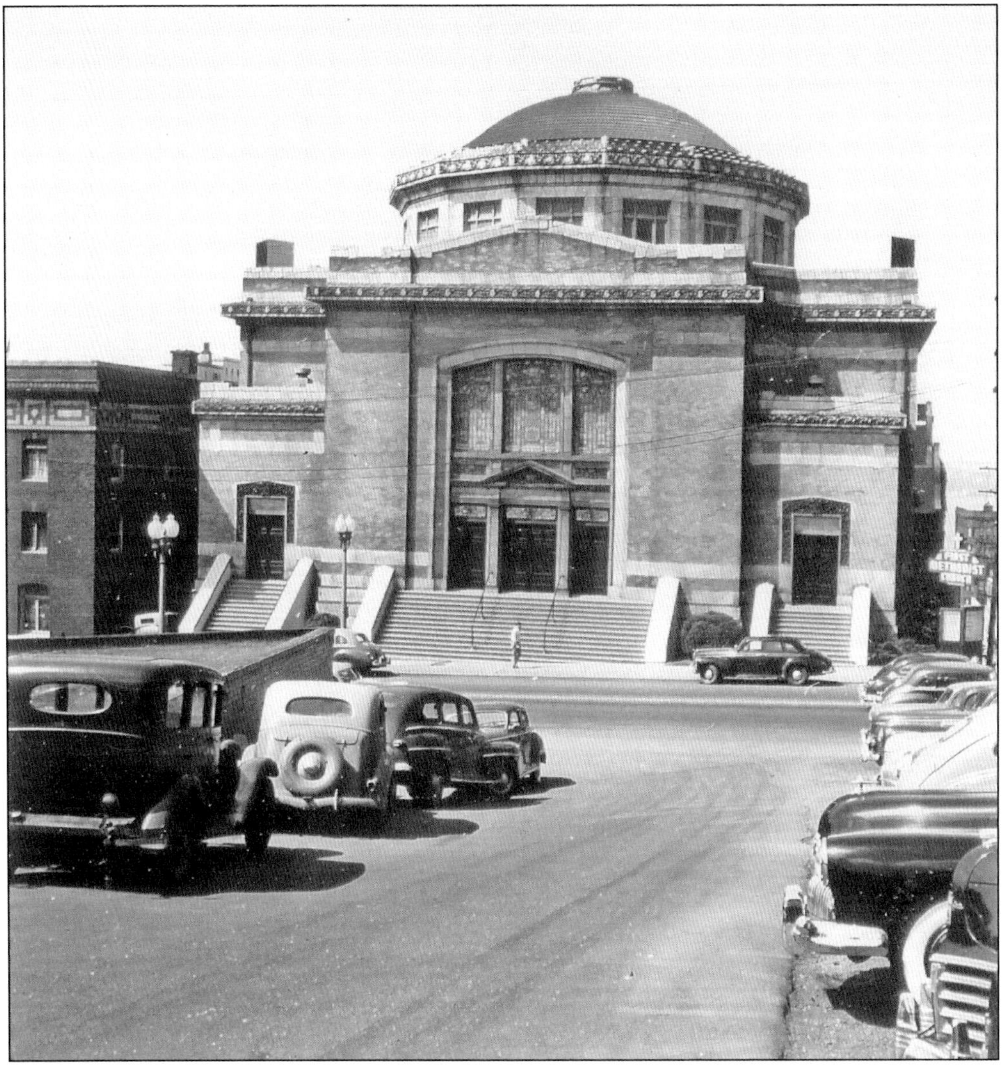

The First Church sanctuary is pictured before the addition in the 1940s. In 1958, the church, under the leadership of associate pastor Rev. Chester Morgan (1957–1959), established the Friendly Club for persons over 60 to address issues associated with the elderly. The Columbia Club for seniors was a result. The Columbia Club offered activities, nutritional programs, and health clinics for the elderly and lasted for 40 years. In the 1980s, the church purchased the Pulliam/Wesley Haven, a low-income housing unit that it operated for 17 years. (Courtesy of First Church Seattle.)

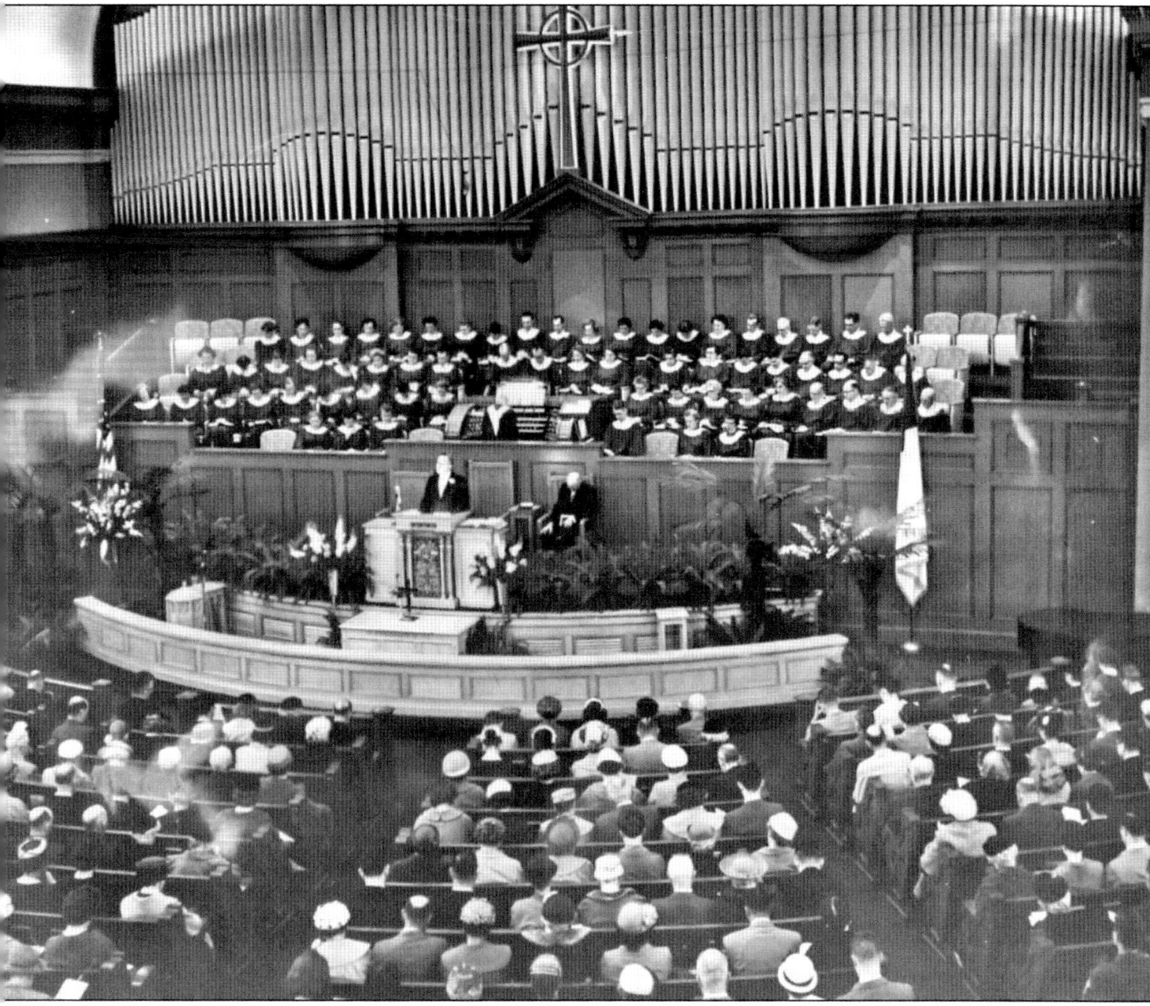

Over the years, First Church has remained a vital part of the Seattle community, and continues to be a progressive and open church that hosts a multitude of groups. Functions at the church are as diverse as Alcoholics Anonymous and the Seattle Men's Chorus. In 2002, the church sold the building at Fifth Avenue and Madison Street and constructed a new church building at Second Avenue and Denny Way. The church continues to serve the Seattle community with inclusiveness and progressiveness and welcomes everyone. (Courtesy of First Church Seattle.)